Studio Culture:
The secret life of the
graphic design studio

& Shaughnessy

Foreword:
Ben Bos

Unit Editions
www.uniteditions.com

Studio Culture
Unit 01

Editors: Tony Brook and Adrian Shaughnessy

Publishing affairs: Patricia Finegan

Production and editorial co-ordinator:
Natasha Day

Design: Spin
Designer: Ian Macfarlane
Design assistant: Joe Carter

Proof reader: Nicola Hodgson
Indexer: Angela Koo
Audio transcriptions: Camilla Shaughnessy

Printer: Granite, UK
www.granitecolour.com

Typeface: Optimo Hermes

Paper: James McNaughton Paper
www.jmcpaper.com
260gsm Incada Silk, 80gsm Colorit silver grey,
90gsm Cyclus print

Unit Editions

Studio 2
33 Stannary Street
London
SE11 4AA
United Kingdom

T +44 (0)20 7793 9555
F +44 (0)20 7793 9666

editorial@uniteditions.com
wwww.uniteditions.com

A catalogue for this book is available
from the British Library.

ISBN: 978-0-9562071-0-4

Images: Every effort has been made to trace
and contact the copyright holders of the
images reproduced in this book. However,
the publishers would be pleased, if informed,
to correct any errors or omissions in
subsequent editions of this publication.

Studio
Culture

The editors owe a large debt of gratitude to the many individuals and studios who helped make this book possible. Special thanks go to the interviewees who generously contributed their wisdom, time and energy to answering our questions and supplying images, and to Ben Bos for his introduction.

Warm thanks to the people who contributed to the Studio Portraits section of this book: Ben Bos, Theseus Chan, Mark Farrow, Ed Fella, Kevin Finn, Paola Fletcher, Raffaella Fletcher, Carin Goldberg, George Hardie, Richard Hart, Jessica Helfand, Mark Holt, Domenic Lippa, Hamish Muir, Flávia Nalon @ ps.2, Peter Saville, Toffe, Niklaus Troxler, Marion Wesel-Henrion.

Heartfelt thanks to the many people who helped with this book and with the launch of Unit Editions: Patrick Baglee, Chris Barrow, Harry Blain, Mark Blamire, Elly Bos, Wim Crouwel, Cartan Finegan, Mark Fletcher, Laurence King, Warren Lee, Graham Southern, Matt Watkins, Marc Valli.

Finally, big thanks to the 'Spin Lab' for numerous suggestions and unflagging enthusiasm: Natasha Day, Ian Macfarlane, Patrick Eley and David McFarline.

Contents

Q: What is the most treasured and well-used piece of equipment in your studio?

A: My head.

Alan Fletcher's reply to a question from design students, taken from *An Audience with Alan* (2005), a film by Patrick Baglee. The film was shown as part of the Design Museum's 2006–2007 exhibition, 'Alan Fletcher: Fifty Years of Graphic Work (and Play)'. It was also shown at 4Designers, for which the film was made.

A Studio can be a Daydream

Ben Bos, AGI/BNO

Ben Bos was the first employee of Total Design. He became a creative director of the famous studio, leaving after 28 years. He has won numerous international prizes, and lectures and teaches in Europe, the US, Israel and Japan.

He is the author of several books, including *AGI: Graphic Design since 1950* (written with his wife Elly).

'*Alleen is maar alleen*' is a Dutch expression. It tells you that being alone can be lonesome, 'just lonely'. In its early days, graphic design was mostly a matter of loners. Even today there are niches in our trade in which soloists are doing fine work. Typeface and book designers, for instance, or those typographers who specialize in the lettering of gravestones and tablets. Designing banknotes doesn't necessarily require more than one gifted man or woman (although in difficult matters of technique, they must work with specialists at the printers).

Studios are for team players. To begin with you need a good balance of capabilities, and not just male or female macho types who are permanently in competition with each other. A real leader (but not a dictator) is welcome. Don't underestimate the climatic, humane value of a good mix of male and female staff. Mutual respect is an essential condition.

Designers are designers, and design managers are a different breed. As soon as a studio has more players than are allowed on one side of a football pitch at the outset of a match, the principal designer should not be banned from his beloved profession at which he excels. Instead he should be relieved by the (temporary?) presence of a design manager with the psychological qualities to deal with sensitive semi-artists.

I have watched the world of design teams since the 1950s, both the successful ones and the losers. I have seen the freshly picked, blooming flowers from the best design colleges, happy to become one of the slaves of 'their famous young designer'. (At that time I spent three months teaching at Ravensbourne College in Bromley. Of course all the girls wanted desperately to get a first job at one of the few HQ design groups; quite willing to work like hell.) And once I stole one of them (from nobody less than Alan). There was great joy for a while in my own hothouse at early Total Design.

Combined play delivers the most beautiful, healthy babies. The interaction of talents and intellect is a great good, leading to brilliant design. Some very successful studios are magnets for the continuous recruitment of the best designers – they have no problems at all with succession.

There was a design group in which all the partners had the same contract. Irrespective of the financial performance of their teams, their salaries were equal. One day one of the partners landed a job with enormous financial potential. He wanted – just for his own team – to change the rule of equal pay. His idea worked like a roadside bomb.

Another design group was dazzled by their unprecedented technological lead; the proud creative director then made the horrible mistake of thinking that he no longer needed to employ talented people because nobody could beat the output of his advanced equipment. But everyone soon caught up...

Still another had the wrong kind of design manager, writing too many boring internal notices, killing the spirit by being an ardent meeting-freak, and torturing his designer colleagues during his tiresome sessions.

Then take the case of the group that became a multinational. Blinded by success, awards and honours, it grew and grew until it was just no fun anymore. Collapse was the only thing that could (and did) happen.

Or the studio without a single bit of interior glamour: it looked like a large, pre-war, bookkeepers' office. Lots of computers, yes, but those don't impress clients or prospective clients anymore, because they have the same kind of equipment themselves. A studio should have space for some glamour, fun, excitement; it should offer an inspiring atmosphere. Show that design is a way of life!

Then there was the downtown studio where the opening party of an AGI (Alliance Graphique Internationale) annual congress was to take place. A cab delivered us at the given address. Confusion: no studio, but a nicely decorated New York downtown fire-station. We wondered what had gone wrong; we were about to go back to our hotel when, to our surprise, a guy came out of a side door. I knew him: a fellow AGI member.

And yet – beware. I remember entering the office of a famous Italian designer. The interior was extremely impressive. A big space behind the front door, occupied only by a receptionist (with good make-up) on a throne. Behind her was a long passage that led to the monumental front door of the designer's own chancellery. Upon entering I told him that I missed the two sentries and the banners on both sides of his entrance. Later, I made a tour through his studio. The units in which his employees worked had the most modest measurements I had ever encountered in the profession. They were rabbit hutches, smaller even than those in Tokyo with the most expensive square footage in the world.

A good studio is a centre of professional pride. Colleagues are amplifying, inspiring, studious. The output is often a collective product, in which several team members can trace their own contribution.

A studio. Handle with care. Don't spoil the Daydream. Beware of Nightmares.

'I think there is a limit to how big a design studio can grow before it morphs into a different creature. I can imagine that above six to eight people the studio would start to fragment, and considering the fact that we like to work in a very collaborative way, it just wouldn't work for us, or be APFEL any more; we would become more hands-off, just managers. Perhaps the optimum size for us is as many of us as can fit round one table to have those initial APFEL studio discussions and brainstorms.'

Kirsty Carter, A Practice for Everyday Life (1)

'A student recently asked me if teaching informs my practice and my answer was yes, in that I have to remain engaged and aware of the demands of professional practice. I need to ensure that the breadth and range of my references and knowledge is far greater than if I were solely focused on my own practice.'

David Smith, Atelier David Smith (2)

1   2   3   4

'Ultimately we are a business, and to run it successfully you have to think ahead in case the phone stops ringing. That could be getting into the psyche of potential clients by producing promotional literature, having the right documents prepared for expressions of interest or simple things like keeping the website updated. As for less money – that just means longer hours to keep the cashflow at a sustainable level.'

Mason Wells, Bibliothèque (3)

'One of the big things we've done is completely organize all the work, which we've never done before. We got a dedicated server that allows everything to be in one place. We've also had the work photographed properly. That's been a huge thing, so when people ask if we can send them some work, we've got a library of stuff. We don't do printed portfolios. It just doesn't seem relevant any more. A couple of times in the past I dropped one off at clients. They'd sit on it for a month and go "Oh, we didn't get a chance to look at it".'

Nicola Place, Build (4)

'We work together but act individually. Any new employee has to merge into this jigsaw, with the ability from day one to also be independent. Finding a new designer at Coast is very difficult. Last time I tried to find someone to become part of the jigsaw, I failed.'

Frédéric Vanhorenbeke, Coast (5)

'One of our designers left and went to Interbrand, the huge multinational conglomerate, but I discovered they don't even have a bandsaw there! Shocking! How do they get anything done? I walk through the studio a couple of times every day. I pull up a chair and breathe down their necks and we review designs on their screens. They like that! Our studio is like a design laboratory, and everyone is trying to prove a theory, or exercise an equation.'

Stephen Doyle, Doyle Partners (6)

5 6 7 8

'You can have 125 people, but the work never gets done by more then five people. The teams are never bigger than that. It's all about group dynamics. More then seven people and you don't increase efficiency or effectiveness, you just have more meetings. If you have 12 people, you don't work twice as much as six people, you work 50% more, so in other words you lose money. Seven people round the table, six people plus a project manager, maybe seven plus an intern.'

Erik Spiekermann, Edenspiekermann (7)

'It would be so awkward having an intern in the studio. We really feel we have to do everything ourselves: DIY. To have somebody do all the "dumb" work for us would make us feel terrible. For example, if we come up with a solution that forces us to spend days and days on kerning, we feel we have to do this kerning ourselves. We came up with the solution, so we have to suffer the consequences, even if this involves days of boring work.'

Experimental Jetset (8)

The graphic design studio:
real estate, psychology
and creativity

Adrian Shaughnessy

In the late 1980s I co-founded the design studio Intro[1]. I had previously worked in design firms where I had felt undervalued and creatively stymied. The new studio was an opportunity to change all that. My business partner and I had a shared determination to create a congenial and productive environment; an environment where everyone felt appreciated and fulfilled.

Achieving this came at a price. The pressure to maintain creativity and profitability was often exhilarating, but it was also exhausting. After 15 years, I felt burned out and decided to quit. Yet I look back on my time at Intro with pleasure and a strong familial feeling. One small event confirms that my rose-tinted view is more than just the warm bathwater of nostalgia. On one occasion a client spent a day with members of the design team going through work. In the afternoon I joined them for a review of the project. The client turned to me and said – 'there's a great atmosphere here; it's the sort of place I'd like to work in.' These words meant a great deal to me.

Today I live a nomadic existence that allows me to visit designers all over the world; I've snooped around studios in the UK, the US, Europe, the Far East and Australia, and I can spot a happy shop within seconds of entering one. Call it a vibe, call it ambience, but it's actually little things like the way you're greeted when you arrive; the way you're offered a cup of coffee (and the cup it comes in); the amount of natural light; the furniture; the layout; the stuff on the walls; the music playing.

In fact, a studio is a combination of three things: the physical space, the people who occupy that space, and the work they produce. By the physical space I mean the premises, the location, the furniture, the equipment, and the way the space is designed; by the people I mean everyone from the studio's leaders to the intern on placement; and by the work I mean the studio's creative output. In other words, studios are a fizzy cocktail of real estate, psychology and creativity. To make a great studio you have to get the balance right between these three elements.

Yet considering how fundamental studios are to graphic design's past, as well as its present, it's astonishing how little literature there is on the subject. You can find writing on every aspect of design, but the studio itself receives scant attention. Even an intellectually rigorous and exhaustive publication like *Design Dictionary (Perspectives on Design Terminology)*[2], which contains entries on a vast array of cross-disciplinary design terms including Design and Politics, Environmental Design, Lighting Design, Urban Planning and Virtuality, doesn't see fit to have an entry on The Studio.

Design history is written from the perspective of the individual designer, and most discussion of contemporary design centres on individual personalities. Yet the image of the lone graphic designer working in solitary isolation is not much more than a romantic legacy from design's remote fine art lineage. As Ben Bos points out in his witty and knowing introduction, it's only highly specialized designers who actually work on their own ('Typeface and book designers, for instance, or those typographers who specialize in the lettering of gravestones and tablets.') Even design's most singular figures – the Rands[3], the Fletchers[4], the Aichers[5] – had studios with helpers and assistants; and by far the most common way for designers to organize themselves is in the collaborative shape of a studio. However, despite the ubiquity of the design studio, it remains a neglected area for serious commentary.

It's easy to see why; although design offices are often run by charismatic leaders who personify their firms (they often have their names over the door), studios are actually made up of the individuals who work in them. Take the studios of star designers, for example. Many contain able lieutenants who, when you investigate what they do, emerge as the true authors of much of the work that the star designers are venerated for. Or, ask the head of a design company for an honest appraisal of his or her studio and you'll find that it differs from the assessment offered by a junior member of the same studio. No wonder, therefore, that historians and commentators prefer the easier target of the individual designer. Besides, we want our design heroes to be stand-alone visionaries, unencumbered by the dull realities of running studios. We don't want to hear about them wrestling with rent reviews, health and safety legislation and employment law, not to mention the efforts required to keep ambitious design staff happy and fulfilled.

In truth, the modern designer is unthinkable without the life-support system of the studio, and furthermore, it is impossible to claim an understanding of contemporary design without also understanding how design studios work and how the individual designer functions within a group sensibility. The nature of modern graphic design, particularly in the digital domain with its need for many specialist skills, means that collaboration and group working have become obligatory.

One voice, many voices

The influential design group 8vo (Octavo)[6] was an example of a studio from the recent past with a collective presence far greater than any of the individuals who comprised the company. Hamish Muir[7], one of the co-founders of 8vo, cites two studios as sources of inspiration for his fledgling company, both of which presented a collective face to the world yet were made up of strong individuals. 'Studio Boggeri[8] in Italy, and Total Design[9] in Holland,' he notes, 'did great work over long periods of time, and the balance between the individuals (some great "names" in each) and the studios would appear to be truly synergistic – the work they produced had an energy and purpose that perhaps would not have been achieved by the same people working in isolation.'

It is impossible to discus the modern design studio and its evolution in the second half of the twentieth century without mentioning Total Design (founded 1963). Its reputation continues to grow as successive generations discover the meticulous and idiosyncratic sense of craft and style that emerged from the Dutch studio. For Hamish Muir, and countless other contemporary designers, Total represents a glittering example of one of the great creative powerhouse studios. Wim Crouwel was one of the founders of Total Design, and remains a towering figure in modern graphic design. Yet for him, Total was a collective venture. He describes it as: 'collegiate and comradely. The studio had a structure of teams, each headed by one of the partners. We all believed in straightforward solutions; the partners had a common philosophy on type, typography and design in general, with strict rules. Structuring the content was the main aim. The work, in its minimal and neutral approach, came as a result of these views. It was nevertheless very recognizable.' Crouwel names two studios that inspired him: 'Pentagram[10], born out of Forbes, Fletcher and Gill[11] for their set-up. We adopted their structure of partner-run teams. And the German-Swiss studio GGK (Gerstner/Gredinger/Kutter)[12] for their striking and intelligent solutions.'

Looking at the great studios, past and present, we see that there is no standard model. No one-size-fits-all template. Yet all studios have one thing in common; they are ongoing transactions between the needs of the individual and the collective needs of the group. This is easily stated, but not so easily achieved. We live and work at a time when the individual is at the centre of everything. Individualism is the new religion. It can be seen in the toxic cult of celebrity and in the way traditions of community, civic responsibility and social cohesion have been eroded in favour of an egotistical culture of me-me-me.

How, therefore, within the context of the design studio, do we preserve the sanctity of the individual, while at the same time protecting the collective aims – and survival – of the group? This is the conundrum at the heart of all studios. It doesn't matter whether it's a studio of two friends working as equal partners, or a giant organization with 300

'It is possible we haven't been offered certain jobs because we are a small company, although we have worked on most types and sizes of project, from complete advertising campaigns to business cards. For us there is a kind of "natural selection" process. Generally our work comes through word of mouth – so we are only really offered work that is right for us.'

Damon Murray, Fuel (9)

'Apart from during a probationary period for new studio members, all full-time members get paid the same. It's a symbolic assurance of equality and solidarity. Everyone's contribution is equally valued, so that individual and collaborative creativity is not just an ethos, but also a real structural imperative. This hopefully makes for an environment where creativity is respected and supported.'

Jason Grant, Inkahoots (10)

9

10

11

12

'We're lucky to have found a charming and cheap backyard studio in a busy neighbourhood that we share with two photographers. During the summer it gets awfully hot in there, but the river is close by. Several swimming sessions are part of a regular working day during the summer months, which results in a nice blend of labour and leisure.'

Urs Lehni, Lehni-Trüb (11)

'I have a really good bookkeeper and a good accountant. I do my own invoicing and paying of bills etc, but thankfully, receipts and shit I shove into an envelope and Jacqui does my basic… whatever it is she does, and tells me what numbers to fill in on what boxes on the quarterly GST payments… and then I give all her stuff to my accountant and he says a bunch of gobbledygook to me and I ask him how much I should pay myself each month, and then I do what he tells me.'

Marian Bantjes (12)

people in offices all over the world, all studios have to find an answer to this question. Finding an answer is made more difficult by the fact that most graphic designers choose a career in graphic design because they are attracted to the idea of having a voice that might be heard above the contemporary din of anonymity and alienation. Even the most self-effacing and pragmatically minded designers, with no interest in self-promotion or personal glory, nevertheless want to derive a sense of authorship from the work they make. But as all studio heads know, if egos are allowed to flow unchecked and designers are encouraged to develop an entirely self-centred approach to their work, then the group will suffer.

It won't come as a surprise to discover that the answer to this big question is for studios to build a sense of communal purpose that nevertheless leaves enough space for the individual to retain his or her own voice. Whether this is achieved by inspirational and enlightened leadership, or through genuine collaborative partnerships of equals, it doesn't much matter. But it has to be achieved. Bad studios rarely manage it, but the good ones, the ones we admire, do it by balancing the three vital ingredients that make up the successful studio: real estate, psychology and creativity.

The real estate

In the art world, the artist's studio has acquired mythic status. Hardly surprising; we romanticize the life of artists and therefore it's a short step to romanticizing the artist's place of work. After the death in 1992 of the Irish-born artist Francis Bacon[13], the entire contents of his London studio were moved to the Dublin City Gallery, where his studio was recreated with sacramental reverence. Archaeologists were employed to map Bacon's workplace, tag every object and log its position. It was then painstakingly reconstructed using the original door, walls, floors, ceiling and shelves, as well as drawings, correspondence, magazines, newspapers and vinyl records in exactly the same position that Bacon had left them. It has become a shrine for Bacon's admirers; a place to worship the relics of the great man's life.

The modern graphic design studio's dual requirement to be a place of business as well as a place of creative production makes it less likely to be an object of interest beyond the purely professional realm. Would the gallery-visiting public pay to see Paul Rand's studio recreated? Perhaps not. Yet among designers there is a deep-running fascination with how other designers organize their space and run their businesses. The 'studio visit' is an established feature of design life, and most designers are happy to show a visiting designer round their secret domains: yet getting them to talk about how they run their studios is not so easy.

One of the few important designers to theorize the studio was Otl Aicher. With doctrinaire thoroughness, Aicher offered a vision of his ideal design office. For him, transparency was paramount: 'My profession requires me to work with other people,' he wrote. 'And so I want to be in the same room as them. Anyone is permitted to see and hear what I am doing. This is the only way to produce the correct network of work and workers. I want to be in sight of them and not to have to open and close doors to get to them.' He goes on: 'with the exceptions of toilets and darkrooms I cannot think of a single room that absolutely has to be separate.'[14]

Aicher's spartan view of studio design contrasts with that of the New York designer Massimo Vignelli[15]. Born in Milan, Vignelli offers a radically different vision of the modern studio. In his book, *Vignelli: From A to Z*[16], he shows pictures of his luxurious Manhattan design office. He writes: '... we found a sensational space in the penthouse of a building on Tenth Avenue ... we had the opportunity to design our offices from a large, empty loft. It was the chance to experiment with unusual materials: Dex-O-Tex for the floors, lead for walls, high-density fibreboard for the furniture, and raw steel for tables and lamps, as well as randomly brushed aluminium to frame frosted glass partitions. Every detail had been designed to achieve a serene, almost monastic space. It was a stunningly beautiful office, a destination for people from all over the world to visit.' Vignelli describes how each designer occupies a cubicle, with studio heads in individual offices facing outwards into the studio. There was a library, archive, kitchen, lunchroom, darkroom and toilets. He goes on to eulogize his own office and that of his wife Lella[17]: 'Her desk, flanked by Brno chairs, was a black granite top resting on four bronze legs by the Italian sculptor Arnaldo Pomodoro[18]...'

Vignelli moved out of his studio in 2000, but looking at pictures of this richly attired space, it's clear that it boldly matches his status as one of the grandees of modern design. It's also apparent that his practice's track record in interior design proved a useful asset when planning his own studio. For most graphic designers, however, planning the layout of even a modest studio takes them into the unfamiliar realms of space planning and the sheer expense of fixtures and fittings – not to mention workplace psychology and data-flow management. We also need answers to dozens – perhaps hundreds – of questions. Productivity vs creativity? Open plan vs partitions? Meetings with clients at the desk, or a lavish conference room? Shelving – Vitsoe or Ikea? And that's before we worry about what magazines to have in reception; whether to have posters on the wall; where to put the bikes; and devising the studio's music policy. Or, in the case of Erik

Spiekermann (see pages 76–85), designing a studio typeface. For many designers, studio planning is more a case of making do and muddling through than realizing a grand vision.

No single factor has influenced the layout of design studios more than the arrival of the computer. In the pre-digital era, designers worked at drawing boards. These cumbersome, space-hungry boards were usually free-standing; they couldn't be shared, and the fact that they had parallel motion bars that required unrestricted space on either side in which to move up and down encouraged insularity as designers built little isolated fiefdoms for themselves. Today, when we look at the layout of the modern studio, we are struck by the fluid, barrier-less use of space and by the sight of designers working side by side in close proximity to each other.

The computer means that studios can occupy a much smaller footprint. And when this is coupled with high real estate values and soar-away rents in most urban areas (not to mention shrinking design budgets and increased competition), the small studio is increasingly the norm all over the world. As a recent report by the UK's Design Council, a publicly funded body responsible for promoting the social and business benefits of design, noted: 'Large design consultancies [in Britain] are relatively rare and the design industry is overwhelmingly characterized by very small businesses: 59% of design consultancies employ fewer than five people and a further 23% employ five to ten people.'[19] Among business leaders and policy-makers, the design world's tendency towards smallness is widely seen as evidence of its lack of business credibility. But design is an activity that withers when it is conglomeratized. Small studios are hyper-efficient organisms; their agility and sense of purpose puts most giant corporations and institutions to shame. To quote Erik Spiekermann: 'You can have 125 people [in a design studio], but the work never gets done by more then five people. The teams are never bigger than that. It's all about group dynamics. More then seven people and you don't increase efficiency or effectiveness, you just have more meetings.'

The greatest advantage of 'smallness' is that everyone sits together and everyone gets to know what's going on. This may seem like a minor benefit, but it's really a priceless asset in client-facing businesses. Small, open-plan offices where everyone sits together allow studio heads to know everything there is to know about their studio. Sitting together in a small confined space has virtues even for such a lordly figure as Milton Glaser: 'The great benefit of this is that you can hear what everybody's saying,' he notes. 'I've never written a memo in my life, because everybody knows exactly who I'm talking to and what I'm doing. Everybody here knows everybody's business. If you have a deep sense of privacy I don't think that you could work for me.' (See pages 130–137.)

When I was creative head of my studio, I boasted that I knew the status of every project in the building. I knew what stage each job had reached and I knew how long it would take to complete. I knew where it stood in relation to budgets and schedules. I also knew where it stood on a creativity index: I knew if it was a winner; if it was in need of urgent surgery; or if it was a total wash-out beyond redemption. I had, as my then business partner and I called it, 'perfect knowledge'.

But as we grew to 20–25 people (a few years later we would briefly have a head-count of 40), I no longer knew everything, and I had to rely on skilled project managers and producers for vital information. I still retained a creative overview, but I no longer knew the administrative or financial status of every project. This necessitated a shift in management style that I found difficult at first, but ultimately it resulted in us offering a more professional (if slightly less personal) service.

Our growth resulted in a move to a larger studio. We were spread over two floors (although the upper floor was a mezzanine that allowed some interchange between both spaces). We put all the designers on the upper floor, and all the production and admin staff on the ground floor. This became feasible due to investing in a fully computer-networked studio allowing files to be bounced around in milliseconds and enabling every aspect of a job to be viewed remotely by anyone and everyone, including clients. Slowly the way we worked began to change from isolated designers running individual projects to a fully integrated system; this had practical and psychological effects. Our studio culture changed. Slowly at first, but over time we adopted a more collaborative and integrated approach to design.

So that individuals didn't feel neglected or usurped by technology, we also invested in professional help and asked an interior designer to draw up some plans to enable us to make the best use of the space. He assisted us to plan important details such as cabling and lighting; creating shared spaces and private spaces; and advised us on access and health and safety legislation. But the bulk of the work was done by my business partner, who had a pragmatic and sensitive approach to what was needed; she had an understanding of the way our studio worked that could never be matched by any external advisor. She made sure that the space planning had a psychological dimension.

But studios are more than workstations. Studios have clients who need meetings and want to review work in progress. Studios need reception areas, kitchens, dining tables and toilets; some need pool tables and bike racks, and not all people who work in design studios are designers; admin staff, receptionists and researchers also need space and equipment. And despite Otl Aicher's admirable desire for total transparency, private areas are also essential. Studios without a room where private meetings can be held are at a disadvantage, yet at the same time, it has to be recognized that closed doors breed suspicion and rumour. Our solution to this question was to have a room that was used for both conventional client meetings and private meetings with staff; this room had a strategically placed glass window through which it was always possible to see what was happening. I also made a point of leaving the door open unless the meeting was genuinely confidential such as a meeting with a sensitive client, a salary review, or the discussion of a personal matter with a member of staff. Leaving the door open and having a window may seem like small gestures, yet they contributed to the overall notion that the studio was an open and unsecretive place.

Every studio, big or small, has to design its space with numerous, often competing, considerations in mind. It doesn't matter if it's a single room or an entire building, if we care about our work then we have to also care about the space our work is done in. Today there is health and safety legislation that if flaunted can lead to penalties; most people insist on working in an environment that has basic amenities – light, fresh air and cleanliness. Furthermore, all of us have an ethical responsibility to run studios that do not damage the environment. And as if all this wasn't enough, we also have to cater for two important and sometimes competing audiences: our clients and ourselves. In other words, human beings.

The people

When I first started hiring designers, I made some terrible mistakes by employing designers purely on the strength of their work. I hired people who had impressive portfolios but whose human characteristics were sometimes less impressive. These were talented people who needed a great deal of maintenance; in other words, they were people who needed to be told what to do.

Telling people what to do doesn't fit with the democratic, non-hierarchical nature of the modern design studio. If you have to constantly remind designers not to stray too far from the brief, or if you have to tell someone to arrive early when the pressure is on, then you've got the wrong person. This doesn't mean that designers shouldn't question briefs, or that it should it be taken for granted that people will turn up early as a matter of course. Designers will avoid self-absorption and will make sacrifices only when they know that their efforts will be acknowledged and rewarded, and if their sense of personal investment in a project is sufficient to create its own momentum. To achieve this, designers need to be self-motivated and they become self-motivated through effective and sensitive leadership and the cultivation of a sense of common purpose. For example, it studio leaders – or business partners – are unwilling to 'share the pain', they can't expect others to share it with them; the boss or partner who walks out of the office at 5.30pm while others carry on working will soon find everyone leaving at 5.30pm. Studio bosses can't act like the bosses of nineteenth-century coalmines and expect to run modern efficient businesses. As the writers of the cult business book *Funky Business*[20] point out: 'The boss is dead. No longer can we believe in a leader who claims to know more about everything and who is always right. Management by numbers is history. Management by fear won't work. If management is people, management must become human management.'

Of course, it is possible to run studios on the autocratic model. There are examples in this book of designers who employ staff purely to assist them in realizing their own personal creative visions. There is nothing wrong with this, so long as anyone entering this autocratic domain knows what to expect from the outset. However, the best design studios work on the assumption that 'the boss is dead', and that the modern design office is a place of mutual respect, relative equality and shared endeavour. In addition, well-run studios know that people become self-motivated when a) they are trusted; b) when their contributions are valued; and c) when their efforts are rewarded.

Let's look more closely at trust, value and reward. What does trust mean in the context of employing designers? In surveys of workplace efficiency, it's a word that appears with unfailing frequency. Workers in all areas of professional life want to be trusted, and they want to trust the people they work for. It means that people have to be allowed to do their work without someone constantly – metaphorically or physically – looking over their shoulder. Until we learn to let people make mistakes and take responsibility for their actions, they will never become self-motivated. It's a view corroborated by Hamish Muir when he talks about working life at 8vo: 'Most of the time the work that resulted from our collaborative approach didn't really suffer from egos and day-to-day arguments. Well, not in the end results. We usually found a way through things; we all knew and accepted that better things would result if ideas were generated, tested and developed in this way. Sometimes we got upset with each other, but

we held to our principles of working as 8vo and not as individuals. It was about learning from each other, and learning from the process. I suppose it was about trusting each other.'

Occasionally, though, I've found that trust requires sacrifices. There have been occasions when I've had to take a stand on behalf of designers rather than take the easy route of backing clients. In well-run studios, this situation shouldn't arise too often, but sometimes, just sometimes, clients behave unreasonably (hard to believe, I know). When this happens, we do everything within our powers to ameliorate the situation. But sometimes, just sometimes, we have to back the people we work with. This has only happened twice in my working life, but on two occasions I've had to trust that the designers working on a project had acted correctly when a client became toxic. I trusted them, so I backed them, with the result that we lost two clients – and money. In compensation, a bond of mutual trust was built that made us all stronger – and, as a small footnote, I should add that one of the clients I refused to back returned as a client shortly after the falling out.

Which brings us to value. Designers, in common with most types of workers, have a perfectly reasonable need to have their exertions and contributions valued. In some cases, this can be an infantile need for flattery and attention, but even the most rational, problem-solving pragmatists crave recognition and possess a need to have their work praised and valued. It is clear, therefore, that withholding praise and failing to show recognition can be one of the most dispiriting forces in the workplace. And it's equally clear that the opposite action – giving praise and showing gratitude – can result in mountains being moved and dragons being slain.

This is not a plea for vacuous flattery. When designers screw up (and we all do from time to time) they need to be told they've screwed up. Ironically, it's easier to tell a designer they've messed up if we've made a point of acknowledging and valuing their previous contributions. This is simple stuff, yet it is alarmingly common to find that people are taken for granted and their work undervalued or ignored. If no one is handing out praise and recognition, it's a safe bet that rancour and dissatisfaction will ensue.

But surely, if designers are handsomely rewarded with large salaries and lots of benefits, none of these problems relating to trust and value will matter a hoot? You'd be forgiven for thinking that cash was enough to keep designers happy, but you'd be wrong. When we employ creative people, we enter into an arrangement where creative fulfilment is often more important than money. I don't want to be starry-eyed about this, or over-

'The great benefit of this [everyone sitting together in a single room] is that you can hear what everybody's saying. I've never written a memo in my life, because everybody knows exactly who I'm talking to and what I'm doing. Everybody here knows everybody's business. If you have a deep sense of privacy I don't think that you could work for me.'

Milton Glaser, Milton Glaser, Inc. (13)

'In the last two years we have started sharing some of the profits at the end of the financial year. The way we do it is by offering our workers opportunities for them to get courses in aspects like photography, 3D design etc. We are planning language courses for next year, if things go well. They are free to choose what they want to learn, but they have to be aspects that we all can benefit from.'

Pablo Juncadella, Mucho (14)

13   14   15   16

'Designers need to keep challenging, but their ideas or opinions often come from a narrow point of view. While they are working in my studio, I ask them to work on my ideas and opinions, and after they leave my studio, they can fly off in any direction they like. I think this is the best way to motivate staff in my studio. On the other hand, I am always hoping my staff will have great futures after leaving my studio. This is a Japanese special custom.'

Hideki Nakajima, Nakajima Design (15)

'The idea of going without pay for a couple of months was more appealing than having to take on dull projects just to pay for the extra staff. We'd always been happy to turn away a project if we didn't feel it would be enjoyable to work on. This is a fine policy for just the two of us, but we couldn't expect an employee to be quite so understanding.'

Jon Forss, Non-Format (16)

'I've become accustomed to working in open space, but really no physical space at all, and in utter disorganization. I can't see my own work over a course of a year (it gets put away) and don't remember a job after it's finished. I have absolutely nothing special in the way of tools, unlike my architect partner Jim Biber, who has really nice pens. If I had nice pens I'd just lose them.'

Paula Scher, Pentagram (17)

'I pretty much discovered everything by trial and error. I think I could have applied for grants and gone to see a lot more designers to ask for advice, but I felt like I couldn't go and ask people for help because they had obviously struggled and fought their own way through to get to where they were.'

James Goggin, Practise (18)

17   18   19   20

'We do a lot of projects that take a significant amount of time with corrections and other implementations. To give an appropriate response, we needed more people. We looked for designers who would feel comfortable being assistants. Actually we have really good ones that enjoy doing that part of the design process, which is very important.'

Lizá Ramalho, R2 (19)

'I've always said that if you're too big to have lunch together, then you're too big. So in London we're still nine or ten people. I never wanted a big, big studio. I didn't want 30 people. But what we decided to do was become a big studio by network.'

Neville Brody, Research Studios (20)

romanticize the creative life – after all, people in most walks of life also crave creative fulfilment. But in this tumultuous era of late capitalism, the desire for creative fulfilment among designers is stronger than ever. Many will forgo opportunities to work in studios where they can earn large salaries producing bland work, preferring instead to join smaller studios where they can do the type of work they most want to do. Others will bravely set up studios with all the inherent pressures and added responsibilities that this entails. None of this means that designers will tolerate being underpaid, or that they don't value money. Rather, it acknowledges the fact that they will always try to balance the need to earn money with the opportunity to do the sort of work that inspires them to get up in the morning. Studios that get the balance right between remuneration and the right sort of work are the ones that prosper.

I said that I didn't want to romanticize the creative life, and it would therefore be misleading to imply that studios – even the best ones – are ever entirely stress-free zones of care-free productivity. Far from it. Compromise, rejection, jealousy, envy and disappointment patrol the design studios of the world, beating up designers who dare to step out of line. As Wim Crouwel notes: 'Designers have by definition great egos. You have to accept a lot without becoming angry. In Total Design we knew the impossible characters of some, and we learned to live with them.'

The psychological hygiene of studios is vital. We need to monitor it constantly, and for me the best way to deal with most, if not all, of the 'psychological' problems of professional life is to constantly acknowledge the contribution of individuals, give designers the sort of work that will inspire them, and give them a salary that reflects their status, achievements and productivity.

The creativity

So – you've streamlined your studio and you've filled it full of happy, shiny, self-motivated people. What next? Do you stand back and watch while your door is trampled down by clients demanding your services? Not quite. Now you have to do the work – and work is king. Everything comes second to the work: personal feelings, personal ambition, even money itself. Especially money. Studios who make money their primary goal end up doing second-rate work for second-rate fees. This is not to say that financial ambition and financial prudence aren't essential. They are: there are no rewards for financial ineptitude. But in my experience, when we put money ahead of the work, the work suffers. Think of all the jobs you've done 'just for the money'. When we look back at these projects, we usually find that they lost us money.

Yet, even when you put the work first, you are not guaranteed great work. You need other things too. You need stamina, energy, talent and – of course – clients. But most of all, you need a vision. A vision? Isn't that something poets and mystics have? Call it what you want – a philosophy, a mission statement, a creed – but you need something you can believe in, and something that clients, staff and partners can also believe in. It's easy to be self-centred about this and say that your vision is to 'win awards', or 'gain a worldwide reputation', or 'appear in the design press'. There is nothing wrong with these ambitions, but what would your clients say if they knew that these were your ambitions? When I had my studio, we had a loose rag-bag of things we believed in. Many of them were as common as grass: creative excellence; faultless service; delivering results. But there was one overriding 'vision' that we all shared. It was something we talked about among ourselves, but it was also something we could stand up and tell our clients about.

We believed that we could achieve the outcomes that our clients desired by avoiding formulaic responses. What do I mean by this? If, for example, a client came to us and showed us the work that their competitors were doing and suggested that we 'do something like this', we'd politely suggest looking elsewhere for a starting point. We explained that our philosophy was always to find new ways of doing things. We did this partly for selfish reasons (no one likes going over the same old ground), but also for reasons of effectiveness. We'd point out to clients that there was more leverage and greater benefits to be had by going for calculated difference rather than sticking with generic sameness. They didn't always agree with us, but many did and in most cases we were proved right.

Creativity is dependent on countless factors, many of them discussed in the pages that follow. Increasingly, one of those factors is the ethical dimension. In recent decades, graphic design has subjected itself to theoretical self-scrutiny, a rigorous period of self-analysis that has its roots in cultural theory, political radicalism and aesthetic politics. But many designers were unmoved by this bout of introspection. These were designers who had entered a profession where servicing clients and solving the problems of others were their sole objectives. For them, the designer was a hired gun who did the client's bidding without demur or comment, or the need for self-expression.

Yet for others, a new set of values and considerations had entered design's bloodstream, and they began to question the role of the designer. Some found the notion of the designer as mute foot soldier in the warzone of consumerism and corporatism to be distasteful. This is not the place to test the merits of either view, but what is undeniable is that an ethical and questioning spirit has entered graphic design where once it had lapped at its outer shores. Its effect can be seen in the rise of social design and citizen designers; it also marks a trend in Western cultures where, after nearly three decades of the predominance of the view that the consumer's needs are all that matters, the notion of working for the 'common good' is making a hesitant comeback. It's a theme brilliantly developed by Michael Sandel, the political philosopher and Harvard professor, in his 2009 Reith Lecture. Sandel calls for an end to illusory market triumphalism and the discovery of a better kind of politics. He says: 'the better kind of politics we need is a politics oriented less to the pursuit of individual self-interest and more to the pursuit of the common good.'

As this notion takes root within the culture, and there is growing evidence that it is, then the design studio of the future will be different from its predecessors. This, and other seismic shifts in global culture – the rise of digital technology, for example – will change the nature of being a graphic designer, which in turn means that creativity and the way studios are run will change too. In fact, the traditional studio is already undergoing a radical overhaul. In a few years from now, it might be unrecognizable from the current models. In a conversation with Ellen Lupton[21], the design writer David Barringer[22] envisaged a new sort of studio: 'I can see a model in which, say, a magazine needs a team to collaborate on its next issue. They need a designer, a photographer and a writer for one or several articles. No one is on staff. They are all freelancers. Using an online find-and-track database, a team co-ordinator could assemble teams in Dallas, Detroit and Dubai. Each team meets to research, photograph and even design the print/web pages, submits the work, gets paid and then disbands. Each freelancer awaits the next call from a new team leader, who also may be a freelancer. It's cheap, flexible, temporary labour leveraged by computer technology, and it can be used for editorial, business or creative outlets, for magazines, books, newspapers, online ventures, whatever.'[23]

This model of the 'virtual' studio already exists. It is now common for a single studio to be based in more than one location. The Anglo-Norwegian design duo Non-Format (see pages 152–161) work in two locations, Kjell Ekhorn in London, UK; Jon Forss in Minnesota, US. To their clients, it hardy seems to matter where Ekhorn and Forss are based. Using the new communications technology, Non-Format are able to work as efficiently as if they were still in the same room that they occupied when they first started out.

Universal Everything (see pages 238–245) also operates on a radical new model. Creative director Matt Pyke is based in his garden in Sheffield, yet works with a global network of talented practitioners producing varied and technically demanding work. Pyke's only full-time employee is a project manger who is also based remotely. Universal Everything thrives as clients from all over the world tap into this fizzing network of talent and skill.

What Non-Format and Universal Everything make clear is that new ways of running studios will continue to emerge – just as they always have done. This change will be primarily driven by technology, but also by cultural forces such as the return to a focus on community rather than consumerism; changes in the way clients do business; changes in the way design school graduates view their career options; the rise of green politics; and new employment law.

But a final note of caution: if the studio of today is destined to mutate into new hybrid forms, I'd like to make a plea for one vital element of studio life to be maintained. I'm talking about an aspect of studio life that is rarely commented on, but which nearly everyone who has worked in one will understand. I'm talking about humour. This really is one of the great unsung resources of studio life. The prevalence of humour as one of the vitalizing forces in design studios has something to do with the superior powers of observation that designers often have. After all, most humour is to do with observation and the ability to see what other people miss – which, when you think about it, is a good definition of what the graphic designer does in his or her professional life.

I began this introduction by saying that I've visited lots of studios. I've worked in a few, too, and humour has been a near constant factor everywhere. In the modern graphic design studio, wit and verbal sharpness are as common as bookshelves and mousemats, and if they are eradicated from the studios of the future, the life of the designer will be impoverished. Laughter is the real secret behind the secret life of the studio.
—

Thanks to Wim Crouwel and Hamish Muir for their comments, made in conversations with the editors.

1 Intro, London design group founded by Adrian Shaughnessy and Katy Richardson. See page 197.

2 Design Dictionary (Perspectives on Design Terminology), Michael Erlhoff and Tim Marshall (eds.), Birkhauser Verlag AG, 2007.

3 Paul Rand (1914–1996), American graphic designer best known for his corporate logo designs.

4 Alan Fletcher (1931–2006), British graphic designer described in his Daily Telegraph obituary as 'the most highly regarded graphic designer of his generation, and probably one of the most prolific.'

5 Otl Aicher (1922–1991), leading German graphic designer. Co-founded Hochschule für Gestaltung in Ulm (HfG; Ulm School of Design) in 1953. Best known for work as head designer for the 1972 Munich Olympics and creating the first Olympic mascot.

6 8vo (Octavo), London-based graphic design firm formed in 1985 by Simon Johnston, Mark Holt and Hamish Muir. Closed in 2001.

7 Hamish Muir, British graphic designer, founding principal of 8vo, editor of *Octavo*, teacher and lecturer.

8 Studio Boggeri, founded in 1924 by violinist and photographer Antonio Boggeri. Pioneer of modernism in Italy. Swiss designer Max Huber joined in 1940.

9 Total Design, highly influential Amsterdam design group formed by Wim Crouwel, Benno Wissing and industrial designer Friso Kramer in 1963.

10 Pentagram, eminent design group formed in 1972 in London by Alan Fletcher, Theo Crosby, Colin Forbes, Kenneth Grange and Mervyn Kurlansky. See page 163.

11 Forbes, Fletcher and Gill, forerunner of Pentagram. Founded in 1962 by Colin Forbes, Alan Fletcher and Bob Gill.

12 GGK (Gerstner/Gredinger/Kutter), begun in 1959 when Karl Gerstner and Markus Kutter founded the agency Gerstner + Kutter. The company became GGK when architect Paul Gredinger joined.

13 Francis Bacon (1909–1992), Irish figurative painter.

14 Taken from the book *The World as Design* by Otl Aicher, Ernst & Sohn, 1994. First published as *Die Welt als Entwurf*.

15 Massimo Vignelli, Italian-born designer, founded Vignelli Associates, working for clients such as IBM and American Airlines.

16 *Vignelli: From A to Z* by Massimo Vignelli, Images Publishing, 2007.

17 Lella Vignelli, born Udine, Italy, received a degree from the School of Architecture, University of Venice, and became a registered architect in 1962.

18 Arnaldo Pomodoro, Italian sculptor, born 1926.

19 www.designcouncil.org.uk/en/About-Design/Research/The-Business-of-Design2/Size-and-shape-of-the-design-industry/.

20 *Funky Business: Talent Makes Capital Dance* by Jonas Ridderstrale and Kjell Nordström, Pearson Education, 2000.

21 Ellen Lupton, writer, curator and graphic designer.

22 David Barringer, author, graphic designer, photographer and artist.

23 www.designobserver.com/archives/entry.html?id=39677.

'The great conundrum with new studios is that you don't have a body of work and therefore putting together a portfolio is difficult. In the early days, I was so embarrassed by the thinness of our portfolio that I developed ways of talking about the work without the need to show it.'

Adrian Shaughnessy, ShaughnessyWorks (21)

'Spin works as a collective entity; everyone who works or has worked at Spin has every reason to feel a sense of connection and ownership with the successes that have made it what it is. Every job we undertake is a Spin job and is credited as such, it is pretty fundamental to the way we work. Spin projects always have a number of fingerprints on them. Designers here do occasional lectures and talk to the design press, but in the end we all have to put our ego and our effort into the collective Spin pot.'

Tony Brook, Spin (22)

21   22   23   24

'There is a lot of discussion in our studio and also criticism about wrong design decisions during our testing of how a specific idea should work. This also includes my work.'

Markus Weisbeck, Surface (23)

'I think it's important that people see you as a model, as a point of reference. They have to really want to work with you. It's a matter of esteem. Unfortunately I'm not in the office often, but I speak with everyone by phone and not only about work, but about the lectures I give, and the ones that I attend, and about the international designers I know. We also organize exhibitions and lectures in the studio.'

Leonardo Sonnoli, Tassinari/Vetta (24)

'For the record, we did not receive one new business call as a result [of publishing a studio monograph]. The same is true when I received the AIGA Chicago fellow and the AIGA national medal. The same was true when I was inducted into the AGI fraternity/sorority. These successes and publications do more to stay within design's discourse than to land business. I must say, however, to hear my existing clients boast that they are working with a published and recognized designer is heartwarming.'

Rick Valicenti, Thirst (25)

'We were approached by a much larger global agency that wanted to buy into our culture. It was tempting to gain that foundation, but any resistance from us in growth would have been met by the needs of the agency's backers to make their investment grow, so we declined the offer. I'm opposed to the traditional model of expansion, gaining staff and offices – clients become needed just to keep it afloat.'

Matt Pyke, Universal Everything (26)

25   26   27   28

'I began my career in academia, so I can't say that I thought I would be leading a studio in the office sense – perhaps a classroom studio. I've always practised design, mostly for cultural clients, so the transition from being a tenured professor to the Walker wasn't the huge leap it appeared to be. The leadership skills one picks up in teaching have worked remarkably well in the design studio.'

Andrew Blauvelt, Walker Art Center (27)

'Talent-spotting is an ongoing process. People tend to stay with us for quite a long time so new spots don't open up all that often. But since we also use a number of freelancers we are always looking for new people to work with. They key is finding people who are extremely self-motivated, who are willing to make mistakes then learn from them and improve.'

Brett Foraker, 4Creative (28)

A Practice For Everyday Life
Founded: 2003
Personnel: 4, plus interns
Location: London, UK
www.apracticeforeverydaylife.com

A Practice for Everyday Life (APFEL)
comprises Kirsty Carter (director), Emma
Thomas (director), Louise Ramsay (studio
manager) and Stephen Osman (designer).
The studio was formed by Carter and Thomas
after they met and collaborated at the Royal
College of Art in London. The famous school,
the only wholly postgraduate university of
art and design in the world, has a successful
track record in preparing students for
working life by encouraging them to mix
professional assignments with course work.

After forming APFEL, Carter and Thomas
quickly established a reputation within the
UK cultural sector for their sharply modern
typographic sensibility. They produce graphic
communication that is coolly dispassionate
and devoid of the showy sleight-of-hand
that has characterized traditional ideas-
led design in past decades. They came to
the attention of many commentators with
their intelligent redesign of the magazine *The
Architects' Journal*.

The interview was conducted by email.
—

Could you give us an idea of the background
to you setting up APFEL?

Kirsty Carter: Emma Thomas and I met at the
Royal College of Art in 2001 while studying
for our Master of Arts in Graphic Design.
We shared studio space as well and became
close friends. The first year we worked on our
own. Coming straight from our undergraduate
degrees, we had our own individual reasons
for being there. But as we both developed as
designers we looked up to and took invaluable
advice from each other, through discussion
in the studio as well as from other people we
were studying with. We gradually began to
work on a few projects together, both live
briefs and personal self-initiated works.
At this point our visual languages were very
different, but we were working with similar
research materials and ideas to form the
basis of a project – both of us were and are
enormously interested in contemporary art.
I think even at this point we always knew that
we would end up working in this area. So our
common interest and different skills set us
on the way to some great collaborations.

By the time the course was coming to an end
and we were about to put on our graduate
show, we realized that it made total sense
to carry on this working relationship and
our tutors encouraged this too. I think they
always knew we both had the same ambition
and enthusiasm to make our own studio
happen, and on top of all that we worked

brilliantly together. I remember at some points there was this really amazing feeling that we were going to conquer the world — to this day that is the most powerful feeling you get in a business partnership. You share everything; the ups and the downs, and that is wonderful and exciting. I know I wouldn't have achieved the same on my own without Emma. We encourage, even push each other, to do things that we wouldn't do if we didn't have the other person there.

There is a long tradition at the Royal College of Art of postgraduate students taking on live projects while still at the College — did you do this?

Yes we did. Emma and I were not the richest students so we had to do this to subsidize our studies. It makes sense (when you are at that stage in your education) to make money through graphic design rather than any other part-time job. It was also a great way to gain practical experience of print and project management, with the help of tutors around to advise and help with these live projects. It was about keeping a balance of both live and personal work as we weren't there to start our professional careers, but to develop a process of working.

A key live project for us was a publication called *Leftover*. It was for the curating students at Goldsmith's College and remains a very important project for us, as it was the first time Emma and I collaborated together at the Royal College, as well as being a fundamental project in getting the studio going. There were six curating students working with us on it; they all graduated the year before we did, in 2001, and went to work in different art institutions across the country. They then became some of our first clients; Miria Swain, who then became assistant curator at Modern Art Oxford, commissioned us to do the invitations and leaflets for a three-year exhibition series called 'ARRIVALS'. It was jointly run by Modern Art Oxford and Turner Contemporary (a new museum in Margate that architect David Chipperfield has been commissioned to build) and culminated with a large publication in 2007. The project had many links to other key clients with whom we have a continuing working relationships. Rob Tufnell, who worked for Turner Contemporary, left and started his own gallery, Ancient & Modern. We designed their brand and continue to design all of their printed material, giving the gallery a very distinctive identity. It is still referenced today by many other clients as a project that made them notice us and often want replicated, which obviously we wouldn't do!

It's a big step setting up a studio; how did you feel about it at the time?

It didn't feel like a big step when we decided to go ahead and do it. It just felt like a

01 |
02 |

01/02/ Project: Performa 05/07.
Date: Nov 2005/2007. Client: Performa,
New York. Designers: Kirsty Carter,
Emma Thomas and Stephen Osman.

natural progression. But very shortly after starting it, it became quite overwhelming. We had never worked for anyone before and no one gave us a manual on how to do things. It is such a steep learning curve and you can never anticipate all the things you need to know; the business side of the company is something that you struggle to learn, but you can only learn as you do it. It is an ongoing learning curve, to be honest; a business goes through many stages as it grows, so there are times of ease when you think you have things under control and then suddenly you are onto the next stage – for example, when you need to employ staff or take on larger projects. Suddenly the help you think you are getting brings a whole new set of challenges to overcome and you have to quickly learn how to facilitate those.

Did you have a vision of how you wanted your studio to be?

We wanted a studio that allowed us to design with our own vision, without being compromised by working for someone else. We had a clear idea of what we wanted to do and the type of client we wanted to work for, so the logical conclusion was to form our own studio and then we would be able to grow in our own direction. We wanted to go on a journey that would excite and challenge us. Each person joining APFEL along the way would add another element and perspective, so there would be other strands and other disciplines, all travelling in many directions but all coming from the same school of thought. That's why we didn't call the studio by our names; we even wanted it to be able to exist without us, for nobody to have a sense of individual ownership.

Where does the name come from?

It was taken from a book called *The Practice of Everyday Life* by Michel de Certeau[1], in which de Certeau describes his way of making sense of the city with eyes open, collecting materials, drawing together stories. We liked the reference of 'practice' as a habit, exercise and pursuit. These practices were the basis of how we wanted APFEL to work.

Where did you go for help and advice?

We were really lucky that we had a good group of people that we could speak to for advice and put questions to – colleagues, peers, critics, business seniors, ex-tutors, friends and family. Most of what we have learnt business-wise has come through discussing ideas together, the process of getting on with things, and making mistakes along the way. The most important thing we did was write a business plan. We downloaded various templates from the internet to give us a start. What the plan did for us was make us ask ourselves some really tough questions, the toughest being what would we do if the

studio didn't work out? How the work would be duplicated? What would happen to our clients? What would happen to the studio's name? It seems so strange to talk about these things before we had even started. But we needed to know if we were thinking along the same lines before embarking on probably one of the biggest commitments each of us had ever made.

Did you employ designers from the start?

We only employed Stephen [Osman] two years ago, and didn't bring many interns into the studio at first, even though from early on we had many requests. I suppose Emma and I didn't feel ready to have interns with us here in the studio; we didn't feel ready to teach and guide them, as we were still consumed and focused on getting the studio up and running. When we did get the first interns into the studio, we had them stay a while. Our first employee, Stephen, started with us as an intern and is still with us now. As we grew, we realized that even with just one other designer, the studio would move on leaps and bounds. However, just through having Stephen and an intern in the studio, we realized we were designing less and less as individuals. It's important for Emma and I to continue practising our greatest passion and skill, doing what we are best at – designing.

You also employed a studio manager – small design groups often delay this until they are bigger. What prompted you to employ someone in this role?

We wanted someone who could help with production, management, administration – and we found that Louise [Ramsay] was perfect for this role (we stole her from a client – she was head of the design studio at the Tate). I don't think you can force finding the right person for your studio or even the right role, you just meet people along the way and these people bring their own skills into the studio environment. Along the way we have learnt to have a more open studio, bring people in to work with us, and if everything fits, they stay. Louise has her own set of skills that are different from ours. She has taken some responsibilities away from Emma and I, and has also added a whole lot more to run a smoother, better and more enjoyable studio.

How did you find clients when you started out?

We thought of all the projects that we would really like to do, wrote a wish list, and actually sent packages to some of them, not asking for work, but just making contact. We didn't get one single project at the time from doing that! But actually, we have since worked with many of them. The process of word of mouth is the most effective. We would meet people through other people, whether it was friends we studied with at the RCA, or tutors who had taught us there. One of APFEL's first breakthroughs (which led us to work with many people within the culture sector) was our long working relationship with the Institute of Contemporary Arts in London. We worked closely with the director of exhibitions, Jens Hoffmann, until 2007. Our working relationship began in 2004, working on 'Becks Futures 2005'. From this great success and enjoyable working relationship we then went on to work on 14 different exhibitions (basically every exhibition from 2005 till 2007). This included the invite, poster design, publication, signage and the exhibition design.

This kind of long, ongoing collaboration with a curator not only got us noticed and allowed us to work on many projects with really great artists, but also illustrated how we could work with an individual and an institution on a level of complete trust; this is something you can only develop over time with a client. We had a lot of creative freedom, as we developed a way of working with the curatorial team at the ICA that was inspiring and challenging. It definitely allowed us to develop a body of work that we were proud of, and marked a certain pathway for our work, both in the quality of our design and the clients we wanted to work with.

Could you tell us about your working process?

When we start on a project, much of the creative thinking is done together directly after a briefing, usually when a project is still fresh. We talk about how the project could work. Sometimes what we discuss becomes clear in our minds soon after that initial briefing. We'll talk through ideas, how they might develop, what our research points can be, and one of us begins working on the project. After a day or two, we sit down together and talk further, looking at where the design is at. This process of working, talking, then reworking continues.

Often we shift projects around so that each of us has input from the other, and the right balance – even to the extent that the project may have been bounced back and forth around the studio before one designer takes the lead. It is difficult for us to pin-point exactly what those touches are, but sometimes we think, OK, it needs a bit more Kirsty, a bit more Emma, or Stephen. Even sometimes, 'OK, it needs a bit more of someone else entirely outside of the studio.'

Can you give an example of how an outside collaboration might work?

As we are now working on larger projects, it allows us a little more budgetary freedom to commission people outside our studio; recently we did the design for an art fair in Dubai called Art Dubai. We commissioned

photographers Adam Broomberg and Oliver Chanarin to shoot a series of images for the advertising campaign and signage for the fair. It was so exciting; it was the first time in our six years of existence that we had the opportunity to commission photography directly for use in a project. We had commissioned photography in some shape or form in the past, i.e. for The Architects' Journal. But it was slightly different, as we weren't designing the magazine on a weekly basis. We were there in the process of designing the first issue and we helped Sarah Douglas (the then art director) to persuade the publisher to give us the budget to commission photography in future issues rather than relying on photography supplied by architects. This sounds minor but for us it was a major breakthrough; we wanted the magazine to have more of a considered and cohesive feel, and you can only do this when you bring some visual consistency through imagery rather than just typography.

Because the majority of projects we have worked on are usually with visual artists, the use of photography (or even illustration), other than installation photography, has not really been required. This has meant that much of our work was very typographic. So, Art Dubai was a major turning point in our studio. We are so proud of what we have produced.

Did you have a print portfolio to back up your website?

Yes! Most definitely, our portfolio of printed work offers much more insight than our website. Being print lovers, much of our work has an 'object' quality to it; you understand it when you hold it, as often process is really important. Especially as much of our work has a pared-back aesthetic, the project only comes to life when you hold the object, whether it is an invite or a publication.

How are things at APFEL structured? How would you define your roles?

Emma and I take the lead on different projects, but the whole APFEL studio has an input into everything. Louise is there to glue it all together and Stephen is there to contribute his brilliant design skills. Obviously Emma and I are often out and about having the conversations, meeting everyone, gathering a clear vision on what the client wants and what APFEL's ideas are. We then relay this back to the studio (I suppose, like editors, we can process what is needed quicker, rather than getting Louise and Stephen in at this stage). The next stage, after the whole studio has discussed and brainstormed the project and we have the go-ahead, is for Louise to structure it all – to do design and production schedules and check to see if our ideas are feasible within the time and budget. She also manages the client and gets information out of them. Having an overview of all our schedules, Louise also helps Emma and I manage Stephen and any freelancers or interns that are in the studio. We try to keep them up to date on all projects – we think it is important that everyone feels involved and knows what APFEL is up to as a whole and can feel a sense of ownership and involvement. We do this by having weekly meetings and discussing what everyone is working on. This can change minute to minute, so sometimes it is hard to keep everyone up to date!

Going back to our working process and how we are structured, I suppose what I am trying to say is that behind the scenes we really all do get involved. However, one single person has to be the main point of contact with the client, otherwise it can get really confusing for them. But within the studio we all have a say, and that is right until the moment it goes to print. If one of us doesn't like something then of course the project would not leave the studio. Each project feels like all of us, and we all celebrate together when the project has finished, whether it's at the private view, at lunch or a drink together outside the studio.

How have you found it being an employer?

We all really enjoy having a team of us in the studio! Especially Emma and I, as for so long it was just the two of us. Even though we are the best of friends and love each other dearly, we perhaps could have sent each other crazy if we had been alone too much longer. Every person brings a new character to the party that changes the dynamics and can make more things possible.

Have you considered expanding your business?

Yes, and we are. We've been very fortunate in finding Stephen and now Louise. When we took Stephen on, we were looking for a designer to help in the studio, and then it got to the point where for every project there was so much admin, production, etc, involved that we really needed someone who was multifaceted – able to assist in the running of the studio, as well as print management and administration. However, I think there is a limit to how big a design studio can grow before it morphs into a different creature. I can imagine that above six to eight people the studio would start to fragment. Considering the fact that we like to work in a very collaborative way, it just wouldn't work for us, or be APFEL any more; we would become more hands-off, just managers. Perhaps the optimum size for us is as many of us as can fit round one table to have those initial APFEL studio discussions and brainstorms.

03/04/ Project: Art Dubai 09 (art fair). Date: Mar 2009. Client: Art Dubai, London & Dubai. Designers: Kirsty Carter, Emma Thomas and Stephen Osman. Photographers: Adam Broomberg and Oliver Chanarin.

05 | 06 | 07 |
08 | 09 |

05/06/07/08/09/ Project: Turner Prize 2008. Date: Sep 2008–Jan 2009.
Client: Tate Britain, London. Designers: Kirsty Carter, Emma Thomas and Stephen Osman.
10/11/12/13/ Project: Art Dubai 09 (art fair). Date: Mar 2009. Client: Art Dubai, London
& Dubai. Designers: Kirsty Carter, Emma Thomas and Stephen Osman.
Photographers: Adam Broomberg and Oliver Chanarin. 14/15/ Project: *The Architects'*
Journal redesign and branding. Date: April 2005. Art Direction: APFEL. Art Editor: Sarah
Douglas. 16/17/18/ Project: Happy Hypocrite. Date: Spring/Summer 2008 – Spring/
Summer 2009. Editor: Maria Fusco. Publisher: Bookworks, London. Designers: Kirsty
Carter, Emma Thomas and Stephen Osman.

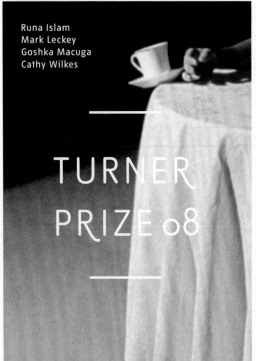

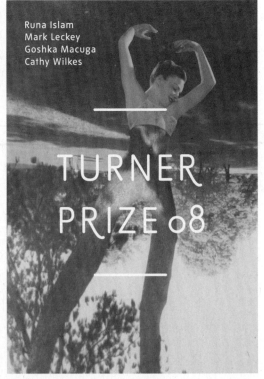

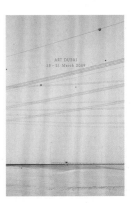

AJ

30.06.05
TONY FRETTON

ISSN 0003-8466

£3.25

THE ARCHITECTS' JOURNAL WWW.AJPLUS.CO.UK

AJ

02.02.06
GM + AD/
CLYDEBANK

ISSN 0003-8466

£3.25

THE ARCHITECTS' JOURNAL WWW.AJPLUS.CO.UK

LINGUISTIC
HARDCORE

HUNTING
AND
GATHERING

What would you say was the worst part of running a studio?

First, being responsible for all the administration of the business. We are so happy to now have help with this, and managing projects and production. Second, and perhaps more importantly, the emotional attachment you have to the business. This is a massive joy and has emotional highs, but there is also the feeling of responsibility you have towards the people that work for you, your clients, the production people who you are working with, and wondering whether the design and business decisions you are making are right. We discuss everything in our studio and try to be as transparent as we can about every aspect of how it is running, so every one of us is responsible in some shape or form for all the important decisions, but the buck will always end with Emma and me. It would be easy to be overwhelmed by the responsibility, so although it is never far from our minds – we always need to keep on our toes – we always keep positive. As my dad would say, 'cream always rises to the top' in these hard times!

And the best?

Being responsible for our own business and the extra satisfaction that the work we produce is born from the studio that we started – choosing the work we do and how we do it, working directly with clients. We actually enjoy the business side too. It's really satisfying to create work that is our own vision and feel that as a studio we are making a great impact on design, producing great graphic design that is respected and making a difference for our generation and hopefully for generations to come.

Do you have any issues maintaining the balance between creativity and profitability?

As we develop the studio, our projects are getting larger, we are learning more, so are able to be more efficient with each process from designing to invoicing, which I guess slowly helps us be more profitable! We are constantly taking on new challenges that keep us on our creative toes, and we now have quite a few regular clients, which means that we are able to keep a good constant flow of work. We really do enjoy the work that we do, and have never had to take on a project that we disagree with just to pay the bills.

Do you socialize together?

Yes we do – we share many friends; many are people we work with or have worked with in the past.

What is your attitude to interns?

We usually have an intern in the studio and they stay two or three months, or longer in some cases. Piero Glina, a great designer, was with us as an intern for four months as part of his course at Karlsruhe and he then freelanced for us for another two months during his summer holidays. Interns learn a lot from being in a studio as small as ours; they have to get stuck in, and get to do some really creative work rather than just making the tea! It is all part of a designer's education to do internships; Emma and I worked at several places while we were students. We really appreciate their assistance, but for the first months you really put a lot of energy into teaching them and them learning from you. We think there is an invaluable exchange going on, but we would never exploit this. Any good intern is up to scratch after a few months, so we then either have to say goodbye, or take them on as a freelancer or employ them. We've had some really great interns. As I mentioned, that's how Stephen started with us.

You do a lot of work for cultural organizations; are there any particular issues involved in this sector?

The budget is usually lower than working for other clients, so we have to keep a certain pace of work. We are often asked to pitch for free, because they are cultural sector clients, but because most of our work is for this area, we can't afford to do that. We don't have one client with a big budget that effectively pays for the studio. But the projects that we do and the variety of work offers us a certain independence and flexibility. We are working on projects that we find interesting, with people we admire, collecting together a group of like-minded individuals that can grow with each recommendation. Working with cultural organizations, we often find that we are working on more common ground, with people who have an understanding of what we are doing and why we are doing it.

Is there any advice you would give to anyone thinking of setting up?

'Work Hard and Be Nice to People.' Anthony Burrill's quote sums it up for us. Anthony is our graphic design dad; we did several collaborations together as APFEL|AB. Anthony was fundamental to us at the beginning; he was full of encouragement to us both and always got us involved in some shape or form. All of our work is born out of a conversation or recommendation by someone.

We found the process of writing a business plan before starting APFEL invaluable. It makes you think pragmatically and rationally about how the studio will work, and to consider and discuss all sorts of eventualities. We also applied for a loan from the Prince's Trust[2] as soon as we left the Royal College of Art; not only was the money a real help, but they also set us up with a business mentor who was a really good sounding board for all sorts of questions we had in the first two years of business. In

2004, a few months after working from my flat, we also won a grant from the Clerkenwell Green Association, a charity set up to help designers for the first 18 months of new business. The grant provides money towards the cost of taking on a studio (the first two years for free and then half-price afterwards), plus a package of business support and advice.

Do you have a music policy for the studio?

Not a policy, but we are keeping on the tradition we started a few years ago of the 'Friday Banger'; exchanging songs with our friends that pick you up on a Friday afternoon. The only rule is that it has to be a 'Banger' – I think that's probably self-explanatory.

How important is the physical environment you work in?

It's really important. We have now outgrown our studio. We were keeping our overheads really low for years, but now we are four people (five with an intern) it is too small. We did outgrow it quite a few years ago but just couldn't leave. It is important to keep overheads as low as possible, but with our business expanding, a move to a larger studio is absolutely necessary. We have found a great new space to move into in April. It's a really bright space, with a garden in the middle and an interesting set up – we are going to be part of a small community of photographers, artists and a publisher in a studio off Princelet Street in East London. We are so happy to move on and have more creative people around us; our studio at the moment is very much a closed door with little contact with our neighbours, but this space is far more open plan and has a communal meeting area that we will share with the other people.

Should all studios have a quiet area for work and contemplation?

We are and still want to be working around one big table – it's important to be able to talk to each other while we are working and share ideas, it is not a solitary process. We have one table with all our computers on at the moment, then a meeting/lunch table on its own where we also cut up and mock up presentations. In the new studio we have designed one big table, but also a separate cutting table and lightbox and then the meeting table is in a whole separate room. Because we are only four people, the studio never gets so raucous that you can't concentrate, although we are looking forward to being able to take a walk or sit in the garden and read or contemplate alone, and get away from the computers.

Note: Since this interview was conducted, the studio off-Princelet Street I mentioned above has fallen through. We are still 'In search of the Incredulous'[3]. The photographs of the studio included with this interview are of a space on Boundry Street in East London. We will share it with a gallery we work closely with. The gallery will be on the ground/shop floor and APFEL on the 1st and top floor (all subject to contract).

1 Michel de Certeau (1925–1986), a French Jesuit and scholar.

2 Prince's Trust is charitable body formed by Prince Charles to help young people. Offers training, skill building, personal development and study support outside school, as well as business loans and grants.

3 Douglas Gordon, *In Search of the Incredulous, in The Studio*, ed. Jens Hoffmann & Christina Kennedy, Dublin City Gallery The Hugh Lane, 2006. A project by Douglas Gordon, where he photographed every studio he went to look at in NYC for many years without finding anywhere he would want to move into.

Atelier David Smith
Founded: 2000
Personnel: 2 designers plus interns
and associates
Location: Dublin, Ireland
www.atelier.ie

Atelier David Smith is described by its
founder as a 'workshop – a place to think
and make'. Based in Dublin, Smith and his
associate Oran Day work for many of Ireland's
leading cultural organizations. Their work –
mainly books and catalogues – exhibits an
abundance of typographic refinement. It is
the work of designers with a firm grasp of
graphic design's formal traditions, but who
also reveal a modern sensibility informed by
the upheavals that have taken place in visual
communication in recent decades.

Smith formed Atelier David Smith after
a European education that exposed him
to the powerful intellectual currents in
contemporary academia. Today he combines
professional life with teaching at IADT (Dun
Laoghaire Institute of Art, Design and
Technology) in Dublin. For Smith, teaching and
maintaining a studio are inseparable: 'I don't
distinguish between being a teacher and a
designer – I have a desire to teach, and a
need to make.'

The interview took place via email.
–

Could you talk about your experience prior
to setting up your studio?

David Smith: Before establishing the studio,
my immediate experience had been with
UNA[1] (Amsterdam). My time at UNA followed
my graduate studies at the ANRT (l'Atelier
Nationale de Recherche Typographique) in
Paris. Prior to doing my postgrad I had briefly
worked in an advertising agency as a junior
designer, which was a chastening experience.
I left the ad agency within a year and at
22/23 years of age I was fortunate to be
able to work independently for clients in the
fashion and music sectors. I was art director
of an independent style magazine that in
attitude and ambition was akin to British
style mags such as *The Face*, *ID* and *Dazed
and Confused*, but without the same level of
influence. At the same time I was also house
designer for a small independent record label
and did design and production for Ireland's
leading music promoter. It was great fun – the
money, the social life – but the work was a bit
too cool and I tired of it quickly. So I did my
homework and opted for the ANRT and went to
study in Paris in 1997.

What was the catalyst that made you set up
your studio?

I returned to Dublin seeking a mentor to bring
me on a bit more, or at least an opportunity
that would allow me to exercise some of my

new thinking and approaches, but which would also provide me with a grounding in running a studio and a business. I mail-bombed all the major studios in Dublin and I got a lukewarm response. However, the few individuals that did take the time to view the work were remarkably positive in one sense, but also quite unsure as to where my type of work and experience fitted in with what they were doing. I had offers to provide typographic master classes, be a surrogate creative director, and be a part time creative and production consultant, but no job offers. It was then that I realized that if I wanted to practise in a way that was faithful to, and consistent with, my European experience, I would have to work independently – not as a freelancer – and develop my own project opportunities.

How did you feel about it at the time; was it daunting?

The most daunting aspect of setting up was the financial side. I had no desire to continue working from the spare room and I needed to have a dedicated space to work and think in. Fortunately, Deirdre Mallon, a former classmate, had recently returned from London and was thinking of going it alone. We decided to pool our resources and get a space to work in, and if we had the opportunity to collaborate we would.

Did you have any clients in place?

No. We both had some teaching hours to keep the wolf from the door. But we eventually got a lucky break when a friend of mine recommended us to the curator of a large public art project in the west of Ireland. We suddenly had six months' work and a client who was open-minded and responsive to our ideas and proposals. Despite the success and breadth of that project our hit rate for new work was still pretty abysmal and things remained hand-to-mouth for the first year or so. Eventually, Deirdre decided to pursue a career as a visual artist, leaving the design studio to me.

Did you have a distinct idea about the kind of work you wanted to do?

It was always going to be typography and print – typographic design.

Initially I had ambitions to do these huge complex information projects. Pure typography. But there were no such projects being undertaken here in Dublin, and the likelihood of an independent studio getting such work was non-existent. I naively pursued a number of complex information design projects including the redesign and development of a new typeface for the Irish phone book, the design of the Dublin Bus timetable, and a typeface design for the city's nascent lightrail system – all to no avail.

01 |
02 |
03 |
04 |

01/ Project: House Projects Books. Date: 2007. Client: Gavin Murphy/House Projects. Designer: David Smith. 02/ Project: Space For Art – Sligo County Council Arts Plan. Date: 2007. Client: Sligo County Council Arts Office. Designer: David Smith. Aerial Photography: Gerry O'Leary, Ordnance Survey Ireland. 03/ Project: Blake and Sons. Date: 2006. Client: Lewis Glucksman Gallery. Designer: David Smith. Editor: René Zechlin. 04/ Project: IMMA Artists' Panel Report 2005/2006. Date: 2006. Client: Irish Museum of Modern Art. Designers: Oran Day and David Smith. Photography; Irish Museum of Modern Art.

Which studios and designers influenced you?

The two-and-a-half-year period (1997–2000) in Paris and Amsterdam shaped and informed much of what I practise today. Hans Bockting[2] and Will de l'Ecluse[3] at UNA and Peter Keller[4], Jean Widmer[5] and Hans Jurg Hunzicker[6] at ANRT marked and inspired me in diverse ways. I had always been 'into' design, but they made me serious about the practice of design. It wasn't always their work that I liked but what I appreciated was the rigour, interrogation and quality that was apparent in everything they did. In Dublin, Niall Sweeney[7] was a friend and an influence. He was, and still is, the most singular designer of his generation; I had the good fortune to be taught by him and work alongside him for a brief time. Obviously I had favourites that impressed me from afar – Studio Dumbar[8], Karel Martens[9], Anton Stankowski[10], Wolfgang Weingart[11] and 8vo (Octavo)[12]. But having to choose, I would have to say that the work of Bruno Monguzzi[13] and Jost Hochuli[14], and the writings of Norman Potter[15] have been among the most enduring of influences.

When setting up your studio, did you seek any help or advice?

No. We were very naïve – no business plan or strategy for new business. It was quite a while before I realized I needed to pay more attention to the business side and it remains one of my weaknesses.

Did you have to borrow money?

We were fortunate that we both had our own kit and we pooled a small amount each to secure the lease, and that was it. To this day I haven't borrowed on the studio – I'm not sure if this is just prudence or an aversion to risk.

This is a recurring theme in these interviews – designers seem to have an aversion to financial risk. Do you think financial risk-taking runs counter to the graphic designer's instinct for the elimination of chaos and the bringing of order and structure to their work?

Possibly. There's no question that many designers crave control – or as you put it 'order and structure' – and maybe this applies also to the financial or business side of our practices. Obviously, having made the decision to work independently, one assumes ultimate responsibility for both the business and design direction of the practice. The fact remains that many, if not all, principals will have greater expertise in design and this will be their primary motivation for maintaining a practice. The time and effort invested in establishing a reputation for quality is also significant; this could also be a reason for the apparently conservative approach to business and financing.

You run your studio in partnership with Oran Day. Are you an equal partnership?

No, we are not a partnership in any formal sense. Oran started in the studio as an assistant and in time became an associate and principal designer for many studio projects. He still retains a small private client list as well as teaching and managing a number of Atelier projects. The creative direction and financing of the studio remains my responsibility.

What are the human and creative qualities that make a successful design business partnership?

Ambition, intelligence, trust, tolerance, clarity and honesty. In the studio we share a common ambition – which is to endeavour to make the best job possible at every opportunity. This can lead to stresses and anxieties if things go wrong or are misinterpreted, but 'shit happens', we move on and hope to improve with the next opportunity.

You combine your working life between your design practice and your role as an educator at IADT in Dublin; how did this come about?

Towards the end of my time at ANRT many of my peers were being offered jobs and referred for design positions ahead of me. This was a real blow and I assumed that the staff had no confidence in me. Eventually I plucked up the courage to ask why I was being overlooked. I was told that it was expected that I would return to Dublin to establish my own atelier and teach. Their absolute confidence that this was what I would do was probably the most significant factor in me becoming engaged in education. So I never set out to become an educator. But equally I didn't (and obviously don't) subscribe to [George Bernard] Shaw's[16] dictum, 'Those who can do, those who can't teach.' Having had professors of the calibre of Jean Widmer, and seen the calibre of staff at undergraduate level in the ENSAD (École Nationale Superieur des Arts Decoratifs), it was clear that the provision of a good design education was contingent on engaging the best practitioners available. So, for as long as the studio has existed I have practised and taught. Initially only in a part-time capacity, but since 2001–02 I have been a full-time lecturer and for some years the programme co-ordinator at IADT.

Is it difficult to balance the two?

Early on it wasn't such an issue, as I could put in as many hours as I liked – nights, weekends, early mornings – before teaching. But now with a young family it can be increasingly difficult to balance both. But I can't separate the two. I don't distinguish between being a teacher and a designer – I have a desire to teach, and a need to make.

05 | 06 |
07 | 08 |

05/ Project: Fire Station 10 book. Date: 2009. Client: Pauline O'Connell/Fire Station Artists' Studios. Designers: David Smith and Patrick Mullen. 06/ Project: Ideas, Craft, Attitude and Desire – ICAD @ 50 poster. Date: 2009. Client: Institute of Creative Advertising and Design. Designer: David Smith. 07/ Project: Klutz Paradiso. Stephen Brandes, Vinyl, Paintings and Drawings. Date: 2006. Client: Royal Hibernian Academy/ Rubicon Gallery. Designer: David Smith. Other: Two-colour screenprinted Kraftliner cover. 08/ Project: Vehicle Mobile Art Venture. Date: 2005. Client: Yvonne McGuinness. Designer: Oran Day. 09/ Project: Fire Station Master Classes 2009 programme, poster and identity. Date: 2009. Client: Pauline O'Connell/Fire Station Artists' Studios. Designer: David Smith. Original Artwork: Nothing Domestic (detail) Malachi Farrell. 10/ Elévate PR 5th Anniversary notebook. Date: 2007. Client: Elevate. Designers: David Smith and Oran Day. 11/ Project: Umbrella Project book. Date: 2006. Client: Rhona Byrne/Atelier Projects. Designer: David Smith. 12/ Project: Foreign Affairs of Dutch Design, Promotional poster for exhibition and lecture series. Date: 2006. Client: Royal Nederlands Embassy/Design Week 2006. Designer: David Smith. 13/ Project: Pallas Heights book. Date: 2007. Client: Pallas Artists' Studios. Designers: David Smith and Oran Day. 14/ Project: Umbrella Project poster and programme. Date: 2006. Client: Rhona Byrne/Atelier Projects. Designers: Oran Day and David Smith.

How does this work on a practical level?
How much time do you devote to the studio?

Currently I'm on a 0.5 contract, so I can potentially give the studio three days per week, including evenings and some time over the weekend. But at the busiest times of the academic year, this can drop to one day at the weekend, with plenty of remote contact and direction. Without question I couldn't sustain or maintain the studio without Oran, who manages many, if not all, aspects of the studio in my absence. We try to ensure that we only take on manageable amounts of work and we predominantly work on a project-by-project basis. This is not an ideal business model but it has worked thus far. Part of this is for practical reasons, as Oran teaches too, but it is also for qualitative reasons. Also, as the studio has grown — not in size but in reputation — we have been fortunate with the steady flow of work; in many instances potential clients have been willing to wait for us to become available for their projects, or they are willing to work to less demanding schedules.

Does teaching inform your practice, and vice versa?

A student recently asked me this and my answer was yes, in that I have to remain engaged and aware of the demands of professional practice. I need to ensure that the breadth and range of my references and knowledge is far greater than if I were solely focused on my practice alone.

Do you think your students take you more seriously because you have an independent practice? Or is it the case that in the era of market-driven education they would prefer to have you teaching 100%?

During the formative stages of their undergraduate education I don't believe they are aware if I (or a colleague for that matter) practised, so it matters little to them early on. Towards the latter stages of their studies, having acquired some knowledge and experience, they have their own opinions, likes and dislikes about professional practice. It is only at this stage that students possibly value the currency of my practical experience and knowledge. But please be aware, this is not the same as taking me more seriously or liking my work.

With regards to my commitment, the students have me 100%. The fact that I maintain a practice on top of fulfilling my academic commitments shouldn't be of any concern to them. I believe that my students are very lucky with the manageable class numbers that are currently maintained. The level of access to staff and quality of resources is very good and is to the benefit of all.

In reference to your point about 'market-driven education' I think research and practice profiles become even more essential at postgraduate level because of the market and competition for places — and yes, I believe the Institute would be mindful of the value of such practices in establishing and maintaining a reputation for their programmes. Within the Institute and more specifically within the School of Creative Arts there is an understanding of the value and necessity of many staff members maintaining a practice — be it a visual arts practice, critical writing, designing or filmmaking. However, the challenges of maintaining a reputable practice and fulfilling your academic commitments are demanding and I can understand why so few colleagues maintain a contiguous practice.

I imagine you have a steady stream of designers from the college knocking on your door. What is your attitude to interns?

Surprisingly, not as many as you would think. We do get quite a few requests from international students but unfortunately we have had to decline as we rarely know if and when we will need the additional assistance. The value of professional placements has never been embedded into Irish design education, which means that many Irish graduates commence their careers without any insight into the workings of a design studio. Apart from a lack of resourcing I think a reason for this is that there is only a limited number of studios who would take students in and afford them the appropriate amount of time and advice during their placement.

You run something called Three x 3 internship. Can you talk about that?

This is a programme we initiated in 2007. The idea is simple — a cluster of three like-minded studios commit to taking on three graduates for three months each. They pay them and give them some decent work to do. It has been a great success and we have benefited from having some of the best young graduates work with us over the last couple of years.

Do you have formal rules about things like time-keeping at the studio?

Early on we used to work ridiculous hours, late nights and weekends. But eventually you realize that this is a consequence of inefficiency. Now its 9.30am (plus or minus 15 minutes) till 6.00pm. Lunch is a moveable feast and is usually just 30 minutes. I may work on an hour or so after the guys have left to clear the desk of admin or prep the next day.

How do you maintain the balance between creativity and profitability?

The studio is not very profitable. It pays its way and facilitates and enables the work that we want to do. The majority of our projects are in the public and cultural sector and the budgets are very tight. We never work 'on the clock' but always to an agreed budget, so more often than not, more of our margin than is necessary is invested in making the work that little bit better, a little more beautiful, and a little more distinctive. When the money is not there, and only if we're taken with the project's needs and the opportunity given to us, we may draw upon the goodwill of our suppliers to realize the project or sometimes co-publish with the commissioner.

How did you go about finding new clients?

Apart from the initial 12 months I've been fortunate enough not to have to make the hard sell and hawk our work around. All our work is by direct referral. Usually an existing or previous client has made the recommendation.

Do you still have a traditional printed portfolio to accompany your website?

We worked with Group 94 on the design and development of our site – having existed for five years without one – and it has made life and promotion much easier. But it is the production values and material quality of our work that really distinguishes our portfolio. I think it is difficult to effectively capture such things online, so we insist that potential clients see our printed work before a project commences.

Do you have any ambitions to grow?

The thought was there recently and efforts were made in that direction, but it didn't happen. It's not an issue, especially in the current climate. We'll continue to work closely with associates and collaborate when necessary.

How important is the physical environment you work in?

It is important to have a dedicated space – a place to think and a place to make. It's important to be able to step away from the screen and work quietly elsewhere. We have a good library – light on eye candy – that is a great resource, and some nice posters.

Does this mean a pristine environment with Vitra furniture and Vitsoe shelving?

Not on our fees. It's more Habitat sale than Milan Furniture Fair. Although it is important that we have good operator's chairs (Ypsilon by Vitra, and Gisberger).

Do you have a music policy?

I don't mind what plays. Oran has incredibly eclectic taste, so he's the boss of the sounds. We listen to quite a few podcasts from the BBC. Stephen Merchant, Radio 4 and 5 Live!

How would you define your studio's culture today?

The studio is quite relaxed, but we're serious about what we do and have great ambition for every project that comes our way. We can be very demanding on ourselves, our clients and our suppliers. If you are making books or something that demands to be read, the content better be good. If it's not, it's a pointless exercise; a waste of time and money. And we don't like wasting either.

1 UNA, important Dutch design group based in Amsterdam.

2 Hans Bockting, owner and partner of Amsterdam-based design agency Bockting Ontwerpers since 2007, with partner Sabine Bockting Reinhardt. Worked at UNA designers for more than 20 years.

3 Will de l'Ecluse, creative director of Total Identity in Amsterdam since April 2009. Formerly a partner at UNA designers for 21 years.

4 Peter Keller, born in Switzerland, head of The Atelier Nationale de Recherche Typographique (ANRT) in Nancy.

5 Jean Widmer, Swiss graphic designer influential in French design. Ran the French agency Visuel Design.

6 Hans Jurg Hunzicker, Swiss graphic designer, trained under Adrian Frutiger.

7 Niall Sweeney, founder of London-based design agency Pony Ltd.

8 Studio Dumbar, highly regarded Dutch studio established in 1977 by Gert Dumbar.

9 Karel Martens, important Dutch designer and teacher, founder of Werkplaats Typografie in Arnhem. His work includes postage stamps, books and signage. His work is celebrated in the books *Karel Martens: Drukwerk/Printed Matter* and *Karel Martens: Counterprint*. Both volumes are highly sought collectors' items.

10 Anton Stankowski (1906–1998), German graphic designer. Best known for designing Deutsche Bank logo.

11 Wolfgang Weingart, internationally known German-born graphic designer and typographer, widely credited as 'the father' of New Wave typography. Published *My Way to Typography* in 2000.

12 8vo (Octavo), London-based graphic design firm formed in 1985 by Simon Johnston, Mark Holt and Hamish Muir. Closed in 2001.

13 Bruno Monguzzi, Swiss-born designer. Well known for his work on the Musée d'Orsay in Paris.

14 Jost Hochuli, Swiss graphic designer and typographer. Co-founded the publishing company VGS Verlagsgemeinschaft St. Gallen, has published numerous books on typography and taught extensively.

15 Norman Potter (1923–1995), British graphic designer and writer. Best known for the book *What is a Designer?*

16 George Bernard Shaw (1856–1950), Irish playwright. First to be awarded both an Oscar and a Nobel Prize for Literature. Well known for plays such as *Pygmalion*.

Bibliothèque
Founded: 2003
Personnel: 5
Location: London, UK
www.bibliothequedesign.co.uk

Bibliothèque are one of the foremost young UK design groups. Formed by a trio of designers – Jon Jeffrey, Mason Wells and Tim Beard – all three served apprenticeships in leading British design companies. Wells and Beard worked at Cartlidge Levene, and latterly at North, while Jeffrey worked at Farrow. In these studios, widely recognized for their thoughtful and meticulous work, the trio completed projects for a varied client list that included RAC, Telewest, the Science Museum and the Hacienda.

The creative output of Bibliothèque is distinguished by a reverence for modernist design principles. Yet despite roots in twentieth-century European traditions, their work is filtered through a contemporary sensibility. They work for a wide-ranging client base that includes Adidas, the Barbican, the Design Council and the V&A.

The group won praise for their self-initiated and rigorously curated exhibition of the 1972 Olympic work of Otl Aicher[1].

The interview was conducted by email.
—

All three of you worked for highly regarded studios where you enjoyed positions of influence and respect. Many designers would give a limb to work for the companies you worked for. But you all quit to set up your own studio. Why?

Mason Wells: Between 1992 and 2003 we were fortunate to work at some of the best London design studios. After an eight-year period in our last studios (North[2] and Farrow[3] respectively), starting up seemed to be the next step – the natural thing to do to gain independence and to have the luxury of doing the work we wanted to do.

When designers leave studios there is usually the messy question of clients. Often clients want to continue with a designer when he or she switches studios. This can cause problems. How did you deal with this issue?

This is a sensitive subject and it is something all studios have to contend with. If the client has severed links with the previous design studio, then there is the tricky conflict between loyalties and business. There was a moment when we were approached by an ex-North client and we had a brief relationship with them – but there was too much baggage from the past and it wasn't working for either party. On the whole it has not been an issue.

Were there studios – past or present –
that you modelled Bibliothèque on?

When we started Bibliothèque we felt a
need to go back to basics, not just in our
work but in the way we approached all facets
of the business. We wanted to keep it simple.
Our studio is a workshop – there is no slick
detailing, there are no big statements. There
is a certain austerity but it is not minimal.
We don't have a particular model but there
are influences – there are certain architects,
product designers and institutions that
we empathise with. The functionality of
Dieter Rams[4], the simplicity of Maarten van
Severen[5], the honesty of Poul Kjearholm[6],
and the intelligent rigour of The Hochschule
für Gestaltung in Ulm[7]. All stuff we love to
connect with.

The name Bibliothèque – where does it
come from?

It was chosen to encapsulate the way our
studio operates. We love to collect and
archive, whether this is work by other
designers, materials and samples, or even
the way we document our own work. It's all
summed up by the name. And the use of a
French name gave us a certain *je ne sais
quoi* [laughs].

Jon, you left your job at Farrow ahead of
the other two and worked in your kitchen for
the first few months. Was this a good move
in terms of setting up the company – finding
premises, acquiring kit, etc?

It was not planned, it was just down to
different contractual obligations. However, it
was very beneficial as it gave me time to start
to pursue potential work, set up systems and
try to find a studio.

What professional advice did you seek?

Once we had announced our intentions to
set up, we had plenty of offers of advice
from designer friends we spoke to, which
was appreciated. However, I think the most
valuable advice we sought was from a very
credible financial advisor friend; he gave
us reality checks and recommended a few
valuable business tips that we still use to
this day.

Can you describe how you operate as a trio
of equal partners? Are there times when you
tread on each other's toes or have you got
your roles clearly defined?

There are pros and cons, but being a
trio means that there is usually a rational
voice on the periphery of creative debate.
We are all on the same page when it comes
to our influences, so for the most part we
all approach graphic design in a similar way.
There are disagreements but we are all
aware of the bigger picture that is

01 |
02 |
03 |

01/ Project: 72: Otl Aicher and the Munich
Olympiad. A self-initiated exhibition
examining the identity program for the
1972 Munich Olympics. Date: Mar 2007.
02/ Project: Dalí and Film. Posters for
exhibition on the surrealist painter. Date:
Sep 2007. Client: Tate Modern. 03/ Project:
Identity for the London contemporary
music ensemble. *The Bulletin* is a quarterly
broadsheet featuring news and events.
Sep 2008. Client: London Sinfonietta.

Bibliothèque, our friendship and design comes first.

If one of you really isn't happy about a decision do you drop it, or is it a vote and the majority decision prevails?

It doesn't happen too often, although we usually run with the majority decision. There have been occasions when if someone feels really strongly about something then we run with their idea and that's fine too.

Tell me about the current Bibliothèque team.

Currently it is the three founding partners and the designer Tom Munckton. Tom made a very good impression on us as a very talented intern in 2006 and then he subsequently joined after his graduation.

Do you have someone working on administration and project management?

A studio of our size has to be adaptable; if a project requires it then we have people who can come in and take on those roles. We mainly handle these aspects of work ourselves as a matter of choice, as direct communication with a client creates a dialogue with the designer – it is also a socially more rewarding process.

The non-designing side of design studios is often neglected by designers. How much attention do you focus on administration, financial management and forward planning?

We see all of these aspects as part of the design process. It is not possible to produce successful design solutions commercially without balancing all of these.

In the early days you expressed a doubt that you wouldn't be able to accommodate other designers within Bibliothèque. This has clearly changed. Why?

This is still difficult; the full-time designers who have joined Bibliothèque share our ideology and make an enormous contribution. There have been times when we have used freelancers and sometimes they have had their own creative agenda. On occasions we have not been right for them and they have not been right for us.

What do you look for in a designer?

Someone who can think laterally – and shape those thoughts (with mutual aesthetic taste) into visual communication.

Bibliothèque has a strong aesthetic and conceptual signature. Where does this come from?

Aesthetically we have an intuitive response to the things we like and this is hard to quantify. We gravitate to a certain material or a typeface, because beyond the objective reasons, such as tactility or legibility, there is a cerebral connection. Most of the design we like dates as far back as 50 years. The products of Braun[8], the graphics of Rolf Müller[9], the architecture of Max Bill[10] – these resonate, not for retro reasons but because they are intelligent solutions that have stood the test of time. We are not interested in aesthetics that are driven by technology or styling; we prefer something more honest. There is a lot of visual sludge out there. The conceptual side of our work is just as important – the expression of content through a captivating idea is key to the way we work. This is probably the area of our work that differentiates each job the most, as the aesthetic outcome is more ideological. The biggest evolution in our work over the last few years is probably in the art direction. We like to make objects that connect with content and this in turn becomes the pictorial element of many of our projects.

What is your policy towards interns?

As previously mentioned, our designer Tom started as an intern. Our policy is one of mutual respect – if they are enthusiastic and want to learn, we will encourage them. However, if they just coast along, we lose interest. We want designers who are hungry, share our passion and want to learn – in return we give them our time. They must also make tea very frequently.

How did you find clients in your early days?

In the early days we were fortunate because there was a bit of a buzz when we started, and this resulted in clients coming to us by word of mouth. We are very lucky in that the majority of our clients want to be involved in a positive way. Good design is about formulating a dialogue with your client so there is a mutual understanding of the visual outcome. One of our advantages is our passion. We love design and we love talking about design – the feedback we get from our clients when they first meet us is that they love our enthusiasm and our discipline.

Can you describe your approach to winning new business today?

We have been very fortunate in acquiring work via word of mouth and recommendations. As we speak there is a global recession looming – and our approach is evolving accordingly.

Can you say what you mean by this? Are you talking about making compromises – or a way of working that takes into account the fact that there is less money around?

No, not compromises – contingencies. Ultimately we are a business, and to run it successfully you have to think ahead in case the phone stops ringing. That could be

04 | 05 |
06 | 07 |
08 | 09 |

04/05/ Project: A limited book celebrating the creativity of adicolor (a range of shoes that come with a set of waterproof markers for individual customization), retail installations of which these lightboxes were a part. Date: Mar 2006. Client: Adidas in collaboration with JJmarshall Associates. 06/07/ Project: Super Contemporary, an exhibition documenting the design ecosystem of London. Date: Jun 2009. Client: Design Museum. 08/09/ Project: An identity for a multimedia design agency. The Moving Brands logo is a black and white geometric abstraction to create the initials M and B. Here it has been applied to a variety of media formats. Date: Jan 2005. Client: Moving Brands. 10/ An array of Bibliothèque projects dating back five years. 11/12/ Project: Le Corbusier exhibition. The solution is a graphic expression of Le Corbusier through the use of typography cast in concrete. Buildings, furniture and other supporting imagery was combined with this in post-production. Date: Feb 2009. Client Barbican. 13/14/ Project: Adidas Olympic Archive – exhibition and marketing materials celebrating the sportswear manufacturers's Olympic legacy. Date: Oct 2004. Client: Adidas in collaboration with JJmarshall Associates.

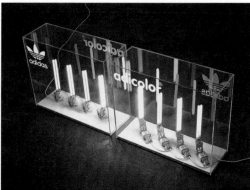

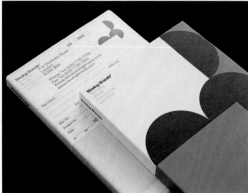

15 |
16 |
17 |

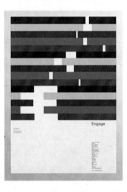

15/16/ Project: Identity for a web
developer. Date: Dec 2008. Client: Engage.
17/ Bibliothèque website launch card.
A schematic design that exploits the
linear nature of the site. Date: Jan 2006.
Client: Bibliothèque.

getting into the psyche of potential clients
by producing promotional literature, having
the right documents prepared for expressions
of interest or simple things like keeping the
website updated. As for less money — that
just means longer hours to keep the
cashflow at a sustainable level.

Do you enter award schemes?

Sometimes.

This suggests a lack of enthusiasm for
the subject.

It is difficult because to voice your
dissatisfaction with awards sounds like sour
grapes. The reality is that judging design is
a subjective process. Some designers are
sympathetic to our work; others don't like it.
So much of it is down to the luck of getting
the right jury.

You set up an exhibition devoted to the work
of Otl Aicher. This clearly took a lot of work,
and for a young company must have eaten
up a lot of valuable resources. Can you
talk about your reasons behind doing this
project?

The Aicher exhibition was primarily done for
fun — to celebrate and share something we
love with the wider design community. Our
secondary agenda was to demonstrate how
good an Olympic design program can be.
Along with doing an airline livery, it's every
designer's dream job. We would have loved
to have had some involvement in the London
2012 creative journey, but from what we could
tell it had been finished at the time of the
exhibition. As far as we know there have been
several recent Aicher/Olympic exhibitions
around the globe.

Do you see yourselves doing more projects
like this?

Hopefully. There are a few ideas on the back
burner. Maybe a book.

You have a big open-plan office with plenty
of natural light. Do you see a link between
your environment and creativity?

Absolutely. Polystyrene tiles on suspended
ceilings create a taste vacuum.

You all sit round a central worksurface.
Presumably this works well for you. Do you
foresee a time when you might need to
change this way of working?

There is something quite egalitarian about
the central worksurface. It works well as
we are all physically connected, no one sits
behind anyone else and we all face each
other. The idea of independent spaces (offices
for account handlers, etc) to underpin
hierarchies doesn't appeal.

Is growth part of the Bibliothèque masterplan? Or are you determined to stay small?

We will grow as the work demands. If we get projects that require more people then we will expand to meet the needs. Our plan is to be realistic while retaining a creative edge. If a global client came to us, and the only way we could look after them was to grow rapidly, we'd consider it. But the work would have to be appealing. For us there is always the balance between enjoying the work we do and the demands of business. We did not become designers just to make money, but because we love it.

How would you describe the Bibliothèque studio culture to a potential client?

Our studio culture is open, friendly and very, very serious about design.

1 Otl Aicher (1922–1991), leading German graphic designer. Co-founded the Hochschule für Gestaltung in Ulm (Ulm School of Design) in 1953. Best known for work as head designer for the 1972 Munich Olympics and creating the first Olympic mascot.

2 North, founded in 1995 by designers Sean Perkins and Simon Browning after both leaving Cartlidge Levene. Famous for their ground-breaking identity for RAC.

3 Farrow, a London-based design company formed by designer Mark Farrow. Worked for Harvey Nichols, Jimmy Choo, British Museum, EMI Records.

4 Dieter Rams, German designer. Chief of design for Braun from 1961 to 1995. Credited with being an influence on Jonathan Ive of Apple.

5 Maarten van Severen (1956–2005), Belgian furniture designer.

6 Poul Kjearholm, Danish furniture designer.

7 The Hochschule für Gestaltung in Ulm (the Ulm School of Design), ran in Germany from 1953 to 1968. Founded by Inge Aicher-Scholl, Otl Aicher and Max Bill. The 'Ulm Model' continues to influence international design education.

8 Braun, German electronics and appliance company. Founded by Max Braun. Created functional appliances in a style linked to the German modern industrial design of the time.

9 Rolf Müller, studied at the Hochschule für Gestaltung in Ulm. He went to Munich in 1967 to work on the design of the 1972 Olympic Games with Otl Aicher.

10 Max Bill (1908–1994), Swiss architect, artist, painter, typeface designer, industrial designer and graphic designer. Studied at the Bauhaus under Wassily Kandinsky and Paul Klee. Moved to Zurich and in 1944 became a professor at the school of arts in Zurich.

18/19/ Project: Annual Review. 3D graphs and charts express growth in the design industry. Date: Jul 2008. Client: Design Council. 20/ Project: Identity. Detail of poster promoting cultural heritage of the Covent Garden area. Date: Jun 2008. Client: Covent Garden.

Build
Founded: 2001
Personnel: 2 plus interns
Location: London, UK
wearebuild.com

Michael C. Place is the designer's designer.' His work is admired around the world. For nine years he worked at the Designers Republic, the influential Sheffield-based design group. But like many designers he had an itch to 'do it all', and in 2001 he moved to London and set up Build in partnership with his wife Nicola, who at the time was working as a digital artist at Sony PlayStation.

Michael Place's highly crafted and intricate work is the product of hours of painstaking labour, and is clearly the output of a designer with a strong sense of personal commitment. As Place says: 'I love doing'.

In the early days of Build there was no plan to grow, but over the years there has been slow evolutionary growth and recently Build began to work with occasional freelance designers. Now with a steady flow of clients attracted to Place's vivid and intense style, growth and all its attendant demands seem unavoidable. The interview was conducted at Build's northeast London studio.
—

What prompted you to start your studio?

Michael Place: I'd worked in small studios as an employee, and after nearly a decade at the Designers Republic, I could see how studios were run and I found it really interesting. I also wanted the experience of actually getting clients, going to meetings – which I didn't get to do very often at DR – and then doing the job and getting paid. Having a studio allowed me to do this. I was 30, so I wasn't exactly young, and I wanted to prove to myself that I could do it. I also wanted to have the opportunity to say – if I don't want to work today then I won't work today.

Did you wake up one day and think 'I've got the confidence, now I'm going to set up on my own'?

MP: The strange thing is that it wasn't a definite decision. Nicky and I both quit our jobs and did a year's travelling before moving to London from the north of England. So we obviously knew that we were going to do something new, but it was a seat-of-the-pants kind of thing, and it built up gradually and organically.

Nicola Place: We'd already made the decision to take time out and go travelling, probably before Mike had made the decision that he wanted to start a studio. Then the natural step was 'let's go away'; then the next natural step when we got back was to set up the studio rather than going back to being employed. But we'd spent all our money travelling, so I continued working for Sony. My role was to bring in the support money to get the studio off the ground. At the beginning I wasn't involved day to day.

Nicky, when did you join Michael full-time?

NP: At the risk of sounding like I hated my job at Sony, I was getting increasingly frustrated, even though I was working on fantastic jobs. But I could see Michael doing his thing, and there was certainly a sense that Build could go a long way. I knew Michael couldn't do it on his own, and it needed more than me bringing in a salary to support him.

You'd previously been a digital artist – what did you think you could contribute to Build?

NP: My background was creative, but over the years I'd become more involved in project management, so I was really in two camps. I knew what Michael was trying to do, so I felt qualified to help him. I certainly didn't feel like I was stepping out and going from a creative role to a business role. I wanted to complement what Michael was doing, but also have creative input as well. My role primarily is the business side of things and I enjoy it.

MP: When Nicky was providing financial support, I knew that I could start to take risks and do a lot of things for free to get the Build name out there. Nicky allowed me to do that. I realize now how important the business side of running a studio is, but at the time I didn't consider it whatsoever, because Nicky was effectively enabling us to eat at night.

Did you at this point have a vision for the studio?

MP: While I was at DR I just focused on my work. But when I set up Build, I realized that I'd learned a lot from how Ian [Anderson][1] ran the studio and how he selected the type of work he took on. I guess I've followed on from that. We did a lot of record sleeves at DR and I wanted to still do them, but I also wanted to do bigger things, and steer away from music stuff, because I knew that was starting to get harder and harder.

You came from a well-known studio – one of the most famous in the world of design. Most people would have traded off that to launch their new studio – but you didn't. Why?

MP: I just wanted to prove to myself that I didn't need a really big name behind me. I didn't show any of the work I'd done at DR to get new work, so of course I wasn't trading on the DR name. All the work I did at DR was credited to Designers Republic, not to me, so I didn't really find it that hard. I'd like to think that my work was good enough that people gave me work on the strength of it, and not because I was ex-DR.

01/02/ Project: Design Museum Shop identity/signage. Date: 2007. Client: The Design Museum. Designer: Michael C. Place. Photographer: Nicky Place.

The name Build sounds like a manifesto. Where did it come from?

MP: I think it was dealing with a lot of band stuff, it felt almost like it was an imaginary band. I just really liked the idea of a cold-sounding name; just a single word. And I like the implications of Build. It has quite a Germanic feel to it. I don't mind getting my sleeves dirty, and I love doing. Also, I didn't want to have a name with an 's' in it. I hate drawing the letter 's'.

In the early days you did experimental work that didn't make much money but that attracted the attention of the design press. Was that a deliberate policy?

MP: One of the things I learned from DR was to just be nice to everybody because they potentially could be clients. You also learn that the design press is a powerful tool, and if you start a young company, you've got to think of any means necessary to get yourself out there. But now we're being a bit more normal. We target people, and we're actually more grown-up about it.

Nicky, you are responsible for getting new clients. What percentage of your workload is new business?

NP: Probably still not enough. It probably should be about 50% of my time, but it's probably about 5%. We did a lot of stuff at the beginning of the year and we got a lot of work from that.

What sort of things did you do?

NP: We built a new website, and we mailed out some promotional material at Christmas. We then approached people and made presentations. One of the big things we've done is completely organize all the work, which we've never done before. We got a dedicated server that allows everything to be in one place. We've also had the work photographed properly. That's been a huge thing, so when people ask if we can send them some work, we've got a library of stuff. We don't do printed portfolios. It just doesn't seem relevant any more. A couple of times in the past I dropped one off at clients. They'd sit on it for a month and go 'Oh, we didn't get a chance to look at it.'

So your portfolio is electronic now?

NP: Yes. It means you can really tailor what you want to show to people, whereas with a print portfolio, you've got to make sure that everything's in it that they might want to see, and you've got to send a courier or take it there yourself. It's so cumbersome.

Since setting up Build, you've worked on your own, but now you've got your first designer and you're hiring interns – has this been a big step?

MP: I think the big step was me realizing that I can't do everything myself. Another step was realizing that getting somebody else in expands our repertoire, and our possibilities of doing more work. Having a junior designer helps with all the stuff that it's not practical for me to do. So for me it was initially about getting that mindset that you need someone else; someone that's good for me and good for the business.

NP: I almost had to force it on Michael. Last year we had a few students doing placements, some were really good and some were less good, which you'd expect, but they were the first step towards having somebody else in the studio. It was quite odd for us. Our first student was probably terrified at the idea of sitting between us both.

Have you had to make adjustments to the way you work?

MP: No, I'm still a grumpy bastard! I have to let go, and that's something I've found really hard, but you have to do it.

How do you deal with the people who approach you looking for work or internships?

NP: The online applications come to me because I'm the point of contact on our website. If there's anything really interesting I'll show it to Michael. At the moment we're not looking for anyone, but when we're hiring we need to know who is around.

Do you feel a sense of responsibility towards your interns?

MP: Absolutely. We try and give them interesting stuff to do. I don't want them to go away thinking that all they've done is make the tea and go to the post office.

NP: When we're busy, there isn't enough time to figure out what our interns should be doing. But we definitely have a sense of responsibility towards them, which is why we haven't got anyone at the moment because we don't want them to sit there thinking that it was a waste of time.

Do you pay the interns?

NP: Yes, we do.

Nicky, can you say what your role is? Can you list the key things you do?

NP: Michael is design, and I'm everything else. If you want some key jobs, I'd list recruitment, project management, new business, bookkeeping, IT, all the studio

03 | 04 | 05 |
06 | 07 | 08 | 09 |
10 | 11 | 12 | 13 |

03/ Project: Helvetica Timeline postcard. Date: 2007. Client: Gary Hustwit/Plexi Film. Designer: Michael C. Place. 04/ Project: AUS Music identity. Date: 2006. Client: Simple records. Designer: Michael C. Place. 05/ Project: Not For Commercial Use catalogue. Date: 2008. Client: Generation Press/Build. Designer: Michael C. Place. 06/ Project: *The Crow* book cover. Date: 2006. Client: Faber Faber. Designer: Michael C. Place. 07/ Project: Not For Commercial Use Manifesto poster. Date: 2008. Client: Generation Press/Build. Designer: Michael C. Place. 08/ Project: Not For Commercial Use Test-card 1 poster. Date: 2008. Client: Generation Press/Build. Designer: Michael C. Place. 09/ Project: Not For Commercial Use Dendrochronology poster. Date: 2008. Client: Generation Press/Build. Designer: Michael C. Place. 10/ Project: Cimatics AV Festival programme. Date: 2006. Client: Cimatics. Designer: Michael C. Place. 11/ Project: Promo One. Date: 2008. Client: Timothy Saccenti. Designer: Michael C. Place. 12/ Project: Scale series One Pence Piece. Date: 2007. Client: Build. Designer: Michael C. Place. 13/ Project: *The Practitioner* magazine redesign. Date: 2006. Client: CMP Publishing. Designer: Michael C. Place.

14/ Project: *Helvetica* film, limited-edition poster. Date: 2007. Client: Gary Hustwit/Plexi Film. Designer: Michael C. Place. 15/ Project: *Friendly Integration* CD cover. Date: 2006. Client: Detroit Underground Records. Designer: Michael C. Place. 16/ Project: *Flying Lotus–Los Angeles* LP cover (front). Date: 2008. Client: Warp Records. Designer: Michael C. Place. Photographer: Timothy Saccenti. 17/ Project: *Friendly Integration* CD cover. Date: 2006. Client: Detroit Underground Records. Designer: Michael C. Place. 18/ Project: *Flying Lotus – Los Angeles* LP cover (back). Date: 2008. Client: Warp Records. Designer: Michael C. Place. Photographer: Timothy Saccenti. 19/ Project: Think Global, Act Local poster. Date: 2008. Client: +81/The North Face. Designer: Michael C. Place. 20/ Project: Cimatics AV Festival programme. Date: 2007. Client: Cimatics. Designer: Michael C. Place. 21/ Project: Refill Seven, laser-etched skateboard. Date: 2007. Client: *Refill Magazine*. Designer: Michael C. Place. 22/ Project: Faber Finds typeface design. Date: 2008. Client: Faber Faber. Designer: Michael C. Place.

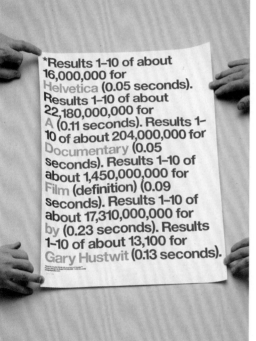

management stuff. In fact, absolutely everything except design.

Are you ambitious? Do you want to grow the business?

NP: Yeah, we do. At the moment we're considering a move to a new studio with more space and room to expand. For us this would be quite a big leap. We'd be making a commitment to the business by investing money that we've earned so far, and not seeing it back for two or three years. Because we're operating as a partnership, we could take that money and enjoy it and just trundle on as we are. But we've talked about it and we feel like we want to reinvest it.

I want to ask you about the studio; it's very tidy and the desks are immaculate. Did you tidy up because you were being interviewed today — or is it part of the philosophy?

NP: For both of us a good working environment is conducive to good work, and I find that if you get rid of the crap it stops you being distracted. When we first moved into the studio it was an opportunity for us to actually build a studio space, as opposed to occupying a room in our house. It was great to have a meeting table and dedicated bookshelves.

Were there any studios that you admired when you were starting out?

MP: The design studio Spin[2] is a really good example of what we wanted to be. I really like their work, and having met Tony [Brook] a few times, he seems like a really decent person with good values. Browns is another one. I've got to know Jonathan [Ellery][3] fairly well. I like the way Browns mix corporate work with Jonathan's art side, which I think is really interesting. Another example is Graphic Thought Facility; they do amazing work and have stayed small. But rather than the specific studios I've already named, it's a certain type of work that I admire, and that tends to be British. I don't know too many other studios outside of England; it's that independent spirit that I really like. People who have a certain attitude; I know Jonathan has a certain attitude in the way that he runs Browns. I think that Tony is a good example of integrity.

NP: Early on, Mike used to talk about Spin and Browns and a few smaller studios, and that helped me to understand what he was aiming for. We don't want to be Interbrand.

It's fairly unusual to be working as a married couple. Are there any pluses or minuses that people should be aware of?

MP: I'll start with a minus. I think the hardest thing is that when you go home, work is still there as well. I'm looking at the same

23 |
24 |
25 |

23/ Project: Phil Harrison bespoke framed piece. Date: 2008. Client: Sony Computer Entertainment Europe. Designer: Michael C. Place. 24/ Project: Think Global, Act Local – Birth/Work/Death triptych. Date: 2008. Client: +81/The North Face. Designer: Michael C. Place. 25/ Project: Think Global, Act Local poster. Date: 2008. Client: +81/The North Face. Designer: Michael C. Place.

person, and as beautiful as Nicky is, I think that's hard. The pluses are that through being partners, we are completely together and focused because we're both essentially helping ourselves to have a decent life and earn decent money. The bond thing is really good, because we know each other so well through being married. We think in a similar kind of way.

NP: You said it was unusual, but there are quite a lot of couples who do it. I don't know if I could work with anyone else so closely. But other people would say 'I could never work with my husband or wife so closely.' And this sense of not having to explain things, because I know what Michael is thinking, I'd say that's a plus.

You live near your studio. Is that important?

NP: Now that we're planning to move, we've discussed moving out of Walthamstow, the area that we are in now. But we feel a loyalty to this area, and not just because we live down the road. Why make life difficult for yourself?

Walthamstow is a fair distance from the centre of London. Do you think this discourages clients from coming to see you?

MP: Not really. It's easy to get here because we're at the end of a major tube line.

Designers Republic famously made Sheffield their base rather than move to London where the vast majority of UK designers are. Are you making a similar stance by staying in Walthamstow?

MP: With DR, it was a very definite declaration of independence, and maybe that's what I'm thinking here. We're a little bit further out, and that was mainly to do with finding somewhere we could afford. We could move now, but I've always said that I find it uncomfortable being among a million other design agencies, and that's not because I lack confidence in our ability, it's just the way I feel.

How would each of you define the studio culture of Build?

MP: We take our work really seriously. We do interesting design, but with a sense of humour.

NP: I think people see us as very serious and quite scary, but actually we're not, or I hope not! I can be quite silly, which is the opposite of the brutalist approach [to design] that Michael has sometimes. Marrying that up as part of the studio culture is still missing, but that's where our new blog will come in. It will be more of a window into what the studio is really like – this is our website, but this is what we're like and we're not so scary.

MP: I think it's fair to say that we have a laugh and I think that's really important.

1 Ian Anderson, founder of Designers Republic.

2 Spin is the studio of this book's co-editor, Tony Brook. www.spin.co.uk. See page 204.

3 Jonathan Ellery, founder of Browns. www.brownsdesign.com. Ellery's art projects can be found at www.jonathanellery.com.

Coast
Founded: 1999
Personnel: 4 designers plus studio manager
Location: Brussels, Belgium
www.coastdesign.be

Based in Brussels, Belgium, Coast describe themselves as a 'European multidisciplinary branding practice.' Founder Frédéric Vanhorenbeke was educated in his native country but after graduation moved to the UK, where he became immersed in British graphic design culture and acquired a lasting affection for many British design studios. In the mid-1990s he worked for the London music design company Stylorouge[1].

In 1996 Vanhorenbeke returned to Brussels to form Coast in partnership with his wife Celia Carrera. Today, the studio works on brand identity, art direction, packaging, print and new media. They have a strong focus on large-scale global branding projects, yet simultaneously relish working on small design-led projects. Their work for clients in both the commercial and cultural sectors reveals a sense of painstaking craft, careful research and high aesthetic standards.

The group share their studio space with web designers and architects. The interview was conducted via email.
—

Where did you study?

Frédéric Vanhorenbeke: Celia Carrera and I met at the Ecole de Recherche Graphique in Brussels, where we studied graphic design and all sorts of things during our four years there. It was the kind of experimental school where multidisciplinary means 'all you can do'. Creativity in any field could be expressed either through visual language, written language or conceptual art. I also spent a year studying economics before going to art school.

What prompted you to start your own studio?

As a student I had already worked on some freelance jobs and wanted to apply to design studios in Brussels. Things have changed now, but back then communication and visually related communication was ruled by advertising agencies and corporate studios with a dated approach to graphic design. So I made the decision to move to London. A lot of design studios inspired me back in 1995 – Why Not Associates[2], Farrow[3], Cartlidge Levene[4]. After contacting some, I met Rob O'Connor[5], founder of Stylorouge, who offered me a placement for a week. This placement became a job, a wonderful job. I worked for some great music clients and I met great individuals who now run their own studios: Christopher Thomson (Studio Thomson[6]), Tony Hung (Adjective Noun[7]), Andy Huckle (1358[8]), Richard Bull (Yacht[9]). I decided to go back to Brussels

01 |
02 |
03 |

01/ Project: Exhibition design.
Date: Sep 2008. Client: Ville de Bruxelles.
Designer: David Nerinckx.
02/ Project: Party invitations and poster.
Date: May 2009. Client: Statik Dancin.
Designer: Peter E Rossi. Illustrator: Peter
E Rossi. 03/ Project: Packaging Death
Disco album. Date: Sep 2003.
Client: News/Ivan Smaaghe.
Designer: Frédéric Vanhorenbeke.
Illustrator: Frédéric Vanhorenbeke

in autumn 1996 to launch my own design studio as I wanted to use this energy for my own clients and projects.

Is it the same people who inspire you now, or have you discovered others?

Yes, they still inspire me, as they are still guardians of quality and intelligence in design. But I have many others now: Spin[10], MadeThought[11], Bibliothèque[12], Graphic Thought Facility[13], Wim Crouwel[14]. I'm also very inspired by information design. Magazines like *Adbusters*[15], *Time*[16] and *Monocle*[17] are very inspiring. The branding and strategic work of agencies like Wolff Olins and Interbrand are also nurturing our current global approach.

It's unusual for a small design company to take inspiration from big brand-focused agencies like Wolff Olins and Interbrand. Do you see a time when you might be more like them, employing dozens of people and working for global brands?

We do not want to be like big brand-focused agencies (employing dozens of people and having offices worldwide), but we can learn from them: their client-focused approach, the value of their methodologies. That doesn't mean we are going for the global look and feel. We see ourselves as custom-made thinkers for clients who want to avoid the global brand approach – something we think will disappear with the reemergence of local interests. When a global brand asks us to develop a project, we always take the path of difference.

We try to focus on results. By understanding the client's needs we are more likely to open up our minds to all disciplines. If these disciplines involve research and strategic understanding, development and implementation, then we deliver it all. As graphic designers we are frustrated by clients asking us 'only' to resolve graphic issues when we feel it is more the substance and the content that need to be challenged. By getting to the source of the problem (the brand, the cultural centre, the magazine content), we can redirect by understanding the needs and shaping the content.

In your early days where did you go for help and advice?

I couldn't really count on anyone for advice. I had help from my mother, who rented me her flat for less than the market rate. This helped me a lot in setting my studio space in my room.

How important was it to find a good studio name?

I wanted a short, strong, English name to send out an Anglo-Saxon message. I wanted to bring back to Belgium my London experience as a graphic designer. The last frontier between England and Belgium is the coast. From the coast you can see the horizon, and anything is possible. I also wanted to show my London friends my English flag was still flying in Belgium. Coast was also a response to Yacht, the studio formed by my friends Christopher (Thomson) and Richard (Bull) in 1996.

Did you have a vision of how you wanted your studio to be?

Not really. I just wanted to do great jobs and be different. At that time I was 25 years old, so very open to any kind of job as long as I could do it differently. I was still very impressed and influenced by the year I had spent in London and the experiences I had there. Nine to five was not an option. I wanted to spend as much time as I could to make the work look and feel good.

Did you have to borrow money?

Yes, for my first computer. It was quite an investment at that time. In our first month as a studio I was still working on an Apple IIvx with a 15-inch screen so I needed to change. I didn't have any kind of business plan or PR vision, so borrowing money for a computer and a car was all I needed.

Can you describe the process you went through to get started?

I remember struggling to find a name and create my own corporate identity. I wanted to have my own identity before going to meet people and start working. As a first piece of design I printed 100 Coast T-shirts, which I sent to all my friends – I remember sending 20 T-shirt boxes to London. I always knew that my friends and relations would talk about my work and maybe get me a project. The first project for which I was paid was the identity of the restaurant L112. The client was a friend of my brother's. This first job gave me the opportunity to express myself. It got people talking about Coast, and also got some press attention. I also got a phone call from the director of a real-estate company to do their business cards. This job was the starting point of a long relationship that is still going on today. I am still very grateful to that person who was one of my first clients.

Can you define your roles within Coast?

My role is multiple. As creative director I have an overview of the studio production, and talk with the team about projects. As client manager I arrange meetings and create project frameworks. As brand analyst I work conceptually on the content of a brief and the values of a brand. We are now in a new interpretation of our disciplines as we are working for bigger clients asking us to think globally about their brands. As my experience in brands has grown, I am able to have a 360-degree view of a project. I'm also still

a graphic designer. Celia is studio manager. She works on the finance and billing aspects of the studio. She is also in charge of the interns and the employment policy. She has just finished a degree in management so she will integrate her new competences to our studio structure soon.

That's a really interesting move. What do you think Celia's management training will bring to the studio?

I think we are now entering a new era in our discipline, and as I always want to move forward, our studio is getting more professional. We are still strongly bound to our graphic roots, but now we are looking for the best practice approach: intelligence, brand consultancy, graphic design, quality production. Celia is helping to structure our teamwork, making us more flexible and avoiding cross-information. She will also be working on our profile, to reach our audience and meet people we could work for and with.

Could you talk about how you find new clients?

I've been lucky since day one as clients come to us. I never had to call people to get work. The only thing we did in 2002 was send out approximately 300 portfolios to prospects and friends. I think that kind of action can bring you clients, via friends or contacts. It's never a stone in the sea.

Today you have a very broad range of clients. How did you achieve this?

There are many reasons. The first is the Belgian market, which is really quite small. With only 10 million inhabitants, Belgium has only a few international brands, in fields like food (chocolate and beers), fashion (Antwerp fashion scene) or banking. So if you want to make a living from graphic design and communication you have to broaden your client sector. Second, I always welcome the opportunity to work with different sectors. I believe that design has a place in any sector or within any brand. Third, we have attracted a broad range of clients by understanding them. Lastly, we never close our doors to anybody. Working for certain brands or institutions can be exhausting, but you get the reward in the end. Working for different sectors is also a good way of understanding the world today.

Can you talk about how you present Coast to new clients?

We are currently rethinking what Coast is. We no longer think of ourselves as just graphic designers. We believe now that our experience of what brands are makes us different and more than just visual artists. I find it hard now just to work on 'beauty' or 'systems'. More and more, we are building up the brief

04 | 05 |
06 | 07 |
   | 08 |

04/ Project: Identity/wrapping tape. Date: Jan 2009. Client: Action+Service.
Designers: Pierre Abergel, Frédéric Vanhorenbeke. 05/ Project: Identity. Date: Oct 2004.
Client: Designed in Brussels. Designers: Frédéric Vanhorenbeke, Ingrid Arquin.
06/ Project: Identity/poster. Date: 2005 Onwards. Client: Lucy Lee Recordings.
Designer: Frédéric Vanhorenbeke. Photographer: Frederic Leemans.
07/ Project: Poster. Date: Sep 2008. Client: Alain Gilles. Designer: Frédéric
Vanhorenbeke. Illustrator: Frédéric Vanhorenbeke. 08/ Project: Branding and packaging.
Date: Jun 2009. Client: Komono. Designers: Frédéric Vanhorenbeke, Ingrid Arquin. 09/
Project: Global communication campaign KVS Theatre. Date: May 2007 Onwards. Client:
KVS. Designer: Ingrid Arquin. Illustrators/Photographers: Various.
10/ Project: Electronic Music Festival identity. Date: Mar 2009. Client: Bozar.
Designer: Frédéric Vanhorenbeke. 11/ Project: Packaging, Four Years, Culture Club
Compilation. Date: May 2005. Client: Culture Club. Designer: Frédéric Vanhorenbeke.

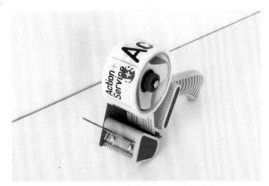

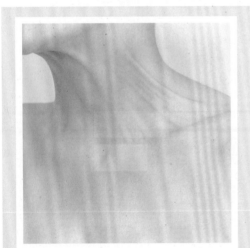

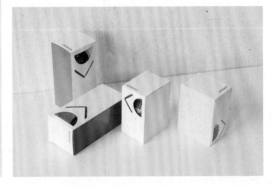

The Penelope[s] Steal This[E.P.]

with the clients, talking about brand analysis, marketing and strategy. We are in the process of being global thinkers. This enables us to work on content and form, building up the best solution for our clients. Therefore we present ourselves as a branding studio, not a graphic design studio.

Employing people is often the most problematical aspect of running a studio. You have to keep talented people motivated and inspired. How do you do this?

Employing the best people is the key to success. We are very lucky to have built a strong team of four people who are now totally independent in their work. We work together but act individually. Any new employee has to merge into this jigsaw, with the ability from day one to also be independent. Finding a new designer at Coast is very difficult. Last time I tried to find someone to become part of the jigsaw, I failed.

What qualities do you look for when employing a designer?

Besides the basics (typography, precision, intelligence, similar reference points), we are looking for an independent, confident individual. They must be a global thinker, a brand-lover, a communicator, and a social being. We are looking for people who are willing to create intelligence. We are looking for people open to discussion and ready for collaboration. We are looking for people who understand the value of time and the value of a client.

What is your approach to designers who want a sense of personal authorship?

Coast is not the kind of studio with a recognizable style, so designers of any background can develop their own personality as long as it fits the brief. I think Coast is stronger as one voice and all designers are art directors. We often act as individuals but sign our work as a group. All jobs are credited to Coast.

Do you have a profit-share policy?

We do not have a specific policy, but when we win an important project – an international pitch, for example – we give a bonus. The bonus can be money or a paid trip. Last year Ingrid [Arquin], one of our designers, went on a trip to New York. This year we had a weekend together in London. I believe deeply that rewarding people is as important as being able to give them a nice job.

Do you socialize as a studio?

Socializing is very important to us, and most of the time we socialize with food! We eat together at the studio (I cook pasta, Ingrid

makes a salad) and sometimes we eat outside. As most of us have young children, we don't socialize as much as before (pub on Friday, studio party once a year with bands and DJs). Socializing means creating an atmosphere of companionship, that we are all in the same boat travelling in the same direction. It's good to know that more than work binds us. It's like being part of a family.

You and Celia have two young daughters. It's often hard for married couples to mix professional and family life. Does this pose any special problems for you?

We think now we have found some kind of balance. Having a family is such a great experience you don't want to mess it up (even if sometimes we are on the edge). Celia picks up our daughters at school after work and I come home for dinner. Having kids pushes you into being 100% efficient between 9.00am and 6.00pm. If you are not efficient, then you have to keep on working between 9.00pm and 11.00pm!

Do you have formal rules about things like time-keeping and timesheets?

We do not have formal rules about work hours as long as the job is done. For example, David [Nerinckx] arrives before 8.00am and I usually arrive at 9.00am. We have a timesheet policy so we can track the time spent on all projects. We have a web-based administration tool that enables Celia to track every aspect of a job, from hours spent to production costs. In these difficult times some clients want to cut costs, so we have to deliver accurate timesheets. Knowing the amount of time spent on a job is a good opportunity to fix an accurate rate for all jobs.

How do you maintain the balance between creativity and profitability?

I believe that being profitable is the only way to develop creativity as a studio. Money makes non-profitable work possible. I always try to maintain a healthy balance between highly creative projects (theatre communications, small visual identities) and profitable projects (global communication for larger brands) because I believe they profit from each other. Small projects enable us to push creative limits and experience new models that will feed bigger clients. Coast is a global communication platform in which brand strategy for a global brand like Belgacom is devised next to a small fashion brand invitation. I think being able to do both is our strength.

What is your attitude to interns?

We get emails with PDF and website links and we offer the best ones an opportunity to work for two months at Coast. Most of our interns come from France, so we don't meet them before they arrive. We do not take as many as we would like. I think it's because it's often exhausting working on projects, and having interns to look after at the same time can be too much. When we have interns they are treated as designers. They get their own studio space and they work on the same projects as the rest of us.

How important is the physical environment you work in?

Very important. This is why we have just moved to our new studio. We wanted the studio to create that sense of individuality we have. We spend at least 40 hours per week at work so having a physical environment that suits us is crucial. I don't really understand blank and meaningless studio spaces. I think it's part of our DNA, being able to translate our values in the space we work in. We asked an architect and an interior designer to create our studio layout. We have a kind of 'John Pawson meets Charles Eames' space. Our previous studio was open-plan, which meant a lot of disturbances. So when we moved I really wanted to keep an open space (vital for communication) but also have some privacy. The result is an open space divided by six-square-meter open cubicles. Each designer now has their own private space.

Do you have a music policy?

As our large studio is shared by web designers and architects, we play music for everyone. We have a stereo playing for all. Each workstation has its own controls, which allows individuals to be the DJ. Music is a key element in the mood of a studio; it plays the social role of unifying, and brings energy as well.

How would you define your studio's culture today?

In Belgium we are at the crossroads of culture. I believe we have influence from the north (Holland, England and Sweden), and from the south (France and Spain). We love Swiss typography but we try to avoid that narrow path of graphic design talking to graphic design. Our culture is to mix our graphic culture background with warm communication. Our culture today is more strategic and communication-led, and we are more open to brands than before.

Do you have any advice to give to someone thinking of setting up a first studio?

Always start with a paying client. Always work for less money for highly creative projects that can bring you press or new creative jobs. Never work for free.

If you could start all over again, what would you do differently?

I think there are many things we should have done differently. Use the word 'no' more often, for example. But the only important thing I can think of is PR. I think PR can connect a studio with its best audience.

1 Stylorouge, London-based design company, founded in 1981 by designer Rob O'Connor. Best know for album covers for Blur and Morrissey.

2 Why Not Associates, British design group run by co-founders Andy Altmann and David Ellis, graduates of the Royal College of Art in London.

3 Farrow, a London-based design company formed by designer Mark Farrow. Worked for Harvey Nichols, Jimmy Choo, British Museum, EMI Records.

4 Cartlidge Levene, formed in 1987 by Ian Cartlidge and Adam Levene. British design group with strong typographic ethos.

5 Rob O'Connor, English designer and founder of Stylorouge.

6 Studio Thomson, English design group.

7 Adjective Noun, English design group, formed 1999, www.tonyhung.co.uk.

8 1358, English design studio, www.onethreefiveeight.com.

9 Yacht, London design studio run by Richard Bull. Established in 1996. Published monograph in 2000.

10 Spin, London design company founded in 1992 by Patricia Finegan and Tony Brook. See page 204.

11 MadeThought, design consultancy, London. Founded in 2000 by Ben Parker and Paul Austin. Clients include Stella McCartney, Yves Saint Laurent, Reiss and Nokia.

12 Bibliothèque, London design company founded by Mason Wells, Jonathan Jeffrey and Tim Beard. See page 44.

13 Graphic Thought Facility (GTF), London-based design consultancy formed in 1990 by Huw Morgan, Paul Neale and Andy Stevens.

14 Wim Crouwel, one of the founders of influential Dutch design group Total Design, formed in 1963. See page 13.

15 Adbusters, Canadian-based anti-consumerist magazine. Edited by Kalle Lasn.

16 Time, long-established US news and current affairs magazine.

17 Monocle, magazine founded by Tyler Brûlé.

Doyle Partners
Founded: 1985
Personnel: 12
Location: New York, US
www.doylepartners.com

Stephen Doyle founded Doyle Partners in
New York in 1985, with William Drenttel[1] and
Tom Kluepfel[2]. He previously worked at *Esquire*
and *Rolling Stone*, and for the great Tibor
Kalman[3]. A flavour of Kalman's quixotic spirit
can be seen in Doyle's cultured and often
witty graphic expression.

Doyle Partners' work has been described
as having a 'distinct design signature and
vocabulary combining a neoclassical (or
what [Doyle] calls "modern classicism") type
aesthetic with an interest in visual puns.'
Humour is a recurring theme in the studio's
work. Doyle has said: 'If something is warm
or friendly, then it actually reaches out to
people; it begins a dialogue, a two-way street.
We try to use humour as a human magnet.'
Doyle Partners work in the retail, music,
editorial, arts and corporate sectors. The
12-strong studio functions as a 'family unit'.
Everyone eats lunch together, and the glue
pot and the bandsaw play a crucial role in
the studio's output.

The interview took place via email.
—

Why did you decide to start a studio?

Stephen Doyle: Honestly, it was to get the
inevitable failure of it behind me. I didn't want
to wake up one day, years in the future, as
someone's employee without having tried it
on my own. This coincided with a would-be
client goading me to start my own shop. I
was working for Tibor Kalman at M&Co[4], and
they accused me of having an 'agent'. If I was
going to be a profit centre, they asked, 'why
not keep the proceeds?' And they offered me
work. Lots of it. The client was Rizzoli, and
they offered me every single book on their
list. Too tempting to turn down, so I jumped.

You use the personal pronoun. Was it just you
at this point?

Not knowing anything about business,
I thought it would be more fun to fail as a
group than as an individual, so I teamed up
with Bill Drenttel, a friend who worked at
an ad agency who promised to bring in lots
of advertising and marketing work, and my
old friend from college (Cooper Union) Tom
Kluepfel, who was working with me at M&Co.
Bill knew business and advertising, Tom knew
institutional design, having worked at Cooper
Union and the Museum of Modern Art, and
I knew editorial design. It seemed like a good
combination.

But to answer the point about the personal
pronoun: the work that we do at our studio

01 |
02 |
03 |

is dependent on a host of staff members, thoughtful clients, and expert collaborators in production, photography, management and all kinds of other expertises including finance. As I write this, I struggle with the editorial usage of the word 'we' because I do not practise alone. However, I'm switching, for the most part to that very American usage of 'I' not because this is about me, but rather that this is a personal reflection of my experience from my own point of view. It is opinionated, and I don't feel like I should foist my idiosyncrasies onto my partners or staff any more than I already have.

So, you started Drenttel Doyle Partners with a regular paying client; did the money roll in from the start?

When I worked at *Esquire* magazine, a financial columnist gave me sound advice: 'Always make sure you have "fuck you" money in the bank.' What's that? It's enough money, he explained, that when you've really had it one day, you can carefully articulate to your employer your reasons for leaving: Fuck you! So I invested my 'fuck you' money, equal to a year's salary, into a new business venture. Bill borrowed his equivalent sum, and I forget about Tom. When Bill started ordering cases of Bordeaux, and having a car service take him to meetings, I had to sit him down and have a little talk. I got him a subway map. We rented space, gutted it, painted it, and waited for Rizzoli to return our calls. They did not.

That must have been a blow – did other work come in?

We started getting small jobs, book covers, posters for small arts organizations, series of book covers, books, and quickly we built a business. It was 1985, Apple had launched the Macintosh. We used messengers to deliver things, type was set at typesetters, and we always had time for coffee and cigarettes in the morning while we waited for the type to be delivered. We made comps from black and white Xeroxes, constructing type from Xeroxes of type showings. We had Photostats made. We glued sheets of 'repro' down after rolling it through the waxer, and every once in a while we'd get a fax. We bought a slide projector to show our carousel of work. We began to draw a salary. At our previous jobs, our pay scales were very unequal, so we devised unequal salary ladders that would all meet in five years. Importantly, though, the three partners shared the business equally. A triangle can be sharp. I insisted on it being equilateral.

It sounds as if you already had a clear idea how you wanted your studio to be. Did you have a clear vision at this point?

Our idea for our studio was that we were going to follow what we witnessed in Britain, which was a merger of design and advertising,

01/ Project: David Byrne CD. Date: 2001.
Client: Virgin Records.
Art Director: Stephen Doyle.
Designers: Ariel Apte, John Clifford.
02/ Project: Uni-Diversity. Date: 2001.
Client: The New York Times.
Designer: Stephen Doyle.
03/ Project: Epidemic Scorecard.
Date: 2003. Client: The New York Times.
Designers: Stephen Doyle, Ariel Apte,
John Clifford. 04/ Project: The Book of
Lamentations. Date: 1997. Client: Marsilio
Publishers. Art Director: Stephen Doyle.
05/ Project: The Druid King. Date: 2003.
Client: Knopf. Designer: Stephen Doyle.
06/ Project: The Stories of Vladimir
Nabokov. Date: 1995. Client: Knopf.
Designer: Stephen Doyle.
Photographer: Geoff Spear.

holistic marketing for companies emerging out of one voice, so that the identity and the marketing were seamless. It was a new idea at the time. But vision is one thing, and clients are another. When you start a studio, you work for your friends. And then you work for your friends' friends. Bill had a friend who was an editor at a publishing firm. Bingo, a book cover. A friend of mine referred me to the art director of a coffee-table book publisher. She was beautiful, so I designed coffee-table books. Then I married her. And so it went, that work led to more work, work and life intermingled and has intermingled since. Within a year we were getting work from strangers, and we were, honestly, lucky. We designed a prototype *SPY* magazine over a six-month period for a fee of $2,000.

Did you take on every job you were offered or did you discriminate?

We learned to balance work for fun that would put us on the map (like *SPY*), and work to keep the business alive. We created a complex algorithm for how to take on or turn away new business. 'The Three Fs' refers to Fun, Fame and Fortune. Pick two, any two, and it's OK to take on. Just one? Forget it. Since I married a client, there was another F that wanted to get onto the list, but that one remains unofficial as *Studio Culture* is a family publication. We keep it at three. We have another maxim to offer: your current business is the path to new business. Which is to say, contacts lead to contacts. Keep your reputation clean, keep your enthusiasm up, and remember that designers get business based on personality, not work.

Was it still just the three of you at this point?

When we started, we were three partners, an assistant and two designers. In two years or so, we grew to 12, and we have stayed at roughly 12 ever since. This size allows us to work on vast projects, yet keeps the partners actively involved with all the work. I don't want to be a new business machine and I don't want to have to 'feed the beast'. I want to be a designer. After ten years or so, Bill Drenttel peeled off to start a much smaller studio with his wife Jessica Helfand.

Splits among business partners can be damaging. Did you have a plan to deal with any of the partners leaving?

We agreed years ago that if one of the partners were to leave, his payment would amount to one-third of the book value of the company. There would be no big buyout, and the emphasis would be for the company to remain healthy for the partners and employees left. Earnings for good work and reputation pays itself out as salary and bonus each year, and we did not want to reward a partner for leaving. Another agreement we have in writing is that spouses

07 | 08 |

09 |
10 | 11 |
12 |

07/ Project: Fresh Dialogue. Date: 2006. Client: American Institute of Graphic Artists.
Designer/Photographer: Stephen Doyle. 08/ Project: Fountain of Life, dedication plaque.
Date: 2005. Client: The New York Botanical Garden. Sculptor: Stephen Doyle.
09/ Project: 19th Amendment. Date: 1996. Client: The New York State Division of Women.
Designer: Stephen Doyle. 10/ Project: Truth. Date: 2001. Client: The New York Times.
Designer/Photographer: Stephen Doyle. 11/ Project: Was/Saw. Date: 1994.
Client: American Center for Design. Art Director: Stephen Doyle.
12/ Project: Machiavelli's Discourses. Date: 2007. Client: Self-Initiated.
Designer: Stephen Doyle.

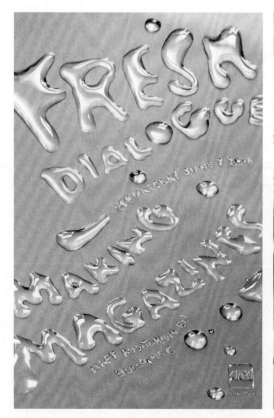

THE RIGHT
OF CITIZENS
of the United States
TO VOTE
SHALL NOT BE
DENIED
or abridged
by the United States
or by any State
ON ACCOUNT
OF SEX

Bill Drenttel
Stephen Doyle

ACD

TRUTH

WAS

Patrons Night

would not be allowed into the partnership.

Lots of studios fail when partners fall out. You and Tom have been partners for a long time. Is there a secret to maintaining a successful business partnership?

I just came back from an enjoyable lunch with Tom. He talked about his daughter, her riding lessons, and how her teacher says it might be time that they 'lease' a horse for Samantha, so that she can 'become one with the horse.' I can't remember laughing so hard as he showed me her progress, with fingertips on the luncheonette counter, trotting in a circle, and then jumping over my ballpoint pen. There is an incredible intimacy and trust that is essential to a successful partnership. I will not liken it to a marriage. It is nothing like it. But for us, it's more like a catamaran: Tom is the hull and I am the sail. He is buoyant and seaworthy, and I pull us forward. (When there is wind.)

Let's come up to date. Do you have a philosophy for dealing with clients?

There is alchemy in design, but the way that we accomplish it is to be careful listeners. When potential clients ask me to articulate what differentiates us from our competition I tell them that they can't go wrong with any of our competitors (assuming they are in a certain league) but that we excel at listening. And the dialogues that we have with our clients, fuelled by our curiosity about their businesses or products or services, makes our work with them actually collaborative. Ultimately then we have arrived at the solution together. We don't spring things on our clients. We bring them along through the process.

Does this collaborative approach extend to the designers who work for you, or are you the sort of studio boss who demands obedience and adherence to your commands?

As an anarchist, it's still hard for me to come to terms with being a boss. Maybe that's why I have a partner. Tom can be the boss, and I can be the petulant child (his words). I like it when the staff are really, really good at designing, at creating, at inventing. I love it when they bring their imagination into play, and show me references that I've never seen. That's when it's fun, when I get to be a teacher and crit the work, help them sharpen it and shape it. I can be disappointed when I have to be the one who supplies the ideas, and then they execute. I like style, but I love substance.

Designers can easily be demotivated. They get discouraged easily. Can you talk about the ways you keep your staff motivated?

I try to let my enthusiasm be contagious. I show them what I'm looking at. I share my

scrapbooks of clippings and wrappers, and photos, and installations, and artworks. The people who come to work here are motivated to begin with. I will never forget the one interview I had with a designer who said she wanted to work for me because our studio was quite close to her apartment.

You do a varied range of work. Does this help to keep everyone stimulated?

If I worked in a studio that did, say, annual reports, I think I might kill myself. What I love about our studio is that we are usually doing a project or two for which we are particularly ill-equipped. In fact, in a sense, it is our own naivety that lets us design with a fresh eye. At the moment, we are working on new packages for Band-Aids. It's a one-billion-dollar global brand of Johnson & Johnson. We are trying to add humanity to a package that is just larger than your business card. We are also working on a new skin for a skyscraper in Toronto. It is one-quarter of a mile high, and we are working on a pattern to be 'fritted' onto its new glass skin; the stone that has been on the building since 1963 is 'failing' (translation: falling off). I was introduced to a roomful of investment bankers (the owners) as one of the 'world's top fritting experts'. Who knew? Somehow I am always over my head, or underwater, or inexpert at what I am asked to do. It is thrilling. This is what keeps me coming into the studio every day. You just never know who is going to call, and what obstacle they are going to throw in your path.

How do you stay personally motivated?

I come to design with an interest in psychology. I am more fascinated with culture and art and architecture than I am with graphic design. I used to think I was interested in typography, but in fact it's language that interests me. My references are more likely to be artists like Tom Friedman[5], Tara Donovan[6], Tony Cragg[7], Martin Puryear[8]. Of course I was influenced and daunted (still am) by my teacher (and first boss) Milton Glaser[9]. I owe a lot of my own design anarchy to my teacher George Sadek[10], who brought a very precise lunacy to the intersection of classicism and modernity. And then, of course, there's Tibor who proved: what's the point of having a personality if you're not going to use it. Sometimes I like to think with my hands. I struggle to create a new visual language, a way of bringing ideas to life in a memorable and human way. In the studio, we spend so much time trying to solve people's problems, it's a welcome relief to create some problems of my own. If inanimate objects could think, what would those thoughts look like? Writing is a visual representation of sounds that, strung together, represent ideas. Is there a shortcut to seeing ideas? That question, that crevasse, is where I thrive, and the way I throw myself into it is with my hands,

because they don't follow the logic of my head.
They have a different scale, and a different
rhythm. Finding time to think with one's hands
is not easy. But neither is finding time to eat.
And you should!

How would you define your studio culture?

I asked the 'studiants' themselves.
They told me that Doyle Partners is like
a family, and that we 'feed off each other',
which conjures up a kind of conceptual
nepotistic cannibalism. But they say they've
never worked in a place where everyone
eats lunch together, and where there is no
rule book. Everyone rises to their abilities,
capacities and interests. They like that
our studio has a focus on the tactile,
and there is room to build, cast, glue and
photograph. (One of our designers left and
went to Interbrand[11], the huge multinational
conglomerate, but I discovered they don't
even have a bandsaw there! Shocking! How
do they get anything done?) I walk through
the studio a couple of times every day. I pull
up a chair and breathe down their necks and
we review designs on their screens. They like
that! Our studio is like a design laboratory,
and everyone is trying to prove a theory, or
exercise an equation. And they quote back
to me the expressions I use: 'Wouldn't it be
more poetic if...', 'Maybe this would be more
beautiful...', 'Make it funner...'

Do you have lots of studio interns?

Lucky kids, they get a double whammy:
both on-the-job training, and a multi-month
interview for a job. In a small studio, interns
get to work on big projects, and a variety
of them. Many, many of our designers here
started as interns, including an art director
who's been here for 15 years, not including
his moves to Texas and Connecticut. But he
came back. Now we pay him.

What advice would you give to anyone starting
a studio today?

It's a different commitment now than
it was in 1985. We needed facilities and
equipment: drawing boards, a waxer, phones,
messengers, a type house, a fax machine,
cigarettes, rubber cement (and thinner), a
carousel projector, Xerox machine, cameras.
Now, all those, except the cigarettes, are
basic items included with everyone's phone.
But it is not about the equipment – remember,
that's the 'book value'. The real value is the
ideas that you can bring to play, and whether
you are actually any different from the kids
next to you in your class. Are you starting
a studio because you believe you can make
a contribution to culture, or is it just another
beauty salon? For sure, there is room for
both, but I would like to salute the designers
who open a studio because they have a fire
burning inside them, and they just can't
put it out.

1 William Drenttel, graphic designer, editor and partner
in Winterhouse Studios. Co-founder of Design Observer.

2 Tom Kluepfel, designer and founding partner of
Doyle Partners.

3 Tibor Kalman (1949–1999) influential American graphic
designer of Hungarian origin. In 1979 he co-founded
design firm M&Co. Best known for his work as editor-in-
chief of Colors magazine.

4 M&Co, influential New York Design studio, founded in
1979 by Tibor Kalman. Designers who worked at M&Co
include Stephen Doyle, Stefan Sagmeister, Alexander Isley,
Scott Stowell and Emily Oberman.

5 Tom Friedman, American conceptual artist known for his
work using everyday materials such as toothpicks and
sugar cubes.

6 Tara Donovan, US artist, recognized for her commitment
to process. She has earned acclaim for her ability to
discover how the inherent physical characteristics of an
object can be used to transform it into art.

7 Tony Cragg, important British sculptor, famous for his
eclectic use of materials and adventurous approach.
Has lived and worked in Germany since 1977.

8 Martin Puryear, African-American sculptor working in
wood, stone, tar and wire. His work unites minimalism with
traditional crafts.

9 Milton Glaser, seminal figure in modern graphic design.
See page 130.

10 George Sadek (1928–2007), former dean of the Cooper
Union School of Art in New York, who transformed graphic
design education by having students work on actual
projects for non-profit institutions. Taught many leading
figures in American design scene including Ellen Lupton,
Emily Oberman, Abbott Miller, Carin Goldberg and
Alex Isley.

11 Interbrand, founded in 1974. Claims to be 'the world's
largest brand consultancy'.

Edenspiekermann
Founded: 2009
Personnel: 100+
Location: Berlin, Germany/
Amsterdam, Netherlands
www.edenspiekermann.com

Erik Spiekermann is one of graphic design's most articulate and highly regarded practitioners. Yet he claims not to be an especially good designer: 'I'm OK when it comes to complex things like grids. I like maths. I like geometry. I like multiples. How things are arranged on the page. I like that because it's all about discipline.'

During the 1970s he worked as a freelance designer in London before returning to Berlin in 1979 where, with two partners, he founded MetaDesign. In 2001 he left MetaDesign and started UDN (United Designers Network), with offices in Berlin, London and San Francisco. Since January 2009 he has been a director of Edenspiekermann.

Unusually among contemporary designers, Spiekermann has a sophisticated set of theories relating to the layout and management of design studios. His theories have been extensively road-tested in the various creative enterprises he has founded and run during a long career.

The interview was conducted in the offices of AIG, London.[1]
—

You have a vision of your perfect studio. You've even got a name for it – The 'Rundbuero' Studio (see diagram). Can you describe it?

Erik Spiekermann: Ideally it's a round space. It's made up of three or four concentric circles. At the centre is a reception area. This is where everybody enters. It is linked to the rest of the studio by a corridor. In the central reception area are the people who answer the telephones, do the emails and make the photocopies. It's where all the machinery is – the printers, the espresso machine. Everybody has to go in here several times a day to pick up printouts, pick up mail, get coffee and so on. Now, the further you go from the centre the quieter it gets. People in the outer rings have windows, others don't. The walls are maybe only shoulder height. If a secretary wants to see if I'm in the outer ring, she can get up and look across and see if I'm actually there.

So the walls don't go all the way up to the ceiling?

Not at all. You can shout across the studio. The people in the third or outer ring are the ones who need privacy. These guys spend time on the phones, and do conceptual work. People like me, in fact. All we have is a desk

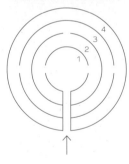

The 'Rundbuero' Studio

1 Noisy activities: reception, printers, copiers, cutting mats, archives, espresso machines, food.

2 Production and planning: people arranging projects, talking to other people.

3 Studio space: designers in front of screens.

4 Quiet area: writing, thinking.

01 |
02 |
03 |

01/02/03/ Project: Hering Berlin Porcelain
visual identity. Date: 2008.
Client: Hering Berlin GmbH, Berlin, Germany.
Creative Director: Ralf Weissmantel.
Design Director: Eva Schekorr.
Graphic Designer: Christian Hanke.
Strategy Consultant: Oliver Schmidthals.
Account: Claudia Baumgartner,
Kristin Laufer.

and a laptop – this is laptop country. In the second ring, there are proper computers with monitors. This is where the designers are; they actually spend all day working on screens. These people do physical work. There might be another ring, where people have cutting tables and boards. These are people who have to make shit.

OK, so looking at your diagram (see page 77), I see four rings joined by a corridor.

Yes, in order to get anywhere you have to cross through the various rings. Every time you do anything, you have to meet other people. So, unless you never go for a pee or a coffee, you have to meet other people at least twice a day.

Have you ever built this idealized studio?

Close enough. At Meta in 1996 we bought a building in Berlin. It was an ex-transformer station, 8000 square meters, or 90,000 square feet, for 250 people. Meta moved in after I had already split off from them. It was not ideal but the ideal was always in our minds. Essentially my vision of the studio was that it would go from noise to quiet. This layout means that traffic goes through the noisy area, you can't duck it. You see people coming in and out; there is always a physical presence.

Clearly you think this traffic and human interchange is important to the life of a studio?

Yes. Something happened to me once that taught me an important lesson. I was with one of my ex-partners at Meta. We had an in-house restaurant run by a proper chef. There were 120 of us, but we could only make about 50 lunches, no more. Some of our people would choose not to come, but our clients would come every lunchtime. I was freelancing at the time and I often dropped by at 12.30pm for lunch. I was standing with five or six people and I said hello to one of them. My former partner was there and actually asked me to introduce this person to him. I said this is so and so from Siemens. But there was another person there and he held out his hand and said 'I'm Michael, I've been working here for two years.' My partner didn't know him. With 120 people, that's a bit embarrassing.

To me, the only way to run a studio is to have perfect knowledge about the people and the work. The idea that you can ignore areas and not get involved is unthinkable. Do you agree?

I would come in at 8.30am and spend the first three hours just walking around the place, and once a day I talked to everybody. Sometimes only just to say hello. I usually knew their names or their sisters or dogs and various members of their family. But in the end, this old-fashioned 'managing-bywalkabout' wasn't popular with my partners. It led to questions such as 'why isn't he at his desk?'

Today, I've got 30+ people in Berlin, but even when I had 100+ I could present any project within half an hour's notice. I knew enough about it. I was involved in the brief. I was at the meetings. People would come to me with questions, often with just a choice of type or whatever, but I always knew enough to do all the presentations. I find that incredibly important, otherwise you're a manager and not a designer. I'm not a very good designer or manager, I'm 'medium' at both. But I'm a good motivator. Designers want to talk shop; they want to talk about design, even to an old git like me. My philosophy is that I want the physical space to inhale the traffic.
I don't want anyone slipping out unnoticed. I want people to know that if they are slackers, or go to the toilet too many times, or take 50 smoking breaks, there is some social control. That's not fascism, that's simply... good management. Whenever I design a space these days, it's the traffic that's important. Circulation for any architect is a big issue. The blood supply has to go in and out. It's very simple but I know so many studios that have no interaction at all.

I was always told that Germany didn't have design studios in the British or American sense, and that most of the commercial work was done by advertising agencies. Is there such a thing as a model for the German design studio?

I hate to say this, but I think I invented it. I started in 1979 while I was working at Wolff Olins[2] in London. We had a few German clients, and I went back and forth to look after them. One day they gave me a project because they just couldn't handle it. Production at British companies was weak, compared to what was the standard in Germany at the time. Michael [Wolff][3] knew this, and Wally [Olins][4] knew this, and so they handed me this project and this is how I started MetaDesign, while commuting between London and Berlin every two weeks. This was 1979, early 1980s even, when the largest German design studio was about six or seven people. It was usually a boss – a famous guy – with a couple of assistants, usually fresh out of school. And more often than not, German designers were also teachers, so they had a regular income to fund their studio. The rest of the people in the studio would be students, usually unpaid.

Was this the model for Otl Aicher's[5] famous studio?

His studio became famous for the Olympics in 1972, but the work started in 1969. All the people he employed were from this school in Ulm. Literally, his entire class. I'm not saying they didn't get paid, but it was a group of kids in their early 20s. For a long time, this was the German model – one guy with a few assistants. The studio layout would echo that. The main guy would be in a corner of his own office, and then there would be the studio floor, but never more than six people. In 1983 or 84 I had eight people, including interns and we were the biggest studio in the country – outside of packaging and advertising. So corporate design was done by advertising agencies and packaging designers. They were the ones who always put the stripes on the packaging, you have this brand and then you make it *like this* [makes diagonal motion with hands], with lots of stripes for the 'light' version. Then you have the specialized people and they tend to be in Hamburg for some reason. All the newspaper and magazine work, until today, was pretty much done in-house.

So you moved back to Berlin with the aim of starting your own studio?

At the time – the late 1970s – Wolff Olins was 75 people. I thought if they can do it in Britain, surely we could do it in Germany? So I came back to Berlin with the intention to build a large studio. It went up to about 16 or 18 people in the middle of the 1980s, which was quite large, and we started getting the projects that we should have been getting before. We got some large signage projects and some large corporate design projects. But the whole market in Germany was one generation behind Britain, which was one generation behind the States. And then in 1989 I realized this was getting too big for myself or too small for the big markets, so I realized I had to do something else because I'm not a businessman. I decided to bring in a businessperson.

I'm guessing you needed a business plan at this stage?

MetaDesign phase 2 started in 1990 and, for the first time, there was a business plan. It allowed for rapid growth to at least 50 or 60 people, because then we could compete with the advertising agencies. And also, at that time a lot of German work went to England – to Wolff Olins and Pentagram[6]. Clients would even go to America. A lot of American and British studios got work mainly because the company was one large design group. I realized this, and I said to my partners 'we need a middle-level management.' The guys we talked to are middle management; they are marketing people, two or three levels down from the CEO. So we needed to have people talking to them on the same level as them – a let-my-people-talk-to-your-people kind of thing. And that worked. Suddenly they were taking us seriously.

Is there a magic number for studio size?

You can have 125 people, but the work never gets done by more then five people. The teams are never bigger than that. It's all about group dynamics. More then seven people and you don't increase efficiency or effectiveness, you just have more meetings. If you have 12 people, you don't work twice as much as six people, you work 50% more, so in other words you lose money. Seven people round the table, six people plus a project manager, maybe seven plus an intern.

We know this from perceptive psychology – the magic number seven – and there's a good reason for that.

By the mid-1990s you were on a rapid growth cycle.

By the end of 1994 we were 70 people at MetaDesign, and we were by far the largest studio in the country. We got Audi and Volkswagen as clients, and that exploded because they needed so much stuff. The first internet work started in 1995, and then grew. It took another four or five years for us to have any real competition. Obviously there were the big studio networks. Landor[7] was doing packaging and airlines; Interbrand[8] was doing large corporate design work out of Switzerland. But in Germany, there was nothing like us – we really did invent the German design studio.

Can you talk about recruitment – was it easy to find all these people?

Until the mid-1990s there were no employed designers in German design. The advertising people employed designers but the designers in the design studios were all freelancers. People wouldn't want to be employed. I had a really hard time finding people. The German scene was very much what the Americans call a 'Mom and Pop shop' – Pop did the work, Mom did invoices. This has perpetuated the idea of a strong studio being one fellow and a couple of assistants until well into the mid-1990s. And if you talk to German designers – designers in their 30s, 40s or 50s – I'm afraid many of them worked with me at one time or another. Every year we do a sort of MetaDesign anniversary, a picnic in the park, and we had up to 300 people. I trained about 600 people in the years I was there. We looked at the personnel files once, and there were always two or three interns, so that would be 20 interns a year over five years. That's already 100 people; over ten years that's 200 people. And if you count those, and if you count all the employees, that's well over 600 people who I've personally employed at one time.

What sort of designer had you become at this point?

Well, I'm not a very good designer; I'm an OK designer. I'm OK when it comes to complex things like grids. I like maths. I like geometry. I like multiples. How things are arranged on the page. I like that because it's all about

discipline. I learnt about type through doing hot-metal typesetting. So I know that what is between the black marks is as important as the black marks themselves. With metal typesetting you have to touch it, it's not just the return key. So that's my discipline. I'm an art historian by trade; I'm slightly intellectual, maybe too intellectual. When it comes to visualizing things I'm too intellectual, it becomes too obvious. Neville Brody's the exact opposite of me. We've worked together successfully. Neville's a digital painter. He just throws it on the page and it looks great, but he can't repeat it. I'm the other way round. I provide the skeleton, I make sure things don't fall down. And he makes it look good, and I'm very happy with that.

When I set up my studio somebody said to me, 'always employ people better then you'. It was the best bit of advice anyone gave me. But I resisted it for a long time. It was hard to accept.

As a mediocre designer, I realized that I could look much better if I had good people. And because I'm good at certain things (I'm pretty good at type, especially the mechanical part of type, and I have a good knowledge of the historical), I can afford to hire good people. Some people are afraid of hiring better people but I've never been like that because actually it makes me look good. So the system was always that I'd hire really, really good people and let them do their shit.

That's the good thing about a large studio. If you had two or three people it is difficult because then you have the egos. When you have 20 or 30 people that evens things out. Also, the one thing I like about having more than 100 people, or more than 70 people, is you suddenly have this little grey area where you can hire two or three people who haven't really got a job description because it doesn't really matter. I hired this American programmer who I never told my partners about. He was doing database programming and C++ in the late 1990s before that really became a necessity, before we had PHP. I hired him because we could afford to.

I had another guy who was a conceptual person. He had no training whatsoever but he was just bright in a slightly weird way. You couldn't put him in a group of people. But you could feed him shit and he'd come out with this amazing stuff. Never to a schedule, never within a group, but I loved the luxury of having these guys who just prance about with bells on their caps. In a small studio you can't afford that.

Designers want to be credited for their best work. What is your view on credits?

I always give everyone a credit and make sure that everybody is in the bylines. I know how important it is to be able to say 'I worked on this'. I don't mind listing ten names in a credit. If the client lets me, I'd put Edenspiekermann, and then list the five or six people who worked on the team. Those people can put this work in their portfolios without lying, or pretending. I've seen portfolios that people have presented to me containing work done by me. They weren't even there. Forgery has become so easy, so if you give somebody a credit, it's out in the open. Of course, a lot of clients won't let you. We have quite a few clients who will not allow any credits whatsoever, which I find very, very difficult. Also credits are not only there for your CV, it's like applause. Designers need applause, they need to be praised and I like praising people.

What do you look for when hiring a designer?

They have to know something really, really well. Something they're really good at. If somebody's good at C++, or someone's really good at drawing, it doesn't matter what it is, they just have to have one speciality. Also, they have to have general knowledge. I hate people who don't read. I hate people who don't cook, or don't know anything about music. I couldn't work with anyone who only goes to McDonalds. I want people who know movies, who know music, who read books. As you know, not all graphic designers are 'multidimensional'. They don't read, they don't do anything else, and I couldn't work with those people. I need team people who have general knowledge because that's what we do, and I want those freaks who can do one thing that nobody else can do.

The most rewarding thing about working in graphic design is that you get to know about other industries. There are a dozen industries that I've worked in that I know pretty well. I know the car industry. I know the public transport industry. I even know the banking industry because I've worked for a few banks. And that's the best thing about our job – that we get to know about all these businesses. And I hate graphic designers who roll their eyes when they find out that we're working for a financial institution. Of course I'd rather only work for world peace. I'd have everything sustainable and green. But I can't just do art books. In fact I'm actually going to retire in four or five years time when I'm 66 or 67, and if I've managed to save some money by then, or sell my shares, then I want to do all the books I've never done. I've got half a dozen ideas, all about design issues.

Is there any work you wouldn't do?

I want people to admit that there is a conflict, that not everything we work for is great. We work for car companies, interesting and fascinating people, but cars are also evil. There are certain things we won't do; obviously, we're not going to work for somebody who makes landmines. I'd rather

04/05/06/ Project: Visual identity, trade fair and advertising concept for Amsterdam housing association Stadgenoot. Date: 2008.
Client: Stadgenoot (merger of two Amsterdam housing associations).
Creative Directors: Hans Booms, Rik Koster. Graphic Designer: Carmen Nutbey, Erwin Slaats, Marion de Backer, Melle Broeksma. Strategy Consultant: Hans Prummel, Joost Mogendorff.
Account Manager: Gerlanda Hoving.
Copywriter: Cathalijne Rodenburg, Pierre Stukker. Interaction Designers: Jack Zwanenburg, Johan Huijkman, Mathijs de Jong, Sonja Radenkovic.
Team Planner: Henrique van der Star.

07 | 08 |
09 |

07/08/ Project: Exhibition about public lighting, traffic management and traffic lights
in The Hague. Date: 2006. Client: The Hague's Traffic Management department.
Creative Director: Arjan van Zeumeren, Jan Dirk Porsius. Account Manager: Nick
Henning, Gerlanda Hoving. 09/ Project: Chocolate manufacturer TCHO visual identity.
Date: 2008. Client: TCHO Ventures, San Francisco, CA, USA. Creative Director: Susanna
Dulkinys. Graphic Designer: Tobias Trost, Robert Stulle, Marcus Scheller.
Illustrator: Francesca Bolognini. 10/11/12/13/ Project: German Railway visual identity
and corporate typeface. Date: 2006. Client: Deutsche Bahn AG, Berlin, Germany.
Creative Directors: Erik Spiekermann, Fabian Rottke, Ralf Weissmantel.
Graphic Designers: Julia Sysmäläinen. Type Designers: Erik Spiekermann,
Christian Schwartz. Strategy Consultant: Oliver Schmidthals.

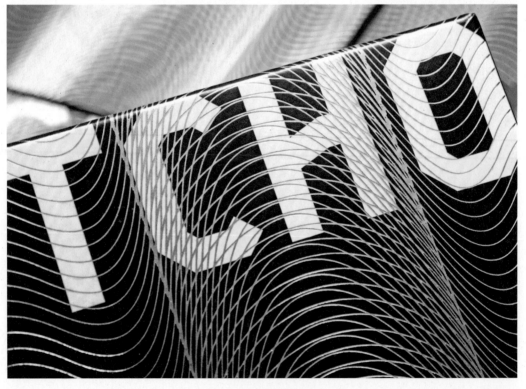

work for public transport than Daimler Benz.
But if they came in tomorrow and gave us a
big project I'm not going to say no. I can't
afford to. So the people I hire need to admit
that they're entering a commercial world.
They don't have to kill for their clients, but
they certainly need to be loyal while they're
working for them.

You touched on the importance of physical
space with your diagram. What about internal
details — does the furniture, the monitors,
the shelving have an impact on creativity and
efficiency?

Oh yeah. There are three or four major
issues. The first is how you feel while you
are working. I spend a lot of money on chairs.
We couldn't save anything there because we
spend 10–12 hours a day at work, and it's our
health. At my age, I know what a bad chair can
be like. Best chairs, best lighting, best desk,
best equipment. I won't buy crap and I won't
buy illegal software. I couldn't always afford
the best furniture, but as soon as I could, I
bought the best for my people. It doesn't have
to look chic. I don't mind Ikea tables. They're
fine as long as they're the right height and
they have the right surface. I want to have
best tools, which for me always included great
espresso machine, clean toilets, good drink,
decent water, that sort of stuff.

14 |
15 |
16 |

The second issue is that it is not necessary
to set out to impress clients. We don't need to
show off. We don't need marble staircases; we
don't need receptionists who constantly file
their nails. But we need to show that we care.

The third part is the communal part of it.
I want a space where people know what's
going on. I want transparency and if we have
a meeting room like the one we are in right
now, with glass walls, we have transparency.
But it's still sound-proof. You do certain
things that need to be conducted out of
earshot. Someone's review, for instance.
So privacy is necessary, but you want people
to see that essentially you have your hands
on the table.

Does location matter?

That's the fourth factor. It's important that
the space is somewhere everyone has an
easy time getting to. Here in London you
could probably get cheap office space out
of the centre, but if you want people to get
to it easily, it has got to be in the middle of
the city. The precise area is important too.
People need to get out. They need to buy
lunch for three or four pounds/dollars/euros,
or whatever, and they also need to see other
people. That's really important, that's why we
get stuck in fairly expensive places. We need
to be where it buzzes. You also need to bump
into peers and colleagues. Wherever I go, even
in London where I haven't lived for almost 20
years properly, I still bump into people I know.

14/15/16/ Project: Exhibition about public
lighting, traffic management and traffic
lights in The Hague. Date: 2006.
Client: The Hague's Traffic Management
department. Creative Director: Arjan
van Zeumeren, Jan Dirk Porsius. Account
Manager: Nick Henning, Gerlanda Hoving.

If I go to a bookshop I bump into people I know. I go to a pub or a restaurant and I bump into people I know. This is important.

So – a studio with good furniture, in a good urban location, near the centre of things. Anything else?

I always go round trying to tidy things. I'm not tidy myself. I'd like to be, but I fall behind like all of us and end up getting piles of paper on my desk. Then I get panicky and I file things into folders. I hate messy offices. I want clean toilets. I won't have posters all over the place. I won't have crappy notices next to the toilets; that annoys me. We don't print out stuff in Comic Sans, and even our office people in Berlin know that when they print out a notice they must use our studio typeface.

Should every studio have its own typeface?

I've always designed the typeface for every studio I've had. Always. It's easier for them to remember which one to use. I designed Unit for United Designers and now we have Espi for Edenspiekermann, and of course Meta had Meta, which I designed for them.

Do you think it's necessary for studios to socialize?

Yes, very important. We have a major crisis in Berlin at the moment; there's hardly any work. Some of the freelancers know they probably will have to go soon. The employees, the people on payroll, also know that it's getting tough. Everyone's getting cut down by 30%, and you can't just send people an email telling them this. You've got to have a get-together.

We have a tradition, when somebody has a birthday they bake a cake or they bring in a cake. Some buy it, some bake it. Now that we have 30 people, that's a birthday every other week. So there's a little email saying 'cake in the kitchen'. Everybody knows, 'oh it's somebody's birthday'. These things are important for team-building and loyalty-building. We have our Christmas parties, and we have our summer parties in between our picnics. We don't go over the top. We don't hire people to plan our parties. But I think they are important.

You've worked in and visited studios all over the world. Do studios exhibit national characteristics?

I've always been fascinated by how studios look different in different countries. Everybody in London works in spaces that we wouldn't even go into. Where British studios have eight people, we'd have two. You work in spaces that are incredibly small. My designers in Germany would just say 'you gotta be joking, there's no way we'll work there.' And they'd probably call some Office of Environment Administration and they'd come and close you down because you are treating people like battery hens. Or you go to Tokyo and they work standing up. Why do Americans love partitions? They love their reception areas, and having their work on the walls. You walk into a lot of American consultancies – design studios or whatever you want to call them – and they look like advertising agencies. And in our case – in Germany – it's much more clinical. It's much more like industrial design. In the UK a lot of studios look more like artist's studios; Britain is still very art-based. British design studios never have a reception area. You always walk straight into the studio.

1 Thanks to Tim Fendley of AIG London, for use of his sunny office.

2 Wolff Olins, design group founded in London in 1965 by Michael Wolff and Wally Olins. Wolff left in 1983; Olins in 2001. Today it is a brand consultancy, based in London, New York City and Dubai. Subjected to international media attention when it launched the controversial London 2012 logo.

3 Michael Wolff, British designer and creative advisor. Co-founder of Wolff Olins.

4 Wally Olins, British co-founder of Wolff Olins, now Chairman of Saffron Brand Consultants. Author of books on visual identity and branding.

5 Otl Aicher (1922–1991), leading German graphic designer. Co-founded the Hochschule für Gestaltung in Ulm (Ulm School of Design) in 1953. Best known for work as head designer for the 1972 Munich Olympics and creating the first Olympic mascot.

6 Pentagram, eminent design group formed in 1972 in London by Alan Fletcher, Theo Crosby, Colin Forbes, Kenneth Grange and Mervyn Kurlansky. See page 162.

7 Landor, founded by Walter Landor, a pioneer of branding, consumer research and modern logo design. Today Landor is a global branding consultancy employing hundreds of people.

8 Interbrand, founded in 1974. Claim to be 'the world's largest brand consultancy'.

Experimental Jetset
Founded: 1997
Personnel: 3
Location: Amsterdam, Netherlands
www.experimentaljetset.nl

Experimental Jetset's resemblance to a conventional graphic design studio is slight. Their work has a robust Modernist-inspired lyricism that is unquestionably Dutch, but that also exudes a radicalism that is derived from their sure-footed understanding of international pop culture.

Their T-shirts bearing the legend 'John & Paul & Ringo & George' have won them legions of fans around the world. Their whip-smart contribution to the movie *Helvetica* added to this global following. If they resemble anything, it's a modern rock band. As they note: 'it is ultimately the band model, and not so much the studio model, that really inspires us. A band is such a perfect socio-economical unit.' This doesn't prevent them from cherishing the tradition of great Dutch design studios. But for them, studio life is 'a way of living, a specific way of looking at the world'. It's a view that can be seen in their idiosyncratic work.

The interview was conducted via email. Experimental Jetset answered the questions collectively.
—

To outsiders there is a strong sense of Experimental Jetset being a trio of equals. Is this the case?

Experimental Jetset: Yes, absolutely. We function best as a group. It's only when the three of us are together that we feel completely safe, that we can deal with the stress, tension and daily deadlines that come with graphic design. We are not only colleagues, but also happen to be neigbours and best friends. At times, it feels as if we are a cult or a gang (to reference The Clash[1]; 'the last gang in town').

We were recently watching the classic *West Side Story*, a musical we've seen a million times before, but only now realized that the gang in the movie was called The Jets. 'When you're a Jet, you're a Jet all the way/From your first cigarette to your last dying day'. Childish maybe, but it gave us a boost of energy.

Most graphic designers become graphic designers because they have an urge to make work that they can call their own. Is it possible to satisfy this need within a studio of equals?

We can call all our work our own, because the three of us have an important input into it. In our view, that's one of the advantages of being a two-, three- or four-person studio: it's small enough for everybody to feel involved, but it's large enough to have the benefit of the collective; that magical feeling when the whole turns out to be more than the sum of parts.

Tell me how you came together to form Experimental Jetset.

We all met when we were still students at the Gerrit Rietveld Academy, Amsterdam. In 1997, Danny was asked by the editors of *Blvd*, a Dutch pop culture glossy, to redesign their magazine. Danny actually wanted to turn down the assignment; he was in his final year, and wanted to concentrate on his graduation project. Linda van Deursen[2], who was our teacher around that time, advised Danny to take on the assignment, and let it count as a graduation project. (Nowadays, this is a common practice at the Rietveld Academy, but back then to do an 'outside-of-school' assignment as your graduation project was unprecedented.) Danny realized the assignment was too vast for one person, so he asked Marieke, who was in the same class, to collaborate with him. (In fact, Danny had collaborated with Marieke before, on flyers and posters for Amsterdam rock venue Paradiso. They also published a small punkzine together, called *PHK*. All this took place between 1995 and 1997.) While Danny and Marieke were working on the first redesigned issue of *Blvd*, they realized they were in urgent need of good illustrations. They knew the work of Erwin, who was in another class (a year below them), and they really liked his illustrations, so they asked him to join. That was the first time the three of us worked together.

Choosing a studio name can be tough. I've always loved your name.

The name Experimental Jetset comes from *Experimental Jet Set, Trash and No Star*, an album from 1994 by Sonic Youth[3]. We have to admit, although Sonic Youth is one of our favourite bands, *Experimental Jet Set, Trash and No Star* is not our favourite SY album. That would probably be *Daydream Nation*, although we certainly like the older albums (*Bad Moon Rising*, *Evol*, *Sister*, etc), and we absolutely love *Goo* and *Dirty* (the SY 'pop' albums, so to speak). Truth is, it was never our intention to name our studio after that particular album. We actually wanted to name our studio 'International Jetset', after a song by The Specials[4]. But when we went to register our name at the Chamber of Commerce, the clerk in charge told us he couldn't accept 'International Jetset', as it was too vague, not specific enough to describe our profession. On the spot, we switched to 'Experimental Jetset', which turned out to be specific enough for the Chamber of Commerce. It is actually a very impractical name, especially in the Netherlands. When asking for a receipt in a store, or trying to order something over the phone, you always have to spell it out several times. We also realize the whole 'Jetset' part might come across a bit tacky, maybe even a bit arrogant: as if we are constantly hopping on and off planes, which is certainly not the case. We even get the odd person coming up to us, complaining that our work isn't very 'experimental' at all (we always tell those persons that Sonic Youth aren't really that 'Young' any more either). But having said that, we are pleased with the name. Although Experimental Jetset shouldn't be taken literally, it does typify who we are in a strange way.

There is a rich tradition of graphic design studios in Holland. Did you model yourself on any Dutch studios?

As students, we were certainly aware of legendary studios such as Wild Plakken[5] and Hard Werken[6] (although those two particular studios were already defunct by then). Another Dutch studio whose work we liked around that time was a trio of designers named Joseph Plateau[7] (and that studio is actually still around today). But the studio that influenced us most is without doubt Mevis & Van Deursen (the studio of Armand Mevis[8] and Linda van Deursen). They provide such a strong model to young design studios. They are fiercely independent, but at the same time really pragmatic. They always work for their clients directly, never through advertising agencies, or other types of agencies, which is something that we also find very important. They made a conscious choice to stay small; while other design studios of their generation transformed themselves into large 'communication agencies', Mevis & Van Deursen always stayed true to the model of the small graphic design studio. They put a lot of energy into education, in stimulating young designers, supporting students: they really pushed Dutch graphic design to the next level. It would be impossible for us to model ourselves on them; we simply lack their relentless energy and raw attitude. But they sure are a source of inspiration. When we're going through rough times, the idea of Mevis & Van Deursen just existing is enough to cheer us up.

Do any other Dutch studios influence you?

Our relationship with Total Design[9], as a model of a studio, is more complicated. Obviously, we are huge fans of the work created by Total Design under Wim Crouwel. Crouwel, despite his disguise as 'functionalist', is one of the biggest visual poets of our time, and his graphic language has shaped us profoundly, so in that sense we find Total Design very interesting. What we also find intriguing about Total Design is the almost 'menacing' character they were projecting around that time. They were really seen as an inhuman design machine, as 'wreckers of civilization', as a totalitarian

entity, which is something we find absolutely fabulous. But at the same time, we also realize that Total Design signalled in many ways the beginning of the sort of studios that we very much dislike: large communication conglomerates, where the actual practice of graphic design is overshadowed by branding strategies, marketing theories, advertising models, etc. In short, all the things we hate.

We understand that for designers like Crouwel, and others of his generation, it was absolutely necessary to break with the 'artsy-craftsy' past of graphic design, to push it into a more professionalized, seemingly more 'scientific' direction. We realize that this was an important step in the emancipation of graphic design. But we feel we are now at a point in history where we actually have to go in the opposite direction. We want to keep that 'menacing' character of Total Design intact, but combine it with a more DIY, lo-fi approach. A synthesis of Crouwel's late modernist language, and the more arts and craft-based ethics of early modernism. Capturing that 'large-scaleness' of TD, and trying to make it work within the context of a small-scale studio. At least, that is what we try to do.

The model of the movement has been very inspirational to us as well. We really like the idea of the studio as a small movement in itself. The studio, not as a nine-to-five job, but as a way of living, a specific way of looking at the world. In that sense, we really see Experimental Jetset as a three-person movement. One movement that really influenced us was De Stijl[10]. Being part of the canon of Dutch history, De Stijl is something every kid learns about in high school, so we knew about De Stijl from a young age, and it made a big impression on us: the idea of a group of people united by their aesthetic beliefs.

Another movement that made a huge impact on us, and still inspires us, is Provo, an Amsterdam anarchist group that existed between 1965 and 1967. Just like De Stijl, Provo is part of the historical canon, so we learned about it in high school. But Provo is very near to us, because Marieke's father, Rob Stolk, was one of the main founders. Provo was an anarchist group that was very much influenced by Dada, had links with the Situationists International[11], and was as much an art movement as a political party. Their performances and actions ('happenings') really influenced Dutch culture; it loosened up a whole generation. We will never have such a cultural impact, but we find the model Provo provided really inspirational.

What about non-Dutch studios?

We remember two particular books that we really enjoyed as students, two books that (each in their own way) projected very strong studio models. The first book had the absurd title *Design or Die! Cash or Charge! Graphic-Men is Coming!*, a sort of overview of the work of a Japanese design group called Tycoon Graphics[12], and it featured really cool pictures of the members of that particular studio walking around in Tokyo wearing American football outfits, in search of 'bad design'. A very bizarre monograph, but very attractive, in a Sigue Sigue Sputnik[13]-kinda way. The second book was *Pure* by Fuel[14], another book that projected a very strong sense of 'studio-ness', almost in a Gilbert & George[15] way. It's not that we modelled ourselves after these two studios, but we do remember that we enjoyed those two titles a lot.

Also, around the time of our graduation, there was a conference on UK design studios at Paradiso. The name of that event was 'Mind the Gap', and the invited speakers were Tomato[16], Peter Saville[17], Fuel, The Designers Republic[18] and Me Company. Maybe also Sean Perkins[19] from North[20] spoke there, but we aren't exactly sure [Eds. He did]. It was a brilliant afternoon, but again, it didn't really provide the model we were looking for. Maybe it was all a bit too British. Having said that, we absolutely love the studio culture in the UK. We really like that idea of hundreds of small studios circling the orbit, almost like bands. Because we really think all these small design groups together form a universe that is very comparable to that whole galaxy of pop and rock groups. We feel very connected with the studio culture of the UK, people are always very friendly to us. In many ways, we feel that we have more in common with groups and individuals such as Åbäke[21], Practise[22] and Sara de Bondt[23] than we have with contemporary Dutch studios. And every Christmas, we receive tons of cards from UK studios we sometimes haven't even heard of. We definitely feel a strong link with the UK.

Talking about bands, when it really comes down to it, we think that it is ultimately the band model, and not so much the studio model, that really inspires us. A band is such a perfect socio-economical unit. Large enough to have the benefit of shared responsibilities, and small enough for every member not to be alienated from the end product.
We sometimes think every human activity should be organized according to this model. Society should be divided in small units, each unit a platform of human creativity, be it baking bread, making music, writing books or curing people.

And the archetypical band is obviously The Beatles, as it was one of the first modern four-piece bands writing their own material. Earlier bands were still divided between a frontman and a backing band (for example, Buddy Holly and the Crickets), but The Beatles broke this whole model open, and pointed to a completely different division

04|
05|

04/05/ Project: Poster, brochure. Date: Dec 2004. Client: Second Amsterdam Film Night.

of labour, a revolutionary change in thinking. The 'John & Paul & Ringo & George' shirt we designed in 2001 should certainly be seen as a homage to the archetypical model of the band.

Can you say how you divide up your workload between the three of you?

We are not really big football fans, but we once saw this interview with legendary player Johan Cruijff in which he explained the concept of 'Totaal Voetbal' ('Total Football', or 'Total Soccer'), and that was really inspirational. Total Football is a system where a player who moves out of his position is replaced by any other player from the same team. So the roles aren't fixed; any player has the ability to be attacker, defender or midfielder. When you think about it, it's a very modernist, modular system. It's also very egalitarian, very Dutch, in a way. There are certainly parallels you can draw between Total Football and Total Design, Cruijff and Crouwel. In short, our ideal is to stay away from fixed roles. When dealing with stress and deadlines, we sometimes fall back into certain roles, but we try very hard to avoid that. Our intention is that the workload is divided equally, and that each one of us has the same set of abilities.

How did you cope with the practical issues of starting a studio – finding premises, administration, finance, etc? Were you able to turn to anyone for help in this area?

Regarding the premises: in the first few years, we actually worked from Marieke's living room. We had some great years there. We can still remember the meetings we had with the Royal Dutch Mail: four men in suits, climbing the stairs, after which they had to sit next to each other on an old couch in a living room, while we presented some stamps to them. Of course they loved it. That seems to us the easiest part about starting out as a graphic designer: you can always work from your living room.

As for administration: we remember that, when we graduated, we received a kind of coupon from an accountancy company specializing in bookkeeping for artists and designers. This coupon was good for one hour of free financial advice. So we turned to this accountant to do our taxes. Since then, we have switched to another accountant, but again one who specializes in artists and designers. We think it's really helpful when your bookkeeper understands your profession. As a designer, your income can be very uneven: long periods of receiving nothing, followed by short moments of receiving vast amounts of money. It's never an even flow of monthly payments. It's nice when your accountant knows about this.

We were also really lucky to receive a so-called 'start stipendium', a grant from the government given to designers starting businesses. It is important to realize that not every designer in the Netherlands gets a stipendium; it's only a really small percentage that receives such a grant, based on the quality of work. This grant enabled us to buy our first computers. Nowadays, every students has his/her own laptop, but when we graduated, in 1997, the question really was how to get your own computer. Computers seemed to be so much more expensive around then.

If we had to mention one specific person who we could always turn to regarding advice and support, it would be Rob Stolk, Marieke's father. As a printer he had a lot of knowledge about a wide variety of things. Sadly, he passed away exactly eight years ago; we miss him every day.

How did you attract clients in your early days?

Clients always know about us through projects we did previously. And we were quite lucky that, even as students, we had done some projects that were quite visible in Amsterdam: posters and flyers for rock venue Paradiso, T-shirts for local punk rock band NRA[24], brochures for fashion label House of Orange, the redesign of *Blvd* magazine. And of course we published our own punkzine, *PHK*. All the assignments we later did as Experimental Jetset can be traced back to these early projects. When you look back at this whole 'chain reaction' of assignments, the real question is: what was the first project, the 'prime mover' that caused all the other assignments? But it's really hard to establish that. Then we really have to go all the way back to our teenage years. For example, in the case of Danny, when he was around 15, he was drawing and Xeroxing small 'comiczines'. Because of these mini-comics he was asked by some local hardcore and metal bands to draw some T-shirts. When, after high school, he moved to Amsterdam to study, he was asked by punk band NRA to design some shirts for them as well. Through these NRA shirts, Paradiso became interested. And through the flyers we did for Paradiso, *Blvd* asked us to redesign their magazine. So yeah, it's this whole chain reaction of projects. And it started right in our teenage bedrooms, drawing comics, making mixtapes, cutting and pasting small zines.

Are all decisions taken collectively?

Yeah, absolutely. But it's not that we officially vote by sticking up our hands. Decisions are taken in a very organic way. The fact that there are three of us might have something to do with that. If two people agree on something, the third person usually just tags along. So we always move in a certain direction. There are never two blocks of people standing against each other.

06 | 07 | 08 |
09 | 10 | 11 | 12 |
13 | 14 | 15 | 16 |
17 | 18 | 19 | 20 |

21 |

06/07/08/09/10/11/12/ Project: Identity, signage, advertising and communication material. Date: Jun 2004. Client: Stedelijk Museum CS, Amsterdam. 13/14/17/18/ Project: Identity, exhibition design, signage and communication material. Date: Dec 2007. Client: 104 (Le Cent Quatre). 15/16/19/20/ Project: Identity and print. Date: Aug 2007. Client: Coming Soon Arnhem. 21/ Project: Poster. Date: Aug 2006. Client: *Helvetica* documentary by Gary Hustwit.

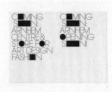

Meet the cast:

ABCD EFGHIJK LMNOP QRSTUV WXYZ

Now see the movie:

Helvetica

A documentary film by Gary Hustwit

A Swiss Dots
production,
in association
with **Veer**

swiss
dots **Veer**

Helvetica
A documentary film
by Gary Hustwit

Featuring:
Michael Bierut
Neville Brody
Matthew Carter
David Carson
Wim Crouwel
Experimental Jetset
Tobias Frere-Jones
Otmar Hoefer
Jonathan Hoefler
Alfred Hoffmann

Lars Müller
Norm
Mike Parker
Michael C. Place
Rick Poynor
Stefan Sagmeister
Leslie Savan
Paula Scher
Manfred Schulz
Erik Spiekermann
Bruno Steinert

Massimo Vignelli
Hermann Zapf

**Produced and
Directed by**
Gary Hustwit

Editor:
Shelby Siegel

helveticafilm.com

**Director of
Photography:**
Luke Geissbuhler

**Additional
Photography:**
Colin Brown
Gary Hustwit
Pete Sillen
Chris Welton
Ben Wolf

Additional Editing:
Laura Weinberg

Sound Editor:
Brian Langman

Sound Mixer:
Andy Kris

Motion Graphics:
Trollback & Co.

**Sound
Recording:**
Nara Garber
Victor Horstink
Dan Johnson
Jörg Kidowski
Sam Pullen
Reto Stamm

Poster by
Experimental Jetset

Music:
The Album Leaf
Battles
Caribou
Chicago Underground
Quartet
El Ten Eleven
Four Tet
Kim Hiorthøy
Motohiro Nakashima
Sam Prekop

**Associate
Producers:**
Andrew Dreskin
John Goldsmith
Sharon Hustwit
Michelle Hustwit
Jakob Trollbäck
Antoine Wilson
Chris Levinson Wilson

(c) 2007 Swiss Dots

You mentioned that you have accountants – do you have any other professional help?

We have an accountant doing our annual taxes. In general, there are two sorts of taxes we have to deal with: income/profit tax, and VAT. The VAT is something we handle ourselves, while the income/profit tax is taken care of by our accountant.

For some of our recent French assignments, we asked a French/Dutch translator to take a look at the contracts. (We can read some basic French, but the jargon used in the contracts was quite hard to follow). But other than that, we have never needed the help of professional advisors such as lawyers (knock on wood).

Experimental Jetset have no employees. Do you ever envisage a time when there will be lots of Jetsetters?

In our 12-year career, there have been moments in which we could have chosen to expand and to employ people. But we have made a deliberate choice to stay small. We know many designers of our generation who have chosen another path; studios that started out with two or three people, and now employ 10, 15, sometimes even 20 people. But we have always resisted this.

We never really understood the point of expanding. As we see it, the reason we exist as a studio is because we have a singular aesthetic/conceptual vision, a very specific language we speak. If we employed people this would mean we had to force this vision upon them, that we had to oblige people to speak our language; we would certainly not want to do that. There's already too much pressure in the world as it is now; we don't want to add this whole system of stress and alienation. We could also leave these people free, and let them develop their own language, but what would be the point of employing them then? Let them start their own studio if they want to speak their own language!

We get offered more assignments than we can handle. We simply don't see that as a problem; we're not megalomaniacs, we don't have to design everything. If a client offers us an assignment while we're busy working on something else, we simply try to direct this client to another small, independent studio. Ultimately, this whole model, of all assignments being done by a lot of different small graphic design studios, is much more interesting than the model of all assignments being done by a few large agencies. If we see two posters in the streets, we would prefer them to be designed by two different small design studios, instead of one large agency. It's as simple as that.

We do realize that there are more and more clients who feel that their project is so special that it should be handled by a large agency. But we think that's nonsense. We really believe that all projects, no matter how large, could in principle be handled by small studios. That's the whole point of printing, of mechanical reproduction: that something small, something created by just a few people, can be blown up to something really big. That's the beauty of it – that the starting point can be small. A few decades ago, it was not uncommon that the whole graphic identity of a museum would be created by just one single designer. It should still be possible. A nice logo, a monthly invitation, some brochures, a couple of iconic posters, a basic website: what else do you need? The reason why it all became so complicated is because there now exists this whole layer of marketing and communication people who are more or less creating work just to keep themselves busy. So instead of efficiently designing good-quality printed matter, you are now wasting days discussing the order in which the sponsor logos on the poster should appear. That is indeed a shame. But the solution of this should not be the design studio growing, but rather this whole marketing sphere shrinking.

What about interns? Do you have a policy towards giving internships?

It would be awkward having an intern in the studio. We really feel we have to do everything ourselves: DIY. To have somebody do all the 'dumb' work for us would make us feel terrible. For example, if we come up with a solution that forces us to spend days and days on kerning, we feel we have to do this kerning ourselves. We came up with the solution, so we have to suffer the consequences, even if this involves days of boring work. (It's probably a Calvinist guilt trip, disguised as a socialist work ethic.)

We are glad that the graphic design department of the Gerrit Rietveld Academy doesn't require any internships. In fact, we dislike this whole notion of giving students a taste of 'the real world', as we simply don't believe there is such a thing as 'the real world'. The world is for students to shape, not to adapt to. Or at least, that is how we think it should be. Four years of study is quite a short time. There's a lifetime of work after that. Why not dedicate those four years fully on investigating new models of design practice? Why waste a couple of months on investigating already-existing companies? Maybe internships make sense in the context of other disciplines, but in the case of graphic design, we really like the idea of students entering the field of graphic design without any preconceived notions about it. It worked for us, so it might work for others. (But then again, we sometimes speak to students who really liked their internships. So we might be completely wrong).

Having said that, it really breaks our heart to receive all these portfolios daily, from students asking for internships. We wish we could help all of them. We know their schools require them to do an internship somewhere; we wished this wasn't the case. Most of these people are really bright, their portfolios look really good; it's a shame they are required to beg for an unpaid job. It's humiliating when you think of it.

In a couple of places you have talked about being 'overworked' and 'stressed.' Why do you think this is? Does the stress come from your own self-imposed demands?

We think that this feeling of being constantly overworked is a very personal problem. We have been designing for 12 years now, and we are planning to do this for the rest of our lives, but at the same time we realize we're not really the right people to be designers. The constant pressure, the daily deadlines, the high expectations that clients have of us; it's very hard for us to deal with. Other people probably thrive on this pressure, but we find it nerve-wracking. So we have a very difficult relationship with graphic design: we wouldn't want to do anything else, but at the same time it sometimes hurts us. It is very much in the nature of graphic design. On the one hand, you are expected to put your soul in it, on the other side, you are expected to compromise, to make concessions. So it's a very difficult balancing act: you have to dedicate yourself fully to your design, while at the same time being prepared to kill some of your babies along the way. It's not something that will ever be easy.

But we fully realize that there are billions of people worse off than we are. We are not working in the mines, or in some sort of third-world sweatshop. In fact, that is exactly what we say to each other continuously: 'at least we are not working in the mines'. We are the lucky ones, and we believe that we don't have the right to feel so bad, which makes us feel bad about feeling bad. Complicated.

Can you talk about the ways you promote yourself? There's a famous picture of your feet [see page 87] – is this an attempt to attract attention by building mystique?

That picture of our feet was not some sort of strategic form of promotion at all. The simple fact of the matter is that we feel very uncomfortable about our own appearance: overweight, sweaty, bad hair, red faces. So, in the beginning of Experimental Jetset, whenever we could avoid showing ourselves, we would do just that. The picture of our feet was a photograph we made in 2001. We were walking from our studio to the printer, which was located on the other side of the park. We strolled through the grass and decided to make a snapshot of our feet; we liked the way they formed a sort of 'witch circle' together, symbolizing an indestructible bond. Later that day, Spanish publisher Actar happened to ask us for a studio portrait for inclusion in their upcoming book *HD: Holland Design*, and we just decided to mail them that snapshot. That's how that picture came into existence.

When we realized that some people thought there was some sort of strategy behind the idea of not showing ourselves, it totally freaked us out. The last thing we are interested in is mystifying ourselves. In fact, our whole design ideology is very much based on the notion of demystification. So the whole concept of turning ourselves into myths would go against everything we believe in. The moment we realized some people actually thought we were trying to come across as 'mysterious', we completely changed our policy of not showing ourselves. Since then, we became much more easy-going when it comes to portraiture, And this idea reached its apotheosis in our appearance in the documentary film *Helvetica* as stuttering, stumbling gnomes.

A couple of years ago, we were attacked on *Design Observer* by an established UK critic. This attack was followed by a string of comments in which an army of jackbooted commentators tried to kick us even further into the ground. One of these commentators was the musician Momus[25], who, around that time, apparently found it necessary to double as some kind of postmodern design critic. We don't have the appetite to re-read all these comments, but if we remember correctly, Momus accused us of being anti-intellectual, using the photo of our feet as proof. His point was that it was typical of us that we showed our feet and not our heads. This argument really shows a lack of dialectical imagination. Momus suggests that the subject of a photograph is automatically that what is shown. While, in the case of the feet picture, it is clear that the subject is not what is being shown, but the viewpoint from which the photograph is taken. And this viewpoint is clearly our heads.

You have strong views on design – for example, your theory that design is about 'turning language into objects'. How do you communicate these opinions to clients?

We believe that the fact that we have strong views on design is exactly the reason why most clients decide to work with us. In general, clients very much expect us to bring something to the table: a specific viewpoint, an aesthetic/conceptual language, an ideological approach. They come to us with a certain question, problem or theme, and they are usually interested in our analysis, our method of solving this riddle. If they are interested in a more marketing-based approach, in which aesthetic choices are made by assuming the tastes of target audiences, they wouldn't have come to us.

They come to us because they expect another way of reasoning, a specific way of looking at things, the web of references and ideas we carry with us. We may be completely wrong, but it is our impression that clients come to us because of our opinions, not despite of them. So a phrase like 'turning language into objects' is not something we try to hide. It is a very clear statement, telling clients exactly what it is we do. In fact, the whole idea of 'turning language into objects' might be the part clients love best. Last year, when we presented a proposal for a logo to the directors of 104 (Le Cent Quatre), we handed out some badges that already carried the logo. A very concrete way of turning language into objects. The directors were absolutely delighted with the badges, and immediately pinned those badges on their jackets, while we continued with our presentation. In fact, every time we returned to their offices, they were proudly wearing the badges. It gave us such a boost of energy.

You've already mentioned your famous T-shirts. Can you talk a bit more about this?

We see the 'John & Paul & Ringo & George' T-shirts as a very concrete design project, for a very concrete client (Japanese T-shirt label 2K/Gingham). In fact, since we graduated, we haven't done any 'non-commissioned' projects at all. All our work has been client-based. At the same time, we see all our work as personal: the moment you say 'yes' to an assignment, you are initiating your involvement in it. This makes all projects self-initiated. The decision to deal with a specific set of limitations and specifications is ultimately a personal decision, whether this situation involves a client or not.

So we certainly don't have a portfolio containing 'personal' projects ('for fun') and a portfolio containing 'corporate' projects ('to pay the bills'). We really dislike the idea of having such a double portfolio. Imagine someone like Hitchcock doing small personal movies in his basement, 'for fun', and doing big movies without soul, 'to pay the bills'. That would be terrible, wouldn't it? The whole point of Alfred Hitchcock is exactly that he managed to inject his personality right in the middle of the corporate movie industry. That is the model we aspire to (in a somewhat less ambitious way – we certainly don't see ourselves in the same league as Hitchcock).

If you could start all over again, what would you do differently?

Regarding our practice as Experimental Jetset: there aren't a lot of things that we would have done differently. We might have made some small mistakes along the way, but we learned from them. In retrospect, we might have said 'no' to a few assignments we should have said 'yes' to, and we might have said 'yes' to a few assignments we should have said 'no' to. But then again, a spotless, perfect career wouldn't really suit us. Two steps forward, one step back: that's pretty much the way we go.

However, we would have done things differently as students. We remember that, at the Rietveld Academy, we were quite impatient: we couldn't wait to get out of school, to enter 'the real world'. After we graduated, we realized our mistake: there isn't such a thing as 'the real world'. Looking back at ourselves, especially now that we are teachers ourselves, we realize we were really mediocre students. We never really seized the full potential of what school had to offer; we never saw school as a useful context in itself. So that's what we usually try to tell students: that they should try to see school not as some sort of 'waiting room', but as a very real context, something that needs to be explored in its own right.

What advice would you give to someone starting up a studio?

It might sound like a cliché, but we really believe in this: 'slow and steady wins the race'. And we'd like to add, there's not even a race to win. There's no rush. Hypes and trends come and go: just stick to your own principles, and you'll be fine. People will predict the end of print, and then its return, and then its end again, etc. Magazines will state that 'minimalism is out, ornamentation is in', or vice versa; critics will attack you, and attack you even more, until they run out of breath and move to another target. Just don't pay attention, and keep on moving forward, step by step. It's all about the long run, not the short-term. Wim Crouwel just turned 80, Jan Bons[26] just turned 90, and both are still designing. These are our role models. It's our plan to keep on designing for years to come.

1 The Clash, English punk rock band, formed London 1976. The track 'Last Gang in Town' comes from the album *Give 'Em Enough Rope*, released 1978.

2 Linda van Deursen, Dutch graphic designer and educator. Head of the graphic design department at the Gerrit Rietveld Academy. Partner in Mevis & Van Deursen.

3 Sonic Youth, ageless New York guitar-based avant rock band.

4 The Specials, English ska-based band. Formed in 1977, made a series of influential singles in the 1980s on the 2-Tone label. Recently reformed for 30th anniversary tour.

5 Wild Plakken, formed by Rob Schröder, Lies Ros and Frank Beekers. Their work was informed by political activism. Clients included the Dutch Communist Party and other political groups.

6 Hard Werken began life as a magazine. Graphic designer Rick Vermeulen was an editor of the cultural tabloid from 1978 to 1982. Hard Werken became a design studio, amalgamating with a packaging design company in 1994. It subsequently changed its name to Inizio.

7 Joseph Plateau, low-profile Amsterdam-based designers. Formed in 1989. No website or monograph.

8 Armand Mevis, teaches at the Werkplaats Typographie in Arnhem. Partner in Mevis & Van Deursen.

9 Total Design, highly influential Amsterdam design group formed by Wim Crouwel, Benno Wissing and industrial designer Friso Kramer in 1963.

10 De Stijl, translates from Dutch as 'The Style'. Art movement founded in 1917 in Holland. *De Stijl* is also the name of a journal published by designer and artist Theo van Doesburg (1883–1931).

11 Situationist International (SI) founded in 1957 by a group of revolutionaries with ideas rooted in Marxism and the twentieth-century European artistic avant-gardes. Exerted considerable influence during the revolutionary fervor of France in 1968.

12 Tycoon Graphics, founded in 1991 by Yuichi Miyashi and Naoyuki Suzuki. Based in Tokyo.

13 Sigue Sigue Sputnik, British rock band led by former Generation X member Tony James.

14 Fuel, English design duo. See page 98.

15 Gilbert and George, London-based art duo, widely regarded as the godfathers of Brit Art.

16 Tomato, launched in London in 1991 as art and design collective by John Warwicker, Steve Baker, Dirk Van Dooren, Karl Hyde, Richard Smith, Simon Taylor and Graham Wood. Work includes television and print advertising, corporate identity, art installations, clothing, and design for Underworld (Smith and Hyde were founding members of Underworld).

17 Peter Saville, English graphic designer best known for his iconoclastic work for Factory Records' recording artists Joy Division and New Order.

18 The Designers Republic (1986–2009), uniquely influential and pioneering design studio formed by Ian Anderson in Sheffield, England. Best known for anti-consumerist sloganeering, radical digital typography and ground-breaking album cover art for the Warp label.

19 Sean Perkins, London-based graphic designer and identity specialist. Founder of North.

20 North, founded in 1995 by English designer Sean Perkins. Inspired by the ideology of design studios such as Otl Aicher's, Zintzmeyer & Lux and Wim Crouwel's Total Design. Famous for ground-breaking identity for RAC.

21 Åbäke, graphic design collective based in London. The four founding members are Patrik Lacey, Benjamin Reichen, Kajsa Stahl and Maki Suzuki.

22 Practise, London studio of designer James Goggin. See page 170.

23 Sara de Bondt, London-based Belgian graphic designer who has been running her studio since 2003.

24 NRA, Dutch rock band formed in 1989.

25 Momus, Scottish born musician and writer. Recorded for the Creation label. Real name Nick Currie.

26 Jan Bons, Dutch graphic designer and artist. Designed postage stamps, books and posters.

Fuel
Founded: 1991
Personnel: 2
Location: London, UK
www.fuel-design.com

Since their attention-grabbing arrival on
the design scene in the early 1990s, Fuel
have always given the impression – first as
a trio, and latterly as a duo – of designers
with a sense of self-directed purpose. They
arrived at a critical point in contemporary
design's evolution: they arrived just as the
heated debate surrounding authorship
got hotter. Yet Fuel seemed to have the
authorship question calmly rationalized.
They emerged from the Royal College of
Art as designers and authors of their own
journal, yet worked on commercial projects
without any sense of disjuncture. Even
today, with their ambitious publishing
venture, the sense of Fuel as a single
creative entity prevails.

They occupy a studio in Spitalfields,
London, surrounded by the creative buzz
of multiculturalism. Gilbert and George are
near neighbours, and it's no accident that
many of Fuel's clients are stalwarts of the
contemporary art scene.

The interview was conducted by email.
–

You emerged from the Royal College of Art
as a ready-formed design entity. Did the
three of you have a vision of how the Fuel
studio should be run?

Damon Murray: At the RCA, through our
magazines (also called *Fuel*), we had developed
a focused vision and strong graphic style.
We were ambitious to produce good work and
were uncompromising. It felt very obvious
to set up a studio when we left college, and
money we'd already made from commissions by
Diesel and Virgin made it possible. We needed
the studio to be an extension of our practice
at college, because we wanted to continue
producing our own projects alongside
commercial work.

There was an unspoken agreement that
we would continue working together. It was
understood between us that we wouldn't be
able to produce the work we were making
anywhere else, and besides, there were no
other design companies we actually wanted
to work for. After we left college it was tough
financially, but as recent graduates we were
used to not having much money. Initially we
could only afford one Apple Mac and huddled
round it to keep warm...

To outsiders you seemed to have a clear and sophisticated sense if who and what you were. You seemed to be part of the new self-confidence surrounding graphic design at the time. How would you define your design philosophy in those early days?

We had a similar attitude that ranged over many different subjects, including graphic design. This is vital, as it makes the group more than the sum of its parts, and automatically leads to a shared sense of identity and confidence. Our driving force was that our design delivered content over style, that it had something to say. This is why we originally started to work on a magazine – as an outlet for ideas that didn't easily fit into traditional graphic design. It seemed like the graphic design industry at that time felt too satisfied with itself, and we wanted to work against that. We wanted to expand ideas of what graphic design could be and still regard this as an important aspect of our work.

I remember you arriving on the scene. You had a well-articulated identity. There were pictures of you dressed in pinstripe suits. Design groups didn't behave like this – it was the way pop groups (or latterly contemporary artists) announced themselves. Was this youthful folly, or a carefully nuanced plan to make Fuel as different as possible from the normal jobbing graphic design studio?

We were always interested in our identity and how we looked as a group. At the RCA for our second *Fuel* magazine (titled 'HYPE') we were photographed with cropped hair, wearing different coloured boiler suits – a kind of utility uniform. After graduating we had pinstripe suits made. Our local tailor, Timothy Everest[1], makes a lot of suits for people who work in the City – London's financial district – and we asked him to make some for us. These were unusual clothes for a design group to wear; it was quite a harsh look and probably scared off as many clients as it attracted, but it did give the company a strong image.

Presumably you were three equal partners. Did this cause any problems when it came to deciding each other's role?

We don't have any designated roles in the studio, preferring a natural evolution of projects where suggestions can be considered equally. This allows the possibility of unexpected solutions to present themselves.

Did you model Fuel on any existing graphic design studios or did the studios of artists that you knew inspire you?

Our studio has very much developed as we have, adapting to work on different projects. We are fortunate that we have been able to work creatively in so many areas, and this is what keeps it interesting. You can't really

01 |
02 |

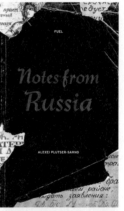

01/ Project: *Notes from Russia*. Date: 2007. Client: Fuel Publishing. Designers: Damon Murray and Stephen Sorrell. 02/ Project: The House of Viktor & Rolf. Date: 2008. Client: Barbican Art Gallery. Designers: Damon Murray and Stephen Sorrell.
03/04/05/ Project: *Russian Criminal Tattoo Encyclopaedia*. Date: 2003–2008. Client: Fuel Publishing. Designers: Damon Murray and Stephen Sorrell.

produce that kind of work using a template, or mimicking others – part of the process is finding your own methods.

You've explained that after graduating you didn't want to work for any of the established design groups of the time. But do you think if you had, you might have gained useful experience in the business of running a studio?

No one really talks about the mundane tasks involved in running a studio, particularly not other design studios, and at college the focus was on artistic development. Some basic knowledge would have been useful, but not essential.

Your studio is near Brick Lane in East London, in a street that is famous because it is where the artists Gilbert and George live. It is also near where many of the stars of the Young British Art movement of the 1990s started out, and you have worked with many if these people. Was it a deliberate move on your part to choose this location?

We found our studio in Spitalfields by seeing a sign in the window. It is a floor of a Georgian house situated between the edge of the City and the Bangladeshi community of Brick Lane. It was this interesting mix of people that we found inspiring. At the time it was an unusual place for a design group but we couldn't afford a studio in the West End or Clerkenwell. Many of the (now famous) artists in this area moved there for exactly this reason. We didn't know them at this time, but have since worked with some of them on various projects. The area has developed dramatically over the past 15 years and is now fashionable and gentrified, with many young artists, designers and galleries.

How important to your development as a studio was your location – would Fuel have been the same company if it had been based somewhere else?

It made sense for us to work in an area outside of a traditional design industry location. Again, it felt like we were finding our own way and this gave us a clearer sense of identity. When we first moved to the area we used a lot of places in the derelict market and around the streets as photography locations.

You are now a fully fledged publisher – we'll talk more about this later – but ever since the *Fuel* magazine at the RCA, you have produced your own books – monographs, surveys, etc. Lots of designers dream of doing studio monographs, and you've done a few. Can you say what effect this has had on your practice? Did each new book have clients knocking on your door?

We've never actually done a monograph of our work. In all our books, magazines and

06 | 07 |

06/07/ Project: *Crime and Punishment*, 60th Anniversary Edition. Date: 2006.
Client: Penguin. Designers: Damon Murray and Stephen Sorrell. 08/ Project: A Process
Revealed. Date: 2009. Client: Waugh Thistleton Architects/Fuel Publishing.
Designers: Damon Murray and Stephen Sorrell. 09/ Project: Jake & Dinos Chapman,
Bad Art for Bad People. Date: 2007. Client: Tate Liverpool. Designers: Damon Murray and
Stephen Sorrell. 10/11/ Project: Kevin Cummins, Juvenes. Date: 2008. Client: To Hell With
Publishing. Designers: Damon Murray and Stephen Sorrell.

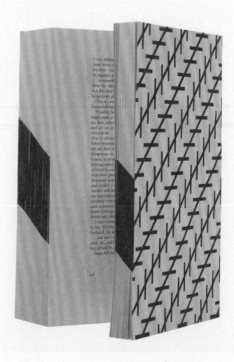

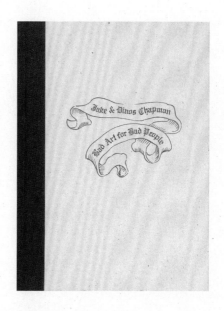

films we've always wanted to do new work in an attempt to push ourselves and our graphic design. This more experimental work can surface commercially later on, but this may take years to happen, if at all. The books never led to a stream of clients wanting to employ us; the work we produce for ourselves is about taking risks, and that's something clients are generally wary of.

Your studio is not the usual temple of surgical whiteness that many graphic design studios are. You have described it as 'a floor in a Georgian house with a big table and a couple of Macs'. Is this working environment conducive to creativity?

Because the studio is in a Georgian period house, it already possesses its own character. In a way it's impossible to turn it into a 'design studio'; it is much more of a relaxed, home environment. In some ways it reflects the area; we loved the whole character of the place and in the early days we'd find bits of furniture just walking around. Other bits have come from Brick Lane market and local junk shops. It was partly all we could afford to buy, but at the same time the idea of mixing old furniture with modern equipment and computers appealed to our sensibility. We didn't want to work in a sterile environment. In some ways this also reflected our taste in design and the influence of vernacular.

Since 2004, when original member Peter Miles left to work in New York, you have been a duo. How did the studio dynamic change at this point? I ask because two-person partnerships can sometimes be hard work, whereas a third partner can often make decision-making easier. Or of course, vice versa. What is your experience?

When Peter left it felt like a good time to make a slight change of direction by publishing our own books as well as being graphic designers. This means we are now involved in every aspect of book production from editing to marketing. Because there are just the two of us we need to be even more efficient with our time, so the decision-making process has become quicker, not harder.

At some point you changed your name from Fuel to Miles Murray Sorrell (Fuel). Now you are Murray & Sorrell Fuel. Could you explain this — and say what importance you place on a studio name?

We took the name Fuel because it reflected our energy and drive to produce work. The name is important and it has worked well for us. Unfortunately several other companies have also liked and attempted to use it. We own the trademark for the name in all the areas in which we work, and have had to take legal action on a number of occasions against other companies to stop them

12 |
13 |

12/13/ Project: Jake Chapman, The Marriage of Reason & Squalor. Date: 2008. Client: Fuel Publishing. Designers: Damon Murray and Stephen Sorrell.

using it. We always win but it is a pain. Our full company name is Murray & Sorrell Fuel but everyone knows us as Fuel.

You have now been together as a partnership for 18 years. What makes a partnership successful? Mutual respect? Intense rivalry? Each knowing what the other does best?

It's impossible to generalize about this as it depends on the individual, but enjoying what you do is the most important factor.

I've got to press you on this. Partnerships are a notorious stumbling block for many design groups. Lots of designers form partnerships early on, and then find over time that individuals change. You say you can't generalize – but you must have some view on what makes your partnership work? It's lasted a long time!

Perhaps the answer is because we are still interested in the same things, and have a similar outlook on design. We respect each other's opinions and don't let egos get in the way.

How do you carve up your professional duties. Can you describe how you work on projects?

We both have equal roles, but of course we work on separate projects some of the time. There is always an ongoing dialogue between us on projects and each other's work. We are not identical designers and the combination of the two is the magic formula: 1+1=3.

If one of you designs something the other doesn't like, are you able to tell each other, or do you suffer in silence?

This situation doesn't arise. Because we are both looking over what the other designs, we both have a hand in every project – although one person may work almost exclusively on a project, that doesn't mean that the other hasn't voiced an opinion. When someone looks at our work, it is the work of Fuel and not us as individuals. This is our approach to work.

Sending out the invoices, debt-chasing and VAT returns; no one ever talks about these things but we all have to deal with them. How do you handle this side of your business?

We have accountants that we've used from the beginning, and they handle all the tax forms. We make sure we always have the money we need to pay our tax bills in the bank. We have never had to borrow money.

That's a pretty impressive feat. It tells me that there is a great deal of financial and business discipline at work here. Would you say you had that discipline?

Yes, we are disciplined in this way. It's essential to running a business.

You have never employed design staff – not even the occasional intern. Why?

Part of the success of our business has been to keep our overheads low and as we don't have other people to pay except ourselves, there is a certain freedom to this. Our studio is quite compact and the dynamic between the two of us is quite tight – student interns have never really appealed. But we would employ help if necessary, and we do work with other specialists such as web programmers, illustrators, photographers and cameramen.

Your clients obviously like the fact that they deal with you both directly and not account handlers or see their work handed down to junior designers. But perhaps others look at you and say, they are just too small to handle our business. Does this bother you?

It is possible we haven't been offered certain jobs because we are a small company, although we have worked on most types and sizes of project, from complete advertising campaigns to business cards. For us there is a kind of 'natural selection' process. Generally our work comes through word of mouth – so we are only really offered work that is right for us.

You are now a publisher. You publish intriguing and unusual books under the Fuel Publishing imprint. Can you talk about how this came about?

We have always been involved in publishing – from our early magazines, books of our own work, and now as a publishing house. We started the imprint after we had co-published the first *Russian Criminal Tattoo Encyclopaedia* in 2003. It felt like a natural development to publish in our own right. We have always had an interest in editing and the content of books as much as the design (from our very first magazine we were art-directing the text to fit the images and communicating our ideas). This involvement gives our books a defining Fuel aesthetic. We are building our list across a range of subjects that retain a consistency of vision. We want all our books to be beautiful objects that are interesting on a number of levels. The design is obviously crucial, but the content and subject matter are just as important.

Do you see the Fuel studio set-up changing over the next few years? Or do you think it will be the same mix of publishing projects and commercial design work?

That depends on the jobs we get offered, and how the publishing side develops. At the moment we are quite happy with the balance of work, which splits fairly equally.

1 Timothy Everest, British tailor who has designed suits for Hollywood stars and the England football team.

Inkahoots
Founded: 1990
Personnel: 6 plus collaborators
Location: Brisbane, Australia
www.inkahoots.com.au

Inkahoots was formed as a public-access poster collective in 1990. In 1995 it became a design company, working for clients in the community and cultural sectors. As the directors note on the studio's website: 'Contrary to the popular premise of commercial visual communication, we don't necessarily see our role as selling the client's product ... we figure the unique qualities of their product or service should sell itself. Our role is to communicate these qualities because anything beyond this is a deception. After all, if the only qualities that differentiate a product are superficial elements of contrived visual seduction, then in a world of rapidly dwindling natural resources, maybe it shouldn't even exist?'

This blunt declaration is no empty boast. For Jason Grant and Robyn McDonald and their small team of collaborators (everyone earns the same amount) it's a way of life: 'Over 15 years we've evolved from a collective of rebel community artists, screenprinting political posters in a union basement, into a multidisciplined design studio that continues to hustle for social change through visual communication.'

The interview was conducted via email.
–

Robyn, can you talk about the personal journey you undertook from being part of an activist-based collective to being part of a fully fledged design studio?

Robyn McDonald: A couple of years before Inkahoots there was Black Banana, a political poster group that I started with a few friends. But it quickly ground down with no wages and exposure to toxic screenprinting inks. We started Inkahoots with a commitment to make a screenprinting collective really work, both creatively and financially. Thanks to good people, hard work and a motivated community we succeeded.

Was the transition to a dedicated design studio a natural progression?

RM: A big shift came with the banning of street posters by the local city council. A lot of community activists utilized the studio's screenprinting facilities to get their messages onto the streets and the new law allowed the organization behind the message to be prosecuted as well as the individual posters, so there was suddenly less of a demand for street posters. Next was the fact that computers and offset printing became more affordable, and a lot of community activists took jobs in the new Labor state government and commissioned Inkahoots to design information material. And finally Jason Grant joined the collective in 1994. While I'd studied illustration at Queensland College of Art, I didn't have a formal education as a graphic designer. Jason started at Inkahoots at the young age of 23 but quickly and efficiently became my mentor — he was then, and always has been, a great teacher.

Jason, can you talk about your own personal journey?

Jason Grant: I started a fine art degree, focusing on printmaking and drawing, before swapping to study graphic design. This was a time when 'art' still saw itself above the marketplace. I remember campus graffiti campaigns slagging off designers as prostitutes. And designers retaliating with accusations of irrelevancy. That was the binary. But the artists definitely had the best graffiti. Studying design in a traditional art college meant there were ideologies clashing in the classroom as well as on the toilet walls. The practical classes, with briefs to redesign toothpaste packaging, rubbed up against critical theory lessons introducing [John] Berger[1], [Ferdinand de] Saussure[2] and [Antonio] Gramsci[3]. The only real integration of theory and practice happened via an excruciating 'marketing' class. I guess I'm just grateful 'branding' wasn't around then.

Since high school I'd been reading philosophy and politics, and would go to political rallies with friends. The corrupt local cops were notoriously violent, and saw teenage socialists as sport. My mum's got a collection of TV news clips with me escaping arrest (and headlocks). I also studied traditional karate, which had a profound impact on my ideas of social justice and aesthetics, but it's too much to get into that here. So anyway, I was never going to accept design as a tool for capitalism. I figured with all of design's power, it could be a kind of resistance.

When I joined Inkahoots it was an artist collective with a raw engagement to the grassroots community. Unfortunately, screenprinting was becoming less and less viable, as cheaper, more accessible technologies prevailed. So my intention for the studio was to stay in that cultural space but embrace the changing media landscape.

The studio still has a strong political and social ethos. This is at odds with most design studios where creative and commercial considerations predominate (you acknowledge this on your website when you pose the question — how many designers only burn to shift a unit, or grow a profit?). How do you maintain your stance in practical terms? You have rent and salaries and overheads to pay; does this mean that commercial demands sometimes take over?

01 |
02 |

01/ Project: Memefest poster. Date: 2007.
Client: Memefest: The International Festival of Radical Communication.
Designers: Inkahoots.
02/ Project: Armchairageddon
(screenprinted fabric/sofa). Date: 2007.
Client: Inkahoots. Designers: Inkahoots.

JG: But every studio has a political ethos. Is ours any stronger than, say, Wolff Olins[4], or Interbrand? They'd certainly be opposed to ours in many ways, and ours might be more transparent, but they're equally as political for sure.

Our clients generally have fewer resources than those of many commercial studios, it's true. But we're a small, relatively efficient studio with aspirations for creative and financial sustainability, not a hunger for profit and growth. And I guess this situation also allows opportunities for independent practice — projects that are self-initiated or collaborative. And really, it's just who we are. We've got rent and salaries to pay, but to what end? If commercial demands ever took over, we'd be a different studio — the reason for our existence would disappear. We started as visual activists and advocates, and Inkahoots has always been a way to avoid dividing our personal and professional concerns.

Let's talk about the Inkahoots studio. Can you tell me how many people work there?

JG: There are six of us all up. Joel Booy and Kate Booy are designers, and Ben Mangan is a designer and works from Melbourne while teaching design down there. Joan Sheriff is our part-time accounts manager. Also Mat Johnston is an unofficial Inkahootser, who does all our programming for interactive stuff. I'm a director and designer. Robyn McDonald is a director and studio manager, but after nearly two decades of incredible commitment, is starting to focus on things outside the studio, such as going back to university to study Indigenous Art. We're based in the inner-city suburb of West End in Brisbane. We feel like we're a part of the neighbourhood, traditionally a vibrant working-class, student and immigrant enclave with a strong activist community. Of course the typical pressures of gentrification are changing the area, but it's still the best place in the world to work!

What is the legal status of the company?

JG: We're a Proprietary Limited Company.

Tell me about the physical space you work in?

JG: The studio is a narrow L-shaped open-plan space designed by our friend, furniture designer Luis Nheu. All the usual equipment.

It's interesting that you had help with the layout of your studio space. Clearly your working environment is important to you. Does the way your space is arranged reflect the way you work?

JG: Sure. We've never been tempted by carpeted cubicles under blinking fluorescent tubes. Natural light, music, a vet next door

for medical emergencies. A democratically arranged space with no special office for the boss. If you want to talk to someone, there's no door to knock on, no appointment to schedule. You might need to turn the music down to answer a phone, but otherwise it's great.

In 1998 you had a devastating fire that destroyed the studio — how did you survive that?

JG: Mainly thanks to the amazing support of clients and friends. And to the hard work and vision of Robyn and the team. We were very generously loaned all the equipment we needed and moved into a great temporary space paying only token rent. People even sent us money in the mail! Fortunately we had offsite file back-up, so we could finish and get paid for projects we were working on. If we'd lost all the archived files I really don't know if we would have made it. Great things can come from having to start again, and one of the ways we survived was approaching it all as a new beginning.

In 2002 Rick Poynor[5] wrote that Inkahoots 'has no stated hierarchy and all the workers earn the same salary, a situation that would be unthinkable in most studios in Australia, and abroad.' Is this still the case, and if so what are the benefits of operating like this?

JG: It's a practical as well as philosophical policy. Apart from during a probationary period for new studio members, all full-time members get paid the same. It's a symbolic assurance of equality and solidarity. Everyone's contribution is equally valued, so that individual and collaborative creativity is not just an ethos, but also a real structural imperative. This hopefully makes for an environment where creativity is respected and supported. I know it's counterintuitive in a hyper-hierarchical culture, but we trust difference can be celebrated without executive bonuses and pay disparity.

Who decides such questions as how much of the studio's turnover can be allocated to salaries? Are these decisions taken collectively or decided by the directors?

JG: They would generally be discussed and decided collectively. We'll raise the salaries whenever we think the studio can sustain it. If there are other priorities for the profit, such as new equipment or a self-funded project, we'll usually make that decision collectively.

How does Inkahoots function creatively? When a client turns up with an assignment, how is it handled?

JG: We'd start by choosing who'll be working on it — one or more designers? Who's got the time? Does someone have a particular interest

03 | 04 |

03/ Project: Bob Dylan poster. Date: 2007. Client: Inkahoots & RedConnect.
Designers: Inkahoots. 04/ Project: Sex poster. Date: 2007. Client: Inkahoots &
RedConnect. Designers: Inkahoots. 05/ Project: It's Not a Crisis, It's a Creed poster.
Date: 2008. Client: Inkahoots. Designers: Inkahoots. 06/ Project: John Berger poster.
Date: 2007. Client: Inkahoots & Redconnect. Designers: Inkahoots.

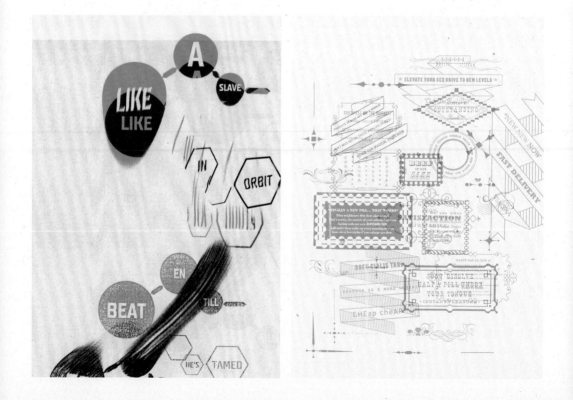

in the subject? We'll often meet to generate ideas, which will then trigger research or more conceptual development. These meetings are always on the brink of descending into farce – which is exactly how it should be. Loose and playful and open-ended. There's feedback from everybody throughout the remainder of the process, whether the project involves a single designer or a group. This is also why traditional studio hierarchy is a hindrance – even the least experienced designer can contribute significantly and benefit the most experienced 'creative director'.

There are many bad creative directors, but it could be argued that a good creative director is someone who makes sure that the 'least experienced designer' gets a hearing. Is there a danger that in Inkahoots' egalitarian, collective approach, certain voices don't get heard?

JG: I suppose so. On the other hand, if it's a genuinely egalitarian collective, it becomes everyone's responsibility to ensure everyone is heard – it's not the lone duty of a creative director.

I'm guessing you don't have account handlers?

JG: We don't have account handlers and all that stuff. A designer will liaise directly with the client and suppliers and see the job through to production – print, fabrication, online or whatever.

And if Pepsi turned up? Would they be turned away?

JG: There's a strange romance that has developed around design. I encounter it among some of my students – it's the romance of superficial creativity enabling participation in consumer myths. That's a certain kind of designer's identity now. It's a designer lifestyle. But it was never my idea of romance. Pablo Neruda[6] testing his poetry on the run in worker's homes, as families hid him from government forces was romantic to me. Or activists living in treetops to prevent ancient forests being turned into toilet paper. Selling cola? Designers Republic courted counter-culture cool with anti-consumer posters, and with the same visual language flogged Coca Cola. That kind of cynicism is just corrosive.

I agree with your comments about the corrosive effects of an all-pervading commercial culture. So do I take it that Pepsi would be turned away?

JG: Yes. They represent an ideology that we've always rejected.

Authorship is a hot subject in many design studios. I'm thinking of the perfectly natural desire of most designers to be personally recognized and credited for their work.

07 |
08 |

07/ Project: Village Twin identity and poster. Date: 2006. Client: Village Twin Cinema. Designers: Inkahoots.
08/ Project: Siren Wall installation. Date: 2008. Client: Department of Emergency Services. Designers: Inkahoots.

How is this dealt with within the collective nature of Inkahoots?

JG: Our experience is that the practical process of design in terms of authorship is actually pretty slippery. Generally, in a studio context, a single designer claiming authorship is an oversimplification of a rich process. If I've had an idea and I'm working away independently for days on a project and someone makes even a slight suggestion, the whole direction and outcome can be affected. It could easily end up as a radically different work. So what does it mean if I claim authorship, when without this input, the ultimate outcome wouldn't exist? Not to mention the many layers of more subtle but just as concrete influence: other people's moods; encouragement; music; client feedback; who's running the country. Attributing work to the studio is just more realistic. It's not to say that an individual's personal sensibility or vision is diverted, but that it's fed by many sources. Usually the most interesting design is fundamentally collaborative.

Then there's a philosophical dimension that aims to downplay the exaggerated and exploited phoney individualism of consumer culture.

Presumably, for the Inkahoots ethos to work, it needs everyone to believe in it?

JG: I'm not sure it requires an act of faith exactly. But like any successful relationship there needs to be shared values and goals. There have been members in the past that probably would have been better off elsewhere – but that's a lesson we've tried to learn. A really important aspect of Inkahoots, and probably any team, is the recognition that everyone has different strengths but that these strengths overlap and evolve. The studio should be a personal and cultural laboratory – a supportive space that encourages creative growth. That's the ideal. Of course it doesn't mean we don't occasionally want to kill each other.

Interns are a morally ambiguous area for designers. They are often exploited by studios. What is your policy towards interns?

JG: Well, massage isn't discouraged. No, there's no coffee-making or car washing. Because we're a busy, relatively small studio we don't pretend to have the resources to properly cater for longer-term interns. And Australia doesn't really have the same kind of intern tradition that the UK or the States has. We'll sometimes take one or two students per year for a two-week period each and try and make it a constructive experience.

What will Inkahoots be like in ten years' time?

JG: Hopefully better at answering questions about the future. I don't know. Your own perspective is never fixed. Sometimes you grandly see the designer's mission as working at the interface of consumption and culture, creating and mediating the messages that become the very idea of who we are. And sometimes it feels like you're just helping out some good people or worthwhile organizations. One of the reasons I'm happy here is that it's always been new. It's always felt like we're just about to catch our own aspirations, but not just yet. Is that an admission of failure? There's just so much to learn and to accomplish.

1 John Berger, essayist, novelist, screenwriter, dramatist and critic. Author of *Ways of Seeing*.

2 Ferdinand de Saussure, (1857–1913), Swiss linguist and one of the fathers of modern linguistics. His ideas have had a lasting impact on literary and cultural theory.

3 Antonio Gramsci (1891–1937), Italian philosopher, writer, politician, political theorist and Marxist. Known for his concept of cultural hegemony as a means of maintaining the state in a capitalist society.

4 Wolff Olins, design group founded in London in 1965 by Michael Wolff and Wally Olins. Wolff left in 1983, and Olins in 2001. Today it is a brand consultancy, based in London, New York City and Dubai. Subjected to international media attention when it launched the controversial London 2012 logo.

5 Rick Poynor, British writer on design and visual culture. Founding editor of *Eye* magazine, which he edited from 1990 to 1997. Print magazine columnist, co-founder of *Design Observer* and author of numerous books.

6 Pablo Neruda (1904–1973), Chilean writer and politician. Considered one of the greatest and most influential poets of the twentieth century.

Lehni-Trüb
Founded: 2005
Personnel: 2
Location: Zurich, Switzerland
www.lehni-trueb.ch

Urs Lehni and Lex Trüb work collectively as Lehni-Trüb, and separately under their own names. Working on art books and on cultural-sector projects, they are part of the new wave of young, mainly Zurich-based Swiss designers whose main characteristic is an aversion to seductive graphic effects. They note: 'As soon as something becomes too slick, we try to saw one leg off to unbalance it again. We like ambivalence more than clarity.'

Lehni-Trüb is barely recognizable as a modern commercial graphic design studio. They themselves use the phrase 'occasional graphic design studio'. They seem almost reluctant to promote their commercial design business, and instead focus on doing only the work that interests them, advancing their independent publishing ventures, and running a project space in Zurich called Corner College – not to mention swimming sessions when their studio becomes too hot in summer.

The interview was conducted via email.
–

Can you give me some background – where did you both train and so on?

Urs Lehni: We both graduated around 1997 at traditional Swiss design and art schools, Lex at the zHdK in Zurich, Urs at the HGKL in provincial Lucerne. By the time we entered art school we had just a vague idea of what graphic design could be and how we would approach it personally.

How did you meet?

After I moved to Zurich, Lex and I met through mutual interests in sports involving boards and wheels, and thereby became friends. At the time I was an intern at Cornel Windlin's[1] studio, working for the Schauspielhaus Zurich. Cornel quit this demanding assignment after one year and Lex agreed to take it over together with Benjamin Sommerhalder. As a surprise to almost everybody, Lex kept standing in the ring for the next three years, and managed to realize brilliant work for the Schauspielhaus during this period. His system involved seasonal collaborations with other Zurich-based graphic designers such as Aude Lehnmann[2], Elektrosmog's Valentin Hindermann[3] and Diego Bontagnali[4]. During this time, Lex asked me to collaborate, but due to bad timing and other circumstances it somehow never worked out.

What did you learn from your period working with Cornel Windlin?

'Design is a lot of work' – C. Windlin.

When did you decide to set up a studio together, and what prompted you to do this?

At some point we realized that all the other designers of our age in Zurich were grouped in small studios. To fight the feeling of being left behind, we thought we might as well give it a try and applied for a couple of jobs under the name Lehni-Trüb.

Were you inspired by any studios?

That's a difficult question to answer. We could respond by dropping a bunch of names of designers and studios, but I think we were much more interested in certain attitudes and forms of practice. As examples we could name a certain approach in recent book design from the Netherlands; conceptual art of the late 1960s; or some playful manifestations of design in Italy during the 1970s: although these are just commonplaces for many designers...

What I like about your work is its lack of showiness – the absence of graphic effects and tricks. This makes it hard to detect your stylistic influences. In what way do the three influences you mention above inspire your work?

We doubt big ideas and concepts. As soon as something becomes too slick, we try to saw one leg off to unbalance it again. We like ambivalence more than clarity. Maybe this results from a lack of security and the lack of a serious attitude, or maybe it is simply questioning the recurring demand to always be inventive and unique. Deception, appropriation and imitation are helpful strategies to find our way out of this, in equal measure good and bad.

As you've said, there are many studios in Zurich. Were there people you could go to for help and guidance?

Zurich is a small town, and graphic designers from the same generation know each other. Ten years ago it became easy to start a studio after school due to the affordability of the technical equipment. By that time studios such as Norm[5], Elektrosmog, later Flag[6], started up and we became friends, exchanged ideas and helped each other with advice or even jobs. And then there was Cornel Windlin, who somehow was the role model for most of us.

One would think that the high density of design studios in Zurich must be an obstacle for another one opening up for business. But actually the contrary is true. The appreciation of 'elaborated' (whatever this means) graphic design has quite a tradition throughout history (also due to economic wealth) by institutions and the private economy. Furthermore, Zurich has a lively and dense art scene (both commercial and

01 |
02 |

01/ Project: Cneai Book. Date: 2007. Client: Centre national de l'estampe et de l'art imprimé. Designer: Lex Trüb. 02/ Project: Peter Saville Estate. Date: 2007. Client: Migros Museum for Contemporary Art, Zurich. Designers: Urs Lehni and Lex Trüb. 03/04/05/06/07/ Project: Silkscreenreprint of Ray Bradbury's *Fahrenheit 451*. Date: 2009. Client: Self-initiated. Designers: Aude Lehmann and Lex Trüb.

non-commercial), which offers numerous possibilities to react to, or interact with. Besides, Zurich is geographically well situated, which makes possible working connections with Germany, Austria and France.

You both work independently under your own names, and you also work collectively as Lehni-Trüb. Can you describe how you run your studio?

We don't really function according to a master plan. Whenever new commissions come up, we decide whether we're interested in doing them; if we are, we negotiate further to find out if we want to work on them together, separately or in combination with other designers. Besides this, the two of us initiate our own projects. Timewise, these non-commissioned projects take up at least half our time.

Let me ask you about the business side of running a studio. It's a subject designers rarely talk about openly. How do you deal with the mundane matters of administration, accounting and financial planning?

It's something we never really pay much attention to. We haven't done accounting for more than a year now and we definitely lack a system of how to handle these matters. Probably the only reason we still can afford to work for no money is that our living costs are pretty low.

I like the idea of designers living a monastic existence. But I wonder if it is sustainable? I wonder if you will feel the same way in five or ten years' time?

We are not living a monastic existence at all. The meaning of 'low living costs' is relative. Hopefully, our current engagement is an investment for the future.

Can you say what you mean by an 'investment for the future?'

We both 'invest' either in our independent publishing ventures Rollo Press (www.rollo-press.com) or Bookhorse (www.bookhorse.ch), and we're looking forward to extending these activities with more financial freedom – in the sense of 'what goes around comes around.'

Your work is mainly books. Books require a great deal of time and effort. Do you share the workload or work independently?

When we designed the publications for the Migros Museum for Contemporary Art, each of us was responsible for one specific project. But these projects took much longer than expected, so after a while we decided to switch responsibilities and this act of 'job rotation' turned out to be quite satisfying.

08 | 09 | 10 | 11 |
12 | 13 |
14 | 15 |

16 |

08/09/12/14/ Project: Tu M'as Volé Mon Vélo. Date: Mar 2008. Client: Linus Bill in collaboration with Rollo Press. Designers: Linus Bill and Urs Lehni.
10/11/13/15/ Project: Polizei Geschlossen Sorry. Date: 2008. Client: Linus Bill in collaboration with Rollo Press. Designers: Linus Bill and Urs Lehni.
16/ Project: Zürich Zine Sezession/One-day Independent Publishers Fair, Poster. Date: 2008. Client: Self-initiated. Organized by Nieves and Rollo Press.

DEC

@ Perla-Mode

VON

BIS

Can you talk in a bit more detail about how
you work together – do you have similar skills
or do you have different strengths
and weaknesses?

We have pretty similar skills, which does not
follow the idea of complementing each other.
Anyway, it still works.

Do you ever disagree about creative matters?

Of course.

Do you have a portfolio to show to potential
clients? How do you handle the question of
presenting the studio?

We have a non-updated website, where
you can get a hint of what we do. We prefer
to meet people first and talk together
generally to find out if collaboration would
suit both sides.

All your clients seem to come from the cultural
and art sectors. What would happen if a big
client turned up from the corporate sector
and asked you to take on a mass-market
project?

Depending on what it was, we would say –
great! It just hasn't happened yet.

Do you employ other designers?

Not at the moment.

Can you see a time when you might have to
employ designers? And if so, do you think you
will be a good employer?

Basically we like to work by ourselves or
temporarily with others. As a lot of decisions
happen throughout the working process it
is very different from delegating work to
someone else. But of course, there is always
work to share and the potential to get
surprised by someone working for, or
with you, would make it worth trying.

What is your attitude towards interns?

We want to start working with interns
more often in the future. Up to now we
couldn't really provide them with a good
situation due to the fact that we didn't
share the same studio space. and that we
are too disorganized in general. But there's
hope that these circumstances will get
better soon.

How important to you is your physical
environment? Does your studio's layout and
its design (its furniture, availability of natural
light and so on) have a bearing on creativity,
or could you work anywhere?

We're lucky to have found a charming
and cheap backyard studio in a busy
neighbourhood that we share with two

17 |
18 |
19 |

17/18/19/20/21/ Project: Stefan Marx,
Zürich Ruins My Nerves. Date: 2008.
Client: Stefan Marx in collaboration with
Rollo Press.

photographers. During the summer it gets awfully hot in there, but the river is close by. Several swimming sessions are part of a regular working day during the summer months, which results in a nice blend of labour and leisure. During winter though, the situation is much more complicated. There is a heating system, but as all windows and walls are very old, we don't really benefit from it. That's the time to stay home and write emails in your kitchen, or go to the studio only if you absolutely have to.

How would you describe Lehni-Trüb to someone who didn't know the studio?

As the children of Lutz and Rivella.

I'm going to press you on this. Imagine a client turned up with a really interesting project and asked you to give a compelling professional reason why Lehni-Trüb should be given the assignment – what would you say?

OK – Lehni-Trüb operates as an occasional graphic design studio. Besides working together on commercial projects, particularly printed matter, both realize their own projects including the independent publishing ventures Bookhorse and Rollo Press, established in 2008. Since 2008, Lehni has co-run the Zurich-based project space Corner College (www.corner-college.com), a small venue that hosts lectures, workshops, movie screenings and culinary experiments.

1 Cornel Windlin, Swiss type and graphic designer. Worked for Neville Brody in London before returning to Zurich.

2 Designer Aude Lehnmann and literary scholar Tan Waelchli, both based in Zurich since 2004, have developed the book series Whyart to examine the current landscape of design, art and popular culture.

3 Elektrosmog's Valentin Hindermann, co-founder of Elektrosmog graphic design studio in Zurich since 1999.

4 Diego Bontognali, Swiss graphic designer, working in Zurich, originally from Geneva. He runs a studio together with Valeria Bonin under the name Bonbon and teaches at ECAL (University of Art and Design Lausanne, Switzerland).

5 Norm, Zurich-based graphics team, founded by Dimitri Bruni and Manuel Krebs.

6 Flag, graphic design studio established in 2002 by Bastien Aubry and Dimitri Broquard in Zurich.

Marian Bantjes
Founded: 2004
Personnel: 1
Location: Bowen Island, Canada
www.bantjes.com

Marian Bantjes doesn't fit into any identikit image of the modern graphic designer. Despite the fact that over the past decade her rich and decorative work has sailed on the cusp of the zeitgeist, Bantjes is an uncategorizable figure. She didn't go to a fashionable design school. She trained instead as a typesetter. She isn't part of any moment, and doesn't live in one of design's urban capitals.

As this frank and revealing interview makes clear, Bantjes is temperamentally and artistically unsuited to life in a conventional studio. She lives and works on a small island off the Canadian coast (pop. 3000), where she produces her distinctive typographic stylings. Her taste for solo working was borne out of an early unsuccessful attempt to set up a studio – an experience that taught her a great deal about herself. Her geographical remoteness does not discourage her clients, many imagining that she is based in New York.

The interview was conducted via email. Requests for interviews, as Bantjes reveals, are a constant and draining demand on her time.
–

You didn't train as a graphic designer – instead you spent ten years as a typesetter before setting up a design studio in partnership with one other person. Were you attracted to the idea of a group of creative people working under one roof, or did you have a feeling that you were really more suited to working solo?

Marion Bantjes: Well, the question infers some kind of planning on my part, and to be honest, at first I was attracted to making a living. Then, as we started to acquire employees, I was attracted to having help. It really wasn't until about our sixth year, when we had a few designers in the office, that I began to feel what it was like to really have a studio, and other people to work with, and a semblance of a culture that I very much wanted to foster. It never occurred to me to work solo at that time because I was a designer, and there are parts of that job that I cannot – even today – bear the thought of handling alone.

Were there graphic design studios you admired back then?

The really stupid and unfortunate part is that I was not involved in the design world at all. I was marginally involved with, or at least aware of, the local firms, and I had a few that I admired for their work, which, looking back, was really nothing too special. It's very embarrassing to me now, but I had absolutely

no sense of the design world at large.
I knew about [David] Carson[1], [Stefan]
Sagmeister[2], [Paula] Scher[3], Pentagram[4],
Studio Dumbar, and a few others, and I
admired them without really knowing how
they related to me or to the world of design,
i.e. how very, very far advanced they were
from where I was. Eventually, in my last year
in design and before I went out on my own,
I found that the more I learned, and the more
I discovered, it was like a universe expanding
with me becoming an increasingly infinitesimal
speck way below all these other heavenly
bodies. That is still happening, actually.

You have written revealingly about the
trials and tribulations of being in a
business partnership. Can you recount
your experiences?

Ha! Whoa. Briefly, I was in partnership
with one of my best friends. We had worked
together at Hartley & Marks where I was a
typesetter and she was an editor. Then she
got a job in marketing, and it was her idea
to start a business. I felt that she 'saved'
me from a potentially miserable death in
some kind of a business card factory after
I had stopped working at Hartley & Marks,
which may have been true. The partnership
worked very well for the first few years.
She managed the clients, and I did the work.
But I was increasingly ambitious creatively,
and that put challenges on her in terms of
the clients, who were very conservative.
Eventually I was pushing her, and instead of
her pushing them, she was pushing me (and
my team) back, and it became a rift in the
company – a very common one, I think – of
designer vs. account manager. I think she
felt that I was unreasonable and eternally
dissatisfied with the work she was bringing
in, and she told me in no uncertain terms
that the kind of work I wanted to do (like the
work I do now) wasn't wanted by anyone. I was
actually a very accommodating designer, and
not a prima donna at all, but I felt that she
was undermining me behind my back (and in
some cases she was). She thought I was a big
whiner, and perhaps I was. It got very, very
bad, and I was overjoyed when she offered
to buy me out.

You have also been frank about the early
mistakes you made with your first studio…
One of the worst seems to have been hiring
a CEO who insisted on 'designing her own
business cards' and who confessed to 'not
liking meeting strangers.' This sounds pretty
disastrous.

Actually the CEO was nothing compared to
the bitterness between me and my partner
in our last two years… the CEO didn't design
her own cards, but she did require a different
(less outrageous) design for her card, which
I created. But it was disastrous in that
aside from the fact that she was incapable
of bringing in the shiny new clients I'd hoped

01 |
02 |

01/02/ Project: Valentines cards.
Date: 2009. Client: Self-initiated.
Designer: Marian Bantjes.
Medium: Pen and ink.

she would, she was just far too corporate for our culture. We were laidback, warm wood and red Persian carpets; she was hard shiny surfaces, steel doors and cubicles. We hired her because we thought we needed someone tough, and she was tough: we were afraid of her... it turned out that so was everyone else.

Do you think if you'd done a stint in an established design studio – going from junior to senior designer – you might have avoided some of the mistakes you made?

Absolutely. Particularly in a good studio, it would have been hugely instructive, and I always used to tell my students to do that before going into business.

What would you say to anyone starting a studio today to help them avoid going through what you went through?

Well first, get some experience in one or two small studios and one big one ... always with a mind that it is not forever, just a few years, and to really pay attention to how people are treated in the company, how clients are treated, make sure they attend client meetings, work on pitches etc. See what works and what doesn't. But also to pay attention to the people around them, how they work, and how personalities mix or don't mix. It's like a kind of kindergarten: learning socializing all over again. It's just super-important. Then start small (and preferably stay small, under four... I'm totally with Stefan Sagmeister on that point, unless one really wants to become a manager), and keep your overhead low.

Always look around and read books on design and the annuals and mags – not to get ideas from, but to keep tabs on who's out there doing what. Have a budget for books, and maybe have some kind of weekly social time for the staff to meet and talk about it all, and quickly weed out the people who aren't interested. Don't work just for the money. Have dignity but at the same time understand your job and that you have to be flexible. But at the point the clients trample on you, just fire their asses and move on. Always do new things, never feel creatively safe, and foster support with the other members of the company.

But here's the hardest one: friendship in business. This is hard because we want to be friends with our employees and our clients, but it also leads to great difficulties when troubles arrive. I think when it comes to new employees, don't go easy on them, throw them right into the fire immediately; the best ones will survive and thrive, I think. We were always soft on people and it would take so long to find out they weren't working out, and we were too nice to get rid of them. With clients it's hard, too, and I would say be professional and businesslike for as long as you can, until you have trust and then be friends. Don't

be palling around with clients before you've completed some good work together.

What did the experience of running a studio teach you about yourself and working as a creative person?

Oh, tons. I learned to trust myself more than I ever had. I learned I could do things I never thought I could. But also that I'm weak, and I'm not a leader of people. That was very important for me to realize.

You now work alone. You have an idyllic-sounding studio on an island off the Vancouver coast. Tell me about your studio? I'm guessing it's not a white-walled Bauhaus-inspired atelier?

True. Which is not to say I wouldn't want a white-walled Bauhaus-inspired atelier! (Actually my architectural preference is for a wood-steel-concrete-glass sort of contemporary modernism.) My studio is in my house, which is an... ahem... Swiss chalet-style house. I never would have built such a thing, but it was what I could afford, and the style has some practicalities for our wet climate, such as four-foot overhangs on the roof. Inside it has been opened up (by myself and my ex-boyfriend), and there is a lot of wood (fir, which has a red-gold colour) with floors, posts, beams and windows, and then white walls. The light is beautiful and changes remarkably during the day, so the atmosphere is very warm and cosy. My studio is upstairs and is usually pretty cluttered, but I use the whole house (photography in the kitchen, which has the best light; drawing in the living room, which has a big window looking onto forest, plus the wood stove), and I'm somewhat anti-knick-knack so the rest of the place is relatively ordered and uncluttered.

Do you need to be surrounded by order?

I like order, I hate clutter, but the clutter happens, especially as my house is small. I do so many things with so many materials, and I have several projects going at the same time, plus bills and notes and scraps... it makes me crazy but I just can't control it in the studio. I hid some of it in six filing cabinets, but I need more: cupboards, paper drawers... ahhhh. One day I will have most of it hidden away, I hope.

Do potential clients ever decide not to work with you because you are so far off the beaten track?

Not that I know of – no one has ever said it. Most people don't ask. They often think I'm in New York. When I first started working for Wired, I thought they were in NY, and they thought I was too, and it was only at some later point we realized we were both in the same time zone when we'd each been mentally adjusting for a three-hour time difference!

03 | 04 |
05 |

03/04/05/ Project: Saks Fifth Avenue Snowflakes, Application. Date: 2007/2008.
Client: Terron Schaefer/Saks Fifth Avenue. Designer: Marian Bantjes.
Medium: Pencil, pen. 06/07/08/09/ Project: Love Stories. Date: 2008.
Client: Creative Review. Designer: Marian Bantjes. Medium: Various.

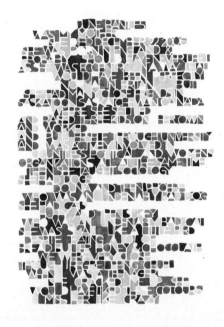

How do you attract clients?

Who knows? They just come to me like flies.
I gotta do something about that, actually,
and start trying to catch some special ones.
This year I'm going to be giving serious
consideration to what exactly I want to do
and how. I've been a bit too passive so far.

I'd like to ask you about working alone. There
aren't many graphic designers who genuinely
work solo. Your work is highly personal and
has a recognizable signature (although I've
noted that you reject this observation!), so it
is perhaps easy to understand why you might
choose to work alone. Can you talk about the
psychological and practical reasons why you
work solo?

I don't really reject the observation that
I have a recognizable signature, more that
I have a 'style'. There's a slight difference;
style usually refers to the curly, swirly stuff
that I now do less and less of. Stylewise I
think my range is broad, but it still somehow
has my signature.

There are times I think about taking on an
intern, or, taking an apprentice to help me
when I get aged and arthritic. But I dread
having to work with someone else. I am
essentially a loner; I always have been.
I like my solitude (while also loving seeing my
friends, and sometimes getting very lonely).
I work on things best when I can concentrate…
distractions make me crazy, and I simply
cannot multi-task. As it is I have too many
distractions with bills to pay and email and
cleaning and feeding myself. Ugh. I wish I were
a creativity machine and someone else took
care of the rest of it.

But also, I'm super-sensitive about other
people's feelings and them getting what they
want or need. When I had employees I was
much more upset that they weren't creatively
satisfied than for myself, and I was constantly
torn between doing the interesting jobs, or
giving it to them because I felt so sad for
them. I'm terrible at giving critiques, I'm just
way too gentle… but at the same time, I have
really high standards and having someone
working on my stuff and not being up to
snuff would be agony for me. I think I would
be reduced to tears with frustration, caught
between being kind, encouraging and gentle
and wanting to beat them about the ears
and shove them off the chair to do it myself.
Awful, awful. And I'm a terrible, terrible art
director. I just don't know how to get what I
want without doing it myself. I do miss having
peers to show work in progress to, because I
often doubt my own judgement. I had someone
I did that with for a while but we have since
parted ways.

You do a lot of collaborative work –
with Stefan Sagmeister, and Pentagram,
for example. When this happens, is it a
refreshing change?

Yes. I love it. I love working with both Stefan
and Michael Bierut[5] at Pentagram. I think we
have mutual respect for each other and trust
in each other's skills and talents. I trust their
judgement implicitly, and when I get criticism
from them I know it's valid. I work really well
with people who really know their shit, and
who have different skills from me. Stefan and
I are really close in our interests and beliefs
about design, Michael and I are a little further
apart that way; but they're both extremely
nice, very smart people. I really think you
can't go wrong with that.

I'd guess that email, Skype and ftp sites
make it feasible for you to work alone and
in geographical isolation?

Yes. Most of my work and communication is
done by email. I rarely have to courier things
or even speak on the phone. The endless
meetings that most people go to I think are
largely unnecessary. If I lived in New York
people would want to have meetings with
me all the time. Thank God I don't… what
an incredible waste of time.

Do you ever visit studios and think – it would
be nice to work with a group of like-minded
creative individuals? Or do you think the
opposite – that it would be hell to have to
fit in around the egos, ambitions and petty
jealousies that are often found in groups of
creative people?

I feel both. I have a strong desire for a
community of friends and like-minded people.
I would love to have them close, get together
socially, even eat lunch together. But I don't
want to work with them and I don't want them
in my working space.

People who work on their own have to be
highly disciplined. It's easy to be disciplined
when you have business partners watching
you, and when you have staff who look to
you to set an example. But when it's just
you there's always the temptation to put
something off. I'm guessing you have self-
discipline?

Well, this is kind of related to the oft-made
comment that I must have patience. I don't
feel either patient or disciplined because
those relate to things you don't really want
to do. I want to work. It's what I want to
do most (and hang out with friends). I'm
completely obsessed. I work every day…
except the days I don't feel like it, and then
don't unless I have a deadline. I actually feel
like a completely lazy tart. I get a lot done,
but it's not that hard. It's fulfilling. The hard
part is all the other stuff in my life. If work
was this task that I needed to do and looked

forward to not doing, that would be hard. But instead I hate Fridays and weekends because my friends are all offline and all I get to read is junk mail.

What's the biggest distraction when working from home? Do you ever feel the need to separate home from work?

My biggest distraction is the weather and the garden in the spring and summer. It's so beautiful here when the sun shines, it's super-hard not to just go out and enjoy it... which I do. And no, if I had to get up and leave the house for work and leave work for home, well I'd never be at one or the other. I like to work late, I like to fall into bed, and out of it back into work. I like to eat when I feel like it, and break for a movie when I feel like it and return to work at 11.00p.m. if I feel like it. You know, I think I'm completely undisciplined!

How do you cope with the business side of Marian Bantjes Inc.? Do you do all your own quoting, invoicing, tax filing, debt chasing and so on?

Yes. I have a really good bookkeeper and a good accountant. I do my own invoicing and paying of bills etc, but thankfully, receipts and shit I shove into an envelope and Jacqui does my basic ... whatever it is she does, and tells me what numbers to fill in on what boxes on the quarterly GST payments. Then I give all her stuff to my accountant and he says a bunch of gobbledygook to me and I ask him how much I should pay myself each month, and then I do what he tells me. I'm a complete idiot when it comes to finances; it's been explained to me many times but I don't understand anything beyond money goes out, and money comes in. Jacqui tells me when people have owed me money for a very long time, and I obsequiously chase after them for that.

But the worst part is, ironically, the part that's connected to my so-called fame. I really hate to complain because I am so, so grateful that people know who I am and admire me, and want me to be a part of their whatever, but I swear to God, the fan mail, and the requests for interviews (sorry!), or to submit something to this magazine or that book; and uploading files, and preparing new images, and updating my bio, and supplying head shots; and filling out forms for travel and expenses and god-knows-what, and oh God, the travel arrangements! It all makes me halfway mad.

Sometimes I get invitations to speak somewhere and I'm just too overwhelmed by the thought of all the work that it will entail beyond the actual going there, speaking and coming back, that I can't decide how to respond. But I'm grateful, I can't wish it to stop, or it will and then I'll be lonely and sad, but it's just so out of control sometimes. And the students... the students! They're so sweet and they look up to me and it's so flattering, but God damn, I just can't answer all their motherfucking questions! So I update my site, and I try to streamline it, but no, there are more, newer questions! This whole thing about my public persona is the part that is so, so hard because I'm so chuffed to have it, but it's driving me insane at the same time.

One of the best things about running a conventional studio is nurturing talent. Do you ever see a time when you might employ an assistant or even the next Marian Bantjes, perhaps?

See above, but also, I have to say that the best thing that came out of my design studio was my two last designers, Brian Morgan and Kirsten Gravkin. I was so proud of them. And yeah... my looming old age is a bit of a worry to me (OK! I'm only 45, but I'm a worrier, all right?). I dunno.

What would you say to a designer today who wanted to start his or her own studio?

It would depend. If that designer has experience, is already doing work they love, has contacts, I'd say go for it; it's gonna be great. If they're just out of school or very inexperienced I'd say earn your chops first, baby. But there are so many factors... what you want, where you live, what your responsibilities are... people with spouses and – God forbid – kids... that gets tougher. Your time is no longer your own anyway, and work probably isn't your priority. Then I guess you need that discipline thing.

1 David Carson, American graphic designer, best known for his innovative magazine design and use of experimental typography. One of the most imitated graphic designers of the 1990s.

2 Stefan Sagmeister, Austrian-born graphic designer and typographer. Runs design company Sagmeister Inc., based in New York. Designed album covers for the Rolling Stones, Lou Reed and David Byrne.

3 Paula Scher, American graphic designer. Partner at Pentagram, New York since 1991. Received four Grammy nominations for her album cover designs and numerous other accolades. See page 162.

4 Pentagram, eminent design group formed in 1972 in London by Alan Fletcher, Theo Crosby, Colin Forbes, Kenneth Grange and Mervyn Kurlansky. See page 162.

5 Michael Bierut, American-born designer. Partner in Pentagram's New York office since 1990. Appeared memorably in the film *Helvetica*.

Milton Glaser, Inc.
Founded: 1974
Personnel: 6
Location: New York, US
www.miltonglaser.com

In 1954, Milton Glaser co-founded Push Pin
Studio in New York. It was to become one of
the most influential and era-defining studios
in graphic design history. In 1974 Glaser
founded Milton Glaser, Inc., from where he
continues to pursue his singular vision of life
as a designer, public intellectual and artist.

For many, Glaser represents the epitome
of the cultured designer – how many graphic
designers quote Horace? Best known for co-
founding *New York Magazine* and designing
the timeless I Love New York logo, his oeuvre
encompasses newspapers and magazine
design, interior spaces, logos, typeface
creation and brand identities, as well as
prints, drawings, posters and paintings
that reveal an artist and draughtsman
of consummate skill and vision.

Glaser is the author of numerous books,
including *Milton Glaser: Graphic Design*. His
most recent book, *Drawing is Thinking*, is a
collection of his drawings and art. He is also
the subject of a recent documentary film
Milton Glaser: To Inform and Delight.

The interview was conducted by phone.
—

It's rare to hear designers talk publicly about
their studios. Can you describe your studio
and your studio philosophy?

Milton Glaser: My office, which has
always been more or less the same, is a big
undifferentiated room. I sit in one place in
the room, in the same relationship to the
rest of the room as everybody else. There is
no visual hierarchy. I think it may have to do
with the fact that when I was a kid my family
lived in a three-roomed apartment. The family
would spend its evenings in the living room. My
mother would knit at one end, my father would
read the paper and listen to the radio, my
sister was at her desk, and I was at the other
end doing my homework. I became accustomed
to the lack of privacy and got used to working
in a place where a lot of things were going on.

For me, the idea of a room with people
doing their work without separation, without
privacy, was quite natural. If your own history
was different, it may be difficult for you
to enter into an open studio situation and
work effectively. It's hard to talk about a
singular ideal studio, perhaps, because when
personalities are arbitrarily thrust together,
a solution that is uniform doesn't apply.

When you started Push Pin in 1954 did you have a studio model in mind?

01 |
02 |

I had an ideal in mind that came out of a visit I made to Donald Brun's[1] studio in Switzerland, when I first went to Europe. I was in my early 20s and very impressionable. I called Brun on the telephone and asked if I could visit him, and he graciously said yes. I went to his house, and at the top was a skylight studio where he worked with two assistants. They each had a desk with a single piece of paper on it, a T-square and a triangle, and that was all. They were wearing lab coats and it was all very Swiss and orderly. I said to myself, 'One day, I'm going to have a place just like this.'

Have you ever managed to get your designers into lab coats?

I've tried on more then one occasion, but of course it never happened [laughs]. At Push Pin we were in a loft in a disreputable building, with stuff all over the place. On our desks, instead of a single piece of paper, a T-square and a triangle, there were a hundred pieces of paper and every kind of pencil, ruler, pen, worn-out brushes, dried-out paint, and dozens of jars of thinners and paints. My ideal model was compromised by life itself. It didn't quite work out.

You didn't have any American models?

The truth is we didn't, and also we didn't even have a model for what a studio did, or how a business ran, or most anything else. We just plunged into this idea that we could continue doing what we were doing at school – play and have fun and talk and listen to music and basically enjoy the day. Over time, we had to modify that a little bit.

That sounds like a pretty good vision, to me. How important is your physical environment?

Actually I have to say that I do like order, but my inclination is to move towards chaos, so it's a case of constantly fixing what exists and every once in a while it stays sort of orderly and understandable for a couple of hours, and then the flow of events catches up. I have finally understood I will never really have the place I dreamed of.

Your earlier description of the studio as a living room where everybody sits together and gets on with their work seems like a very resilient and workable model for a studio.

The only job I ever had, which only lasted about eight months, was for *Vogue*, in their promotion department. Magazines derive their ethos from the world of newspapers and journalism, and this world has always been conducted in big 'sitting rooms' where everybody is thrust together without any privacy. The great benefit of this is that you can hear what everybody's saying. I've never

01/ Project: Poster, Camus: Rebellion, Resistance and Death. Date: 2007. Client: School of Visual Arts. Designer: Milton Glaser. 02/ Project: Book cover, *Plot Against America* by Philip Roth. Date: 2004. Client: Houghton Mifflin Harcourt Publishing Company. Designer: Milton Glaser.

written a memo in my life, because everybody knows exactly who I'm talking to and what I'm doing. Everybody here knows everybody's business. If you have a deep sense of privacy I don't think that you could work for me.

Do your clients come to the studio?

Yes. We have a separate room, a little so-called conference room with table and chairs. So it's possible to leave the studio and go to this adjoining room and have a conversation. But it's looked upon as something that is not part of the culture. If somebody is talking to somebody else in another room, everybody is alerted to the fact that something is going on that is aberrant.

When you set up Milton Glaser, Inc. in 1974 you were working on big projects – supermarkets, that sort of thing. Was there a moment when you thought you might become Landor[2] or Interbrand[3]? Or was it never really part of the plan?

No, it was never part of my plan. I've never felt comfortable in that world. It involves too much time spent with clients rationalizing your decisions and not enough time spent doing the work. For me, the only purpose of being in this field is to do the work, not to give it to others and then work as the salesperson. That fills me with horror. I did the supermarket – Grand Union – with James Goldsmith[4]. Funny man. Mad right-winger, but I liked him very much.

What was he like as a client?

He was the perfect client for me. Fundamentally he agreed with almost everything I wanted to do. The scope of the job was really enormous. We did 2500 packages, and it was stimulating knowing that you were doing work that would be seen by ordinary people, and not the kind of specialized audience that most of our stuff involves. So I geared up, and ran the studio with 45 people and made a lot of money during that period. I also learnt that I didn't want to run that kind of studio. We did the job and then Grand Union was sold (I was on the board of directors, which is an odd place for a designer to be, but it meant that I got a terrific payoff when the company was sold). But I also realized that it had in part taken me away from the work I really enjoyed doing.

So you rejected the move towards becoming a big powerhouse studio. How many people are at Milton Glaser, Inc. today?

We have a very small office. I have a personal assistant, a bookkeeper, three designers and usually an intern, and that's it. And we do a lot of work with that many people.

Elsewhere in this book, Erik Spiekermann points out that in the big studios with 125 people and upwards, the work is only ever done by teams of four or five people.

That's probably true, and in an office like ours, you collectively sit down and talk about how to approach the problem.

I guide the direction, but I like everyone to participate. It's very much a studio, and depends on having a kind of idiosyncratic view of what design is. The only reason clients come to us is because they want some difference from what a commercial design studio would do.

Do you see it as part of your job to nurture and develop talent?

I think the job of a successful studio director is indeed to pass on their knowledge. I've been teaching for half a century and in many cases my students have gone on to work for me. I try to ensure that people who are working for me are also learning something that is useful to them.

What are you looking for in the designers you hire?

More than anything else, an attitude. I want people to know that they can learn here and that it is an opportunity for growth and understanding. And my principle is always that the way you learn is by observing someone who knows how to do what you aspire to. The old apprenticeship system appears to be from a different time, but it is still the best way. More then anything, what you learn is the devotion that people have to the pursuit of their work. I always say that what I learnt from [Giorgio] Morandi[5] when I was living in Bologna[6] was how totally committed he was to the idea of being a painter and an etcher and discovering what the possibilities were. And I think that's what happens when you work with somebody good – your experience is not what they tell you, but what they are.

Here you are, one of the most celebrated and famous graphic designers in the world; can you tell me how work comes to you?

Well, I don't really know. I've never done very much solicitation. We're at a point in professional life where design activities have slowed to a walk and I have to recognize that at this point my reputation is not entirely beneficial. People assume I have plenty of work, that I'm very expensive and difficult to deal with. Which may or may not be true. I have no idea.

I get a lot of editorial coverage that serves to alert people to the fact that I'm still around and still working. But I've never known how to solicit work. I've never known how to send out promotional brochures… and anyway,

03 | 04 |
05 | 06 |
07 | 08 |

03/ Project: Limited-edition silkscreen, appliqué. Date: 2004. Client: Rubin Museum of Art. Designer: Milton Glaser 04/ Project: Limited-edition silkscreen, The Dance. Date: 2004. Client: Rubin Museum of Art. Designer: Milton Glaser. 05/ Project: Poster, The Secret of Art. Date: 2007. Client: School of Visual Arts. Designer: Milton Glaser. 06/ Project: Poster, Tomato: Something Unusual Is Going On Here. Date: 1978. Client: Tomato Records. Designer: Milton Glaser. 07/ Project: Poster, We Are All African. Date: 2006. Client: School of Visual Arts/International Rescue Committee. Designer: Milton Glaser. 08/ Project: Poster, Darfur. Date: 2006. Client: School of Visual Arts/International Rescue Committee. Designer: Milton Glaser.

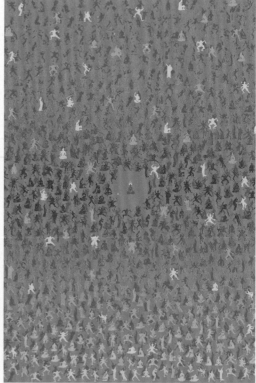

The Secret of Art

TOMATO: **SOMETHING UNUSUAL IS GOING ON HERE**

DAVE BRUBECK / THE NEW BRUBECK QUARTET / JOHN CAGE / CLIFTON CHENIER / LINDA COHEN / DICK GREGORY / JON HASSELL
LIGHTNIN' HOPKINS / JOHN LEE HOOKER / ALBERT KING / LEADBELLY / MAGMA / GARY MC MAHAN / JORGE SANTANA / TOWNES VAN ZANDT

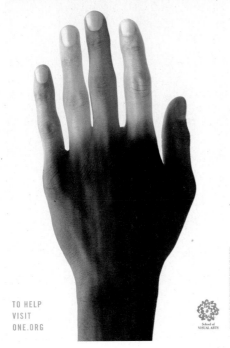

WE ARE ALL AFRICAN

TO HELP
VISIT
ONE.ORG

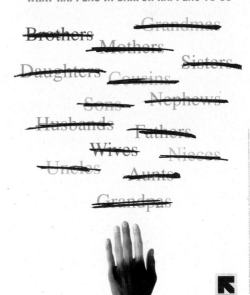

DARFUR

WHAT HAPPENS IN DARFUR HAPPENS TO US

~~Brothers~~ ~~Grandmas~~
~~Mothers~~
~~Daughters~~ ~~Cousins~~ ~~Sisters~~
~~Sons~~ ~~Nephews~~
~~Husbands~~ ~~Fathers~~
~~Wives~~ ~~Nieces~~
~~Uncles~~ ~~Aunts~~
~~Grandpas~~

WE ARE ALL AFRICAN   TO HELP: theIRC.ORG

I don't have the appetite for it. I also don't like the idea of looking for work. Existentially, it puts me in a position I don't like to be in – looking for people to support your efforts and keep you in business, as opposed to people coming to you because you have the answer to their problems.

Most designers imagine that if they become famous, work will flood in. But can fame be a discourager as well as an attractor?

One assumption is that if clients go to someone famous, they wont be able to control the job as well as they would like to. They also think they will pay more. And they're not sure that it's going to be any better. Somebody said that being famous was like being the beautiful girl who never has a date on Saturday night.

Are there any studios from the modern era that you admire?

There are many good people, but I've never really paid much attention to what's going on in the field because it never interested me that way. I have people I admire like Massimo Vignelli[7], and many people who are of my generation. I like Stephen Doyle's[8] work very much. I like Stefan Sagmeister's[9] work. But I have to say that other designers have not been the major source of my inspiration. I've always looked towards history more than what is current. There have been so many great masters and so many extraordinary people. Although at this particular moment, I'm not sure we are at a particularly elevated level.

Among young designers there is a lot of interest in the past. A real reverence for the Swiss guys, for example. I've noticed it more then I ever did before. Have you come across this?

From time to time. At Push Pin, and through my own efforts, I tried to make design less ideologically and stylistically limited. I grew up as a child of modernism and for years that was really the centrepiece of my work, until I realized it was just not interesting enough. You got to a certain point where you understood principles. In many cases they were eminently employable, but there were so many other things one could refer to that were alternatives to that vision. It became like eating the same lettuce and tomato sandwich everyday. At a certain point, you want a thick soup. The Swiss school, and the idea of modernism, became so overwhelming. And academic in the sense that it was being repeated over and over again without examination. It seemed to me that the time had come to open up the subject a little more, and be a little more generous in what things could look like.

I've always thought that one of the great contributions you make is to constantly bring

09 |
10 |

09/ Project: Logo, Tony Kushner's Angels in America. Date: 1993. Client: Tony Kushner. Designer: Milton Glaser.
10/ Project: Book cover, Milton Glaser and Jerome Snyder's The Underground Gourmet. Date: 1975. Client: Simon & Schuster. Designer: Milton Glaser.

the great artists – Picasso, Matisse and others – into the graphic design discourse. Was that deliberate?

It was deliberate in the sense that if you were developing a vocabulary of form you have to look at everything from the Renaissance, to Picasso, to cave paintings. They are all explorations of form and meaning, so why would you as a designer feel that the only reference that was appropriate was to what was happening in your own time.

I see from pictures of your studio that you have the words 'art is work' written over your doorway. What do you want visitors from your studio to take away from that?

Visitors can take away whatever they like from this, but it's intended to say, let's not be so parochial about distinctions between high and low forms. What we discover late in life is that things that are called art are sometimes arbitrarily defined, and things that are called work sometimes become art. The distinction between art and non-art is a complex and fascinating subject, often reduced to style, opportunity and money. Fundamentally my idea is that you need to pay attention to what's in front of you without too many preconceptions.

OK, last question. Somebody has just arrived in your studio from Mars and you have to describe Milton Glaser, Inc. to them; what are you going to say?

Well, first they'd have to understand the nature of capitalist enterprise, and they'd have to understand what a business is, and they'd have to understand what you are communicating, and to whom and for what purpose. The thing about our practice is that it is bound by utility and success. You have to produce ways of communicating to others that move them to action and understanding. That's what we do. Primarily we do it visually, though we use language as well. But we basically move people to action by virtue of images and words.

Having said that, I found a quote that I love from Horace[10]: 'the definition of art is something that informs and delights'. I used part of that quote for the title of a film that was made about me[11]. I like that definition as much as anything I've heard, particularly because of the word 'informs' rather than 'persuades.' My great distinction when thinking about our professional life is that I would rather inform then persuade, and the problem I always have with advertising is that it basically does the opposite.

So I would say to a visitor from Mars, if he spoke our language, that fundamentally we are part of the business and economic structure of the country. That capitalism is the economic form and that we affect both the culture and the economics of the country

by encouraging people to buy things and to do things. That's our job. I don't know if that would be understandable to a Martian.

1 Donald Brun (1909–1999), Swiss graphic designer, exhibition designer and poster artist. Taught at the Basel School of Design (1947–1974). Founder member of AGI.

2 Landor, founded by Walter Landor, a pioneer of branding, consumer research and modern logo design. Today Landor is a global branding consultancy employing hundreds of people.

3 Interbrand, founded in 1974. Claim to be 'the world's largest brand consultancy'.

4 Sir James Goldsmith (1933–1997), Anglo-French financier who maintained three families and homes in four countries. Spent billions fighting the European Union.

5 Giorgio Morandi (1890–1964), Italian painter who concentrated almost exclusively on still lifes and landscapes, except for a few self-portraits. One of the few Italian artists of his generation to have escaped the taint of Fascism. His work was featured in the film La Dolce Vita by Frederico Fellini.

6 Glaser won a Fulbright scholarship and spent a year (1952–1953) in Bologna, Italy, studying with Giorgio Morandi.

7 Massimo Vignelli, Italian-born designer, founded Vignelli Associates, working for clients such as IBM and American Airlines.

8 Stephen Doyle, New York designer. See page 68.

9 Stefan Sagmeister, Austrian-born graphic designer and typographer. Runs design company Sagmeister Inc., based in New York. Designed album covers for the Rolling Stones, Lou Reed and David Byrne.

10 Horace, (65BCE–8BCE), leading Roman lyric poet during the time of Augustus. Best known for his Odes.

11 Milton Glaser: To Inform and Delight, a film about Glaser directed by Wendy Keys.

Mucho
Founded: 2003
Personnel: 7
Location: Barcelona, Spain
www.mucho.ws

Mucho is one of the leading lights of the
new wave of young Spanish design groups.
Like many of their compatriots, founders
Pablo Juncadella and Marc Català worked
in the UK, where they took inspiration from
the vibrant London design scene. Juncadella
and Català both trained under Fernando
Gutierrez[1], and when Gutierrez joined the
London office of Pentagram, they went with
him as 'his team'. After a stint on their own
designing the broadsheet Sunday newspaper
The Observer in London, Juncadella and
Català returned to Barcelona to set up
Mucho (the studio's name is explained below).

Today, they run Mucho as a 'creative
agency focused on graphic design, packaging
and art direction'. Their clients include local
and international names. Their work has the
intelligent sheen of a modern European design
group, yet retains an unmistakable Hispanic
flavour. They describe their studio's contents
as 'Star Wars memorabilia mixed with Ikea
and some Vitra...'

The interview was conducted via email.
—

Could you tell us a little about your
background – where you studied and your
work experience before you set up?

Pablo Juncadella: My partner Marc Català
and I studied in Barcelona at an art school
called Eina – Escola de Disseny i Art, in
Barcelona. Our teachers were Pablo Martin[2]
and Fernando Gutierrez, at the time partners
of an up-and-coming graphic design firm
called Grafica[3]. We joined the company around
1998 as part of their team. In 2000 Fernando
Gutierrez joined Pentagram and we moved
with him as his team to London. In 2003 we
decided to move back to Spain and start
our own company (Mucho). At the same time
we got an offer to art-direct *The Observer*,
in London. So for about three years we
combined running Mucho with working on
the *The Observer*. In 2006 we returned to
Barcelona to dedicate all our attention to
the company.

What prompted you to start your own studio?

Marc Català: It came to a point where we
were not growing as designers, so it seemed
the natural step forward to start our own
company. We both had this idea of where we
wanted to get to, and the kind of relationship
we wanted to have with our clients. We are
still far from that original idea, but we are
closer to it now.

Tell me about your partnership – what makes it work?

MC: It is based on the mutual respect that we have for each other. Often this means going to design places that you would not go on your own. We try not to agree on everything; disagreements often make the workplace more interesting and challenging. Good partnerships are not the ones built on agreements, but on the capability of admitting certain disagreements and building on them.

Did you have a vision of how you wanted your studio to be?

PJ: Our vision of the company is influenced by our previous experiences in other companies. We always thought that we would keep it small, and if we were to grow we would do it with more partners so that we could continue to focus our attention on design.

What inspired the name?

MC: We started without a name, and it took us some time to come to an agreement on one. In Spanish, 'Mucho' is sometimes used as an expression to praise a particular act of skill. If at a concert the band has performed nicely you might say 'Mucho!', or if a football player has produced a good trick, you could use it.

PJ: Many people think the name Mucho ('much' in English) is an anti 'less is more' statement. In fact, it refers to the effort we put into every project, and the will to try and do projects of many different disciplines with a reduced structure. At the beginning it was very ironic because it started as just us in a very tiny space, so it was everything but 'Mucho'. It also sounded good in every language and it is almost a universal word in Spanish that everybody understands.

Where did you go for help and advice?

PJ: Our experiences prior to starting our company gave us a lot of contact with good and experienced designers, so we always took every chance to ask questions. Most of the time we had good advice from them and we feel very grateful for that

Did you have to borrow money?

MC: No. We always had this idea that the biggest investment that the company needed was our full attention, and that economic investment should go to the amount of projects we had and not the other way around.

Can you describe the process you went through to get started?

PJ: The first step was like many others. We were in one room in my flat. Then we moved

01/ Project: Graphics for BMW Awards. Client: BMW. 02/ Project: Identity for Motion Production Company. Client: Boolab. 03/ Corporate identity for restaurant of traditional Catalan cuisine. Client: Petit Comitè.

to a tiny studio, but this was while we were flying to the UK every week to art-direct *The Observer*. When we moved to Barcelona for good we got a more professional structure, more organized and with space that would allow our team to grow.

How is your studio organized?

PJ: The two partners each have their own teams. Depending on the size of the projects we sometimes put the two teams together. Many times the project gets started by both partners and then one of the teams finishes it off. We have a studio manager who is shared by both teams. This person allows the designers to concentrate on design and takes care of many aspects of the daily tasks of the studio. We also have a team of external collaborators like product designers, project managers, copywriters and freelancers.

Were there other studios and designers that influenced you?

PJ: We were influenced by Fernando Gutierrez of Pentagram and Grafica, and Pablo Martin, but also designers like Peter Saville, Mario Eskenazi[4], Vince Frost[5], Simon Esterson[6], Mark Farrow[7] or 'classics' like Josef Müller-Brockmann[8], Saul Bass[9], Massimo Vignelli[10], Jan Tschichold[11] and Tibor Kalman[12].

Are they the same people who inspire you now, or have you discovered others?

MC: We admire the same designers, but in later years we have discovered the work of studios like Experimental Jetset[13], Spin[14], GTF[15], A2/SW/HK[16], NB:Studio[17], MadeThought[18], Work in Progress, Studio Astrid Stavro[19] and others.

Can you define your role?

PJ: Our role is to lead the design teams and make the business decisions that need to be taken at Mucho. We would like to think that some of our work could last longer than its purely commercial purpose.

Could you tell me about the type of clients you have?

MC: Our clients vary from chocolate-makers to car manufacturers, cultural projects, animation and music production companies, restaurants, cosmetics multinationals, and often friends with small projects. Pablo and I always say that we want to work with whoever wants to work with us. This looks like a very simple statement but quite the contrary. It is difficult to achieve. Some clients think they want to work with you but in fact they want a designer who follows their directions blindly.

Could you talk about how you find new clients?

PJ: We have been lucky because many of our projects have been successful and have brought more work. It has come to the point now where clients who want to work with us call the studio out of the blue. But obviously not all the projects have popped up just like that. Lately we have been doing some networking in order to be able to do some more institutional and cultural projects for the city of Barcelona.

Can you talk about how you present Mucho to new clients?

MC: We have a leather-bound portfolio that shows our work nicely printed. We try to get it updated on a weekly basis, and also have low-resolution PDFs to send out quickly by email.

Let's talk about employing people. How do you go about keeping your designers happy and motivated?

PJ: This has been hit and miss from the start. We always try to hire based on talent, and we try to make them part of Mucho. We want them to feel proud of the work we do and the place they work. Many times it works and the experience becomes interesting for our designers. But other times it doesn't. I guess it has to do with personalities.

Do you see mentoring as part of your job? Say for example there was a designer in your studio who had lots of talent but had a bad attitude — would you see it as part of your job to try and turn that person into a good team member, or would you decide that it wasn't worth the effort?

MC: Yes, our ethos is to try to get the best from our designers. In some cases it has proven impossible, but in most of the cases it pays off at the end. When we started out, we were lucky to have people around who had the patience to teach us, and get the best from us. So we see this process as our duty towards the next generation.

What qualities do you look for when employing a designer?

PJ: As I said, talent is the key aspect, but everything counts. Speaking languages is important for us because it means that they can work with other cultures and that they are open-minded. Lately we have been teaching and we have a tendency to recruit designers out of college. We believe there is a better chance to get it right when you have been working in class for a whole year. Another difficult aspect is that we are very careful about being overloaded with stuff. It is easy to fall into a situation in which you end up taking jobs that are not interesting just because you have to pay salaries. So

04 | 05 |
06 | 07 |

04/05/ Project: Annual for the Art Directors Club Of Europe. Client: ADCE.
06/ Project: Christmas card for lingerie brand. Client: Andrés Sardá.
07/ Project: Promotional leaflet for fashion trade fair. Client: Demano.
08/09/ Project: Posters for exhibition of number seven. Client: Powers of Seven.
10/11/ Project: Corporate identity for Japanese restaurant chain. Client: Sushi Itto.

having the right number of people in your studio is crucial in many aspects.

What is your approach to designers who want a sense of personal authorship?

MC: Designers always get credited, and so do Pablo and I. We do this to avoid authorship issues. Work from Mucho is done by Mucho, but the people behind Mucho are as important as the brand.

Giving individual credits to designers in studios is unusual. Does it ever cause problems with potential clients? Do they see a name and decide they want to work with that designer?

MC: As long as Mucho comes first, so far it has not been a problem.

Do you have a profit-share policy?

PJ: In the last two years we have started sharing some of the profits at the end of the financial year. The way we do it is by offering our workers opportunities to take courses in photography, 3D design etc. We are planning language courses for next year, if things go well. They are free to choose what they want to learn, but they have to be subjects that we all can benefit from.

How important is the physical environment you work in?

PJ: It is very important! It needs to be comfortable and inspiring, because we spend a lot of time in it. It also has to be flexible and useful. We are constantly thinking of ways in which we can make it a better, more useful space. A friend of ours regards his working space as a massive thought space, a bit like a computer. I quite like this idea. In our studio we now have a small photography studio, a mounting space, an archive, and we are looking into building a small silkscreen printing space.

So it's not a pristine workspace?

MC: Not really, more like Star Wars memorabilia mixed with Ikea and some Vitra, but very little. It is set in the middle of a Barcelona interior space, with lots of natural light, and has a beautiful floor. It is open-plan so that we all have a close relationship, with a separated meeting room and spaces for specific work as mentioned above.

Do you have a music policy?

MC: Yes, never two iPods at the same time. It gets confusing otherwise.

Do you have formal rules about things like time-keeping?

MC: It's something we have never been good at, but I really think it should be done.

Do you think this is a case of your studio growing and therefore the need for more 'professionalism' grows too?

MC: Yes, it is exactly that. At the beginning it was only us, and two computers. So from the beginning it has been about being more effective, and in the end giving a better service to our clients.

How do you maintain the balance between creativity and profitability?

PJ: I believe that it is easier with two partners, because when a project is not profitable the other partner can balance it with a project that is. We try to be aware of our economic results on a monthly basis, but it is key that profitable projects are not only profitable, and it's important that creative projects give us the chance to make an impact and therefore bring other kind of assets.

What is your policy regarding entering design awards?

MC: Awards always affect one's ego in one way or another, and, after all the work that goes into a project, the enormous effort of finding creative and surprising solutions and the hard task of convincing clients to use them, it is important to any designer to get some sense of recognition. Having said this, there is another important side to awards that has nothing to do with personal aspirations, and which relates to Mucho as a brand. Awards are vital to our industry as our reputation as designers is our only advertising. Clients we have never heard of call us up because somebody who knows the Barcelona design scene has directed them to us. This exposure comes in no small measure from the public recognition we have received when winning design awards.

You take a positive attitude to awards – there are some designers who don't approve of design awards…

MC: Design awards are the tool the industry uses to show itself to the public. They do not set a standard of excellence. How could they? They do not design. The design community, and its sense of self-improvement, will always set the state of design quality. Awards are a way of showing to the rest of the world the present standard. No matter how different we might find our criteria is from that of a certain jury, or how many awards we win or fail to win, as long as our work has been selected to be in the annuals, our goal has been met. I believe as designers we must always remember what awards are for. This is why I find it stupid to fail to give an award – something that happens when a jury doesn't think there is any work deserving of an award. It is a pompous act of contempt on the part of any jury to do this.

Which awards do you enter?

PJ: The Laus Graphic Design and Visual Communication Awards; ADG-FAD, Spain; The Art Directors Club of Europe awards; D&AD; The Type Directors Club. Mainly we enter our work into the Spanish awards as it is the area where our reputation has developed. But we are starting more and more to submit to international awards, as we have always intended to have an international projection.

What is your attitude to taking on interns?

MC: We always have interns. In fact we have an agreement with an art school. It is very good for them and it helps us immensely.

What do you say to people who accuse studios of using interns as cheap labour?

MC: I say everybody deserves a first chance, and if you are patient with them and take the time to make sure they have a good experience, then it is definitely not cheap labour.

If you could start all over again, what would you do differently?

PJ: I would have listened more to my instincts when designing and when dealing with clients. But this is a hard thing to do when you are starting out.

How would you define your studio's culture today?

MC: I would say our studio is ambitious creatively, it is ideas-based, and it reflects the amount of effort of a whole team. It is experimental but acknowledges the commercial side of our work. Essentially, we try to keep our minds and ideas as fresh as possible, and offers images we think can be interesting to the community.

Any advice for someone thinking of setting up a studio?

MC: At the beginning you have to set high standards in what you do. You cannot sacrifice creativity in favour of profitability. This means you will have to suffer for some time but you will see how, with time and patience, profits will come. Once you have set up those standards they become somewhat sacred to you. Also it is key to listen to your clients. Many times the solution comes from them without them knowing. Ask the right questions.

1 Fernando Gutierrez, co-founded Grafica in 1993. Became associate director at Pentagram in 2000. Opened his own studio in London in 2006.

2 Pablo Martin, manager and co-founder of Barcelona design studio Grafica.

3 Grafica, design studio founded in Barcelona in 1993 by Fernando Gutierrez and Pablo Martin.

4 Mario Eskenazi, Barcelona-based graphic designer.

5 Vince Frost, founder of Frost Design with offices in Sydney and London.

6 Simon Esterson, notable editorial designer. Director of Esterson Associates and art director and proprietor of Eye magazine.

7 Mark Farrow, founder of Farrow Design in London. Noted for his designs for the Pet Shop Boys.

8 Josef Müller-Brockmann (1914–1996), highly influential Swiss graphic designer. Founding editor of New Graphic Design.

9 Saul Bass (1920–1996), American graphic designer and Academy Award-winning filmmaker, best known for his design of movie title sequences, including The Man with the Golden Arm, Vertigo, Psycho, Goodfellas and Casino.

10 Massimo Vignelli, Italian-born designer, founded Vignelli Associates, working for clients such as IBM and American Airlines.

11 Jan Tschichold (1902–1974), Swiss typographer, book designer, teacher and writer. Leading advocate of modernist design.

12 Tibor Kalman (1949–1999), influential American graphic designer of Hungarian origin. Co-founded design firm M&Co in 1979. Best known for his work as editor-in-chief of Colors magazine.

13 Experimental Jetset, design company based in Amsterdam. Founded by Marieke Stolk, Danny van den Dungen and Erwin Brinkers. See page 86.

14 Spin, London design company founded in 1992 by Patricia Finegan and Tony Brook. See page 204.

15 Graphic Thought Facility (GTF). London-based design consultancy formed in 1990 by Huw Morgan, Paul Neale and Andy Stevens.

16 A2/SW/HK, London-based design company founded in 2000 by Scott Williams and Henrik Kubel.

17 NB:Studio, founded in London in 1997 by Alan Dye, Nick Finney and Ben Stott. Clients include Knoll, Land Securities and the Tate.

18 MadeThought, London-based design consultancy. Founded in 2000 by Ben Parker and Paul Austin. Clients include Stella McCartney, Yves Saint Laurent, Reiss and Nokia.

19 Studio Astrid Stavro, independent company based in Barcelona.

Nakajima Design
Founded: 1995
Personnel: 5
Location: Tokyo, Japan
www.nkjm-d.com

Hideki Nakajima's character is like his work: restrained, introspective and disciplined. Ask young Japanese designers about him and they talk with a sort of quiet awe.

Nakajima is the son of a kimono tailor and grew up surrounded by traditional Japanese design motifs, which awakened his embryonic sense of design and pattern. In a recent interview he said: 'I believe graphic design is originally a Western art. That is what I was taught and that is why I am influenced by lots of Western forerunners in most of my creative life. I am inclined to believe that my intuition is my major source of inspiration. I have never admired work based solely on concepts or marketing strategies.'

He runs Nakajima Design with quiet determination, demanding that his designers follow his vision. When they leave, he notes paternalistically, 'they can fly off in any direction they like'.

The interview was carried out by email.
—

What prompted you to start your studio?

Hideki Nakajima: I wanted to have my own studio before I became 30 years old. I knew that it would be necessary to gain a lot of experience with many clients before setting up on my own. When I was 30 years old, I got a job as an art director at a publisher called Rockin'on, which focused mainly on music. Rockin'on established an in-house design department at that time and I was the first art director. I worked mainly on the art direction and design for magazines such as *Cut*, *Rockin'on Japan*, *H* and *Bridge*. But it wasn't until I reached the age of 34 that I had my own studio.

Can you talk about design studios in Japan? Were there Japanese studios that inspired you?

There are different kinds of studios in Japan. Some of them are modelled on the London studios of Alan Fletcher[1] or Pentagram[2]. The Japanese studio that inspired me most was Tsuguya Inoue's[3]. He was doing 'on-the-edge' design work for [fashion retailer] Comme des Garçons. I visited his small studio with my portfolio several times trying to get hired, though there wasn't a job on offer. I didn't receive an offer.

Were you able to turn to someone for help and advice when you started your studio?

Mr. Youichi Shibuya, who is the CEO of

01 | 02 | 03 | 04 |
05 | 06 |

01/ Project: Re-CitF. Date: 2008. Client: ginza graphic gallery. Designer: Hideki Nakajima.
02/ Project: Library of Dreams & The Library of the Sky. Date: 2008. Client: G/P gallery.
Designer: Hideki Nakajima. Writer: Gustavo Alberto Garcia Vaca.
03/ Project: Biographical Library. Date: 2008. Client: G/P gallery. Designer: Hideki
Nakajima. Writer: Gustavo Alberto Garcia Vaca. 04/ Project: The Library of Sacred Texts
& Library of Fragrances. Date: 2008. Client: G/P gallery. Designer: Hideki Nakajima.
Writer: Gustavo Alberto Garcia Vaca. 05/ Project: About the Author. Date: 2006.
Client: ginza graphic gallery. Designer: Hideki Nakajima. 06/ Project: dpbq. Date: 2006.
Client: ginza graphic gallery. Designer: Hideki Nakajima. 07/ Project: Seven Exhibition #2.
Date: 2005. Client: Pao Galleries, Hong Kong Arts Centre. Designer: Hideki Nakajima.
Writer: Rainer Maria Rilke. 08/ Project: Seven Exhibition #1. Date: 2005. Client: Pao
Galleries, Hong Kong Arts Centre. Designer: Hideki Nakajima. 09/ Project: The Library
of the Moving Image. Date: 2008. Client: G/P gallery. Designer: Hideki Nakajima.
Writer: Gustavo Alberto Garcia Vaca. 10/ Project: Science Library. Date: 2008.
Client: G/P gallery. Designer: Hideki Nakajima. Writer: Gustavo Alberto Garcia Vaca.

About the author:

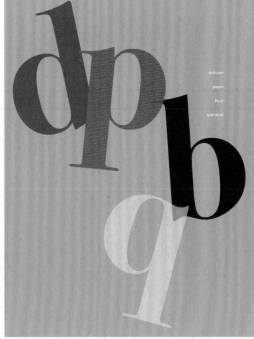

delicate
paper
bear
question

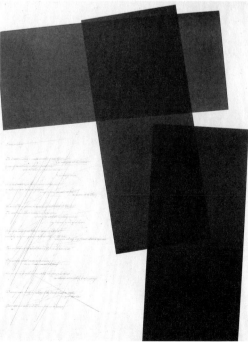

Rockin'on. When I started my own studio, he
kindly let me keep working on the art direction
and design for *Cut* magazine. Having my own
studio with staff costs and rent was more
expensive than I expected. Having a monthly
job with *Cut* magazine helped me a lot, both
economically and mentally. The relation
between Mr. Youichi Shibuya and me continues
today and I'm still working on the art direction
and design for *Cut* magazine.

Keeping ambitious designers motivated is
a difficult task. Can you talk about the
techniques you use to get the best out
of designers — are you a sympathetic art
director or do you demand obedience?

I never ask my staff for their opinions.
But I don't think I demand obedience. To
keep the studio productive and healthy
there is no need to be overly sympathetic.
Designers need to keep challenging, but their
ideas or opinions often come from a narrow
point of view. While they are working in my
studio, I ask them to work on my ideas and
opinions, and after they leave my studio, they
can fly off in any direction they like. I think
this is the best way to motivate staff in my
studio. On the other hand, I am always hoping
my staff will have great futures after leaving
me. This is a Japanese custom.

How do you attract new clients?

I'm not sure, but one of the reasons may be
winning prizes worldwide. Being featured in
many books may be another reason. In Japan,
these accolades can raise a studio's profile.
But actually, I don't believe in such value.

Do you mean that the 'value' is superficial?
Are you saying that studios should be judged
on their work, and not the number of times
that they win awards or appear in magazines?

Yes, I think so. It used to be important to
me to increase the number of awards I won,
and the number of times I was featured in
magazines. But I soon got used to it and
it became less important. To keep my
motivation, I need to keep re-creating
new starting points.

What is your attitude to interns? Is there
a tradition in Japan of employing them in
studios?

It is not common in Japan, and because my
studio is small, it is difficult to employ them.
Also, I think usually they will leave the studio
before they get used to the job. I want to
take enough time to develop my staff.

So does this mean that you see part of your
job as educating staff?

Yes, it does. My staff need to get used to
the way I work and how my studio is run.
But on the other hand, they are not robots.

11 |
12 |

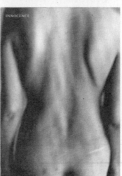

Through working in my studio, I believe they need to face the truth that life can be richer but at the same time it is lonely, sad and tough.

Tell me about the physical environment of your studio. Is the environment you work in important to you?

My studio is messy. The working space is important, but I don't have time to keep it tidy.

I'm surprised! The Japanese tradition of interior design is famous all over the world. I thought you might have incorporated some traditional Japanese thinking into your studio?

It is a shame but my studio is very small and untidy. My staff know where everything is, I do not.

1 Alan Fletcher (1931–2006), British graphic designer described in his *Daily Telegraph* obituary as 'the most highly regarded graphic designer of his generation, and probably one of the most prolific.'

2 Pentagram, eminent design group formed in 1972 in London by Alan Fletcher, Theo Crosby, Colin Forbes, Kenneth Grange and Mervyn Kurlansky. See page 162.

3 Tsuguya Inoue, Japanese graphic designer. Established Beans Co. in 1978. Has produced major works for Suntory, Comme des Garcons and Asahi. Member of the Tokyo ADC, Tokyo TDC and JAGDA.

11/ Project: Playing the Piano 2009 Out of Noise. Date: 2009. Client: Commons. Designer: Hideki Nakajima. Artist: Ryuichi Sakamoto. 12/ Project: Innocence. Date: 2007. Client: AKAAKA. Designer: Hideki Nakajima. Photographer: Miyako Ishiuchi. 13/ Project: I Wanted to Make a Beautiful Paradox. We Were Drawn Together Like Magnets. Date: 2006. Client: ginza graphic gallery. Designer: Hideki Nakajima. 14/ Project: Koshoku Painting. Date: 2008. Client: Rat Hole Galleries. Designer: Hideki Nakajima. Photographer: Nobuyoshi Araki.

Non-Format
Founded: 1999
Personnel: 2
Location: London, UK, and Minnesota, US
www.non-format.com

Non-Format are Jon Forss and Kjell Ekhorn.
They have a passionate following among
designers, art directors and design fans
who respond to the duo's fluid and luxuriant
style, and their apparent freedom from the
normal constraints that renders most graphic
design into bland statements of the obvious.
Yet despite the seeming autonomy of their
work, Forss and Ekhorn regard themselves
as following in the noble tradition of problem-
solving graphic designers. They reject the
notion that they are part of the we're-only-
here-to-please-ourselves wing of design.

Their studio set-up is as eye-catching as
their work. Forss (a Brit) lives and works in
Minnesota, US; Ekhorn (a Norwegian) lives and
works in London. Up until Forss's departure
to the States in 2007, they occupied a studio
in London, where they sat side by side with
their monitors turned inwards so that each
could see what the other was doing. Despite
being separated by the Atlantic Ocean, they
still work in much the same way, using Skype
to talk to each other constantly.

The interview with Jon Forss and Kjell Ekhorn
took place via email.
—

When did the desire to start a studio hit
you — was it there from the start?

Kjell Ekhorn: Both of us were pretty much
in full-time employment in the publishing
industry when we were introduced socially
by a mutual friend. We soon found that not
only did we like to discuss design and ideas
with each other, we also had overlapping
perceptions of what we regarded as good
design. After a year of meeting sporadically
we decided to try working together on some
freelance projects to see if we were as
compatible when it came to tackling actual
design briefs. Jon had already established
a relationship with The Leaf Label and
Lo Recordings and we used the next few
record sleeves for those labels as a bit of a
collaborative moonlighting exercise. At that
point the underlying thought was that if
it worked out we would start up something
on our own, since we were both keen to exit
the world of full-time book cover design
and pursue clients with a more diverse and
complex range of design briefs.

For nearly all designers who eventually
start their own studio, there is a moment
when something happens that causes them to
know that the time has come to make a move.
Can you recall your moment?

Jon Forss: We'd already designed quite a

few record sleeves together when we were approached by the independent music monthly *The Wire* to take on the art direction of the magazine. Given that we both had day jobs at the time and the job of designing a magazine was simply too large to take on, we really had no other option but to make the leap. At the time, *The Wire* staff were in the process of buying the magazine from the previous owner, so there was a bit of an entrepreneurial spirit going on that we were happy to tap into. In fact, we received a lot of help from the accounting firm that was working for *The Wire* and it was on their advice that we established ourselves as a limited company. We had no grand scheme or elaborate business plan – it was more a matter of changing circumstances and pieces falling into place around us.

Did you have a studio that you wanted to model yourself on?

KE: We couldn't really say we had any designers or studios we wanted to model ourselves on, but we had a few design heroes at the time that were running successful studios – the likes of M/M Paris[1], Graphic Thought Facility[2] and Designers Republic[3] to name a few. We looked at and discussed their output and had a tangible dream that one day we might manage to produce work of equal impact and quality.

Where did you go for help and advice in the early days?

JF: The advice we felt we needed most was on the day-to-day running of our company; from the handling of the accounts to tax laws, VAT and how we were going to pay ourselves. Creatively, we were pretty much just continuing our working relationship and naively thinking that if we kept up the good work, clients would come our way and that would be that.

You started off working under the name EkhornForss, then you changed it to Non-Format – can you explain this?

KE: Once we'd completed our first collaborative piece of work we found ourselves sitting in front of the Mac wondering what to type in as our design credit. We were amused that we both had Scandinavian surnames so we simply chose to adopt EkhornForss as the name. It must have been inspired by advertising agencies who often base their names around the founders' surnames, and it certainly felt pretty honest and straightforward. This was in the early part of 1999 and the internet had yet to play a major part in our design lives, so the thought of it being a pretty incomprehensible web address didn't strike us as a potential problem at the time. Non-Format came about once we'd completed an illustration for *The Wire*, quite soon after we'd started art-directing the magazine.

We didn't want to credit it to ourselves so we chose the name Non-Format – which we thought sounded like some kind of creative-problem-solving robot sitting in the corner of our studio.

JF: The name comes from an article in an issue of the US design magazine *Emigre*. The article dealt with the inherent obsolescence of data-storage formats and suggested that even the mighty DVD might one day be replaced by a 'mythical non-format'. Being a couple of fairly introverted people we instantly connected with the anonymity that the name suggested. Besides, we'd been using the name EkhornForss for quite a while and not only were we getting rather tired of having to spell out the name every time anyone called up, but we'd started to notice that of all the work we had in our portfolio it was the more illustrative stuff, credited to Non-Format, that seemed like the most successful work. It was time to ditch EkhornForss and start using Non-Format full-time.

Designers rarely like talking about money – but I have to ask you: did you borrow money to launch the studio?

KE: We had little or no idea about how to start a design company, but the advice we got from our accountants was to borrow a few thousand pounds to ensure that the first few months would run smoothly, so we decided to ask the bank for a £10,000 loan. 'And how much are you putting in yourselves?' the bank manager asked. 'Oh,' we countered, 'we believe £10,000 will be more than enough.' 'In that case we'll lend you £5000 and you'll have to put in the other half yourselves,' she said. And with a sweaty handshake and the paperwork for a company bank account in our bags we were on our way back to where we wanted to be: behind our Macs.

As you've already mentioned, you 'co-habited' with the *The Wire* for the first few years of your existence. At that time you were also designing the magazine; was this a way of growing cautiously or was it just the way it happened?

KE: The cohabitation set-up was a soft option for both parties: we had *The Wire* as the only reliable paying client and *The Wire* had their designers on hand seven days a week. Most of our other work came from small independent record labels that were dealing with us more as friends than business associates and, although they always paid up in the end, the stretch between the invoice and payment was, to put it mildly, very elastic. Therefore, renting a space from *The Wire* felt like the safest option – the rent was deducted from our design fee and regular earnings effectively removed the overheads of renting a studio.

JF: For *The Wire*, having us on site meant

a lot more control and dialogue with their new art directors, which was both practical and cost-effective for them. If a photoshoot needed to be arranged we would suddenly find an editor standing in the doorway blurting out a brief. Although irritatingly intrusive at first, over time we got used to this kind of open-door policy, and it probably did much to oil the wheels, which in turn earned us a lot of creative freedom with our editorial design. They ended up treating us as an integral part of the daily running of the magazine and trusted our judgement on design issues. Would we have stayed with them for four years if we'd had a remote studio? Who knows?

After four years you gave up designing *The Wire* and moved out of their office to set up in your own space – what prompted this?

KE: As we were approaching our fourth anniversary as art directors we felt we had pretty much taken the magazine as far as we could in the direction it was going. Either we had to rethink our whole approach or we simply had to walk away and let a new art director push the magazine in a fresh direction. The previous art director had stayed with the magazine for five years and, when we took it on, we were so sure there was no way that we'd still be there five years later. Of course the next thing we knew four years had past and we'd completed nearly 50 issues. By then we'd begun to build a client list from outside the publishing and recording industries and we'd enjoyed working on some lucrative jobs. We felt there would be more of these lurking in the wings if only we weren't committed to *The Wire* for two weeks out of each month. All these factors converged to give us the push we needed to finally strike out on our own without relying on the safety net of *The Wire*.

Despite a growing international reputation, lots of awards and the publication of a handsome monograph, you are still only two people and you employ no staff – not even an occasional intern. Can you talk about this?

KE: There are quite a few reasons for this. Here are a few: first, neither of us could be described as astute businessmen. We didn't set up the studio as a means of becoming rich – all we ever wanted was to produce good work and be in control of our careers. We felt that if we produced strong work, moneyed clients would eventually come our way and we weren't all that keen on the idea of having to go out and find them. We figured that if we were to employ other designers we'd have to focus more on making a healthy profit, or at least make enough money to pay our employees. In truth, the idea of going without pay for a couple of months was more appealing than having to take on dull projects just to pay for the extra staff. We'd always been happy to turn away a project if we didn't feel it would be enjoyable to work on. This is

01/ Project: Front cover of the Non-Format monograph *Love Song*. Client: Die Gestalten Verlag. Cover image: Non-Format/Jake Walters. Art direction and design: Non-Format.

02 | 03 |
04 | 05 |
06 | 07 |

02/03/04/05/06/07/ Project: Complete book design for Los Angeles-based architecture firm Greg Lynn Form. Client: Rizzoli. Art direction and design: Non-Format.
08/ Project: Music packaging series for The Chap. Client: Lo Recordings. Imagery: Non-Format/Eskimo Square. Art direction and design: Non-Format.
09/ Project: LP sleeve for Black Devil Disco Club's album *Eight Oh Eight*. Client: Lo Recordings. Illustrator: Géraldine Georges. Art direction and design: Non-Format.
10/ Project: CD packaging for Jean-Jacques Perrey and Luke Vibert's album *Moog Acid*. Client: Lo Recordings. Miniature models and photography: Dan McPharlin. Art direction and design: Non-Format.

11 |

a fine policy for just the two of us, but we couldn't expect an employee to be quite so understanding.

JF: The other factor is that we're pretty much total control freaks, especially in the early days. We knew if we were going to aim high we had to be very critical of our own work and we adopted an understanding that either one of us could ask the other to scrap an idea if we felt it didn't meet the standards we were aiming for, no matter how far into the process the piece of work had progressed, or however painful it might have felt to do so. If we'd had a team of people working for us, we would have had to be far more nourishing of their talents; we would have had to give them the freedom to grow by making their own aesthetic decisions without us constantly hanging over their shoulders. Our somewhat fascistic attitude to design would have offered little more than pain, sweat and only a modest economic reward for any employee.

KE: We've certainly mellowed somewhat as we've found our feet over the years, but we'd still much rather work with freelancers when we need to than take on young designers on a more permanent basis and risk a dysfunctional working relationship. The very fact that we now work on different sides of the Atlantic makes the prospect of being a larger design studio even more remote. Maybe we'd benefit from working within an environment where there are other designers, illustrators, photographers and resources we could draw from, but any thought of the traditional design agency set-up doesn't really appeal to us.

Do you think this is viable in the long term?

JF: Any business model can work so long as it plays to its strengths while being aware of its weaknesses. Sometimes we've involved ourselves in projects and collaborations where we've thought, halfway through, that this is not why we started this business or became designers in the first place. There might be a fairly good paycheck at the end of the day but feeling ashamed of what we've produced is too high a price to pay. We hate having to take any of the projects we've worked on and hide them under the bed.

KE: We like projects with a fast pace and a sense of urgency. We like the work to be emotional and have immediacy. We like it to be contemporary and out on the streets making an impression as soon as it is produced — not being diluted through focus groups, vox pops and rigorous marketing strategies. So far we've found a niche for ourselves that stretches between work for record labels, fashion clients, magazines, cultural institutions and advertising agencies. We have a few more avenues we want to pursue as we aim to be less reliant on print media, but we still think we can do this best by

11/ Project: Poster for Nike Basketball. Client: Nike. Design: Non-Format. 12/13/ Project: Fashion story for *Cent* magazine. Client: *Cent* magazine. Photography/digital imaging: Non-Format/ Jake Walters.

staying small, so we're in control. When it's all
over, at least we'll know we had a good crack
at producing the kind of work we believed in.

What is your attitude to growth?

KE: We have every desire to grow and
develop as designers. Beyond that, growth
seems like an abstract concept that – at
least in the Western world – seems to have
become a position of merit in itself. Growing
a business that isn't injecting anything
worthwhile into society isn't growing and
developing but is merely becoming obese.

You've mentioned the importance of doing
work that has some value beyond just making
a profit. Yet you can't make a loss on every
job you do. How do you maintain the balance
between creativity and profitability?

JF: We have to be very selective with the
projects we choose to accept and those we
turn away. One of the toughest decisions that
we face is deciding which projects will offer us
the best opportunities. Of course there are
many kinds of opportunities, so we make sure
to balance our workload between projects
that offer the greatest creative freedom
and those that offer the greatest financial
rewards. We figured out fairly early on that
it's important to take on as many projects
as we can that offer complete creative
freedom. That way we have a focus for
developing as designers, which in turn leads
to more commissions from clients that want
to see those developments applied to their
own projects. In effect, a high-paying client
(usually an international brand or advertising
agency) allows us the freedom to pursue the
projects that offer far less money but gives
us the chance to progress and explore new
creative avenues. As a two-man team we have
to be very careful not to bite off more than
we can chew. It's important to us that each
project is given the attention it deserves, so
we have to make sure we can devote the time
it needs. This has meant we've had to turn
down projects with potentially high financial
returns, simply to ensure we keep the
standard of our work as high as possible.

You have made a really dramatic and unusual
move. One of you is based in the US, and the
other remains in London. How does this work?

JF: Now that we've been working like this for a
couple of years, it feels like we have more of a
handle on the situation, and so far it seems to
work out quite well. It's certainly true to say
that more of the business calls come in to the
London studio, but we've long been advocates
of conducting business via email, which
means that both of us can keep track of each
project as it's progressing. One of the great
advantages of working with six time zones
between us is that the combined studios have
a much longer working day than we used to.
Whereas we once used to work side by side

14 |
15 |
16 |

from 10.00am to around 6.00pm every day, we have a situation where, for example, a project that Kjell has been working on all day can be handed over to me at the end of his day so I can continue to work on it. In effect, Non-Format has something like a 14-hour working day, which comes in handy sometimes.

KE: It's certainly true that we can no longer glance over at each other's screens, but we do still swap files freely between us, and with the use of Skype, the VoIP application, we can video chat with each other for as long as we like, for free. We sometimes sit working together on projects with our Skype connection on in the background. We aren't necessarily chatting all the time, but it's reassuring to know the other is there if we need to ask them something. That window into each other's world is something of a lifeline. We owe a great deal to our high-speed internet connections. Without them, it would be hard to imagine how we could continue to work together so effectively.

Do you split studio duties between each other? Does one look after finance while the other updates the website?

KE: When it comes to the website, we update it whenever we have a new project to showcase and that can be handled by whichever one of us is less busy at the time. When Jon was still in London he handled the finances, simply to avoid any confusion about whether or not something had been taken care of. Now that he's in the US, he still generates the invoices but I have to handle the day-to-day banking and deal with the accountants and quarterly VAT and so on.

JF: I actually quite enjoy the financial side of things. I put together a pretty tight system when we started so that we'd avoid a situation where, for example, we might end up with a pile of receipts and no idea what they were for. So long as everything is put into the right folder straight away, keeping track of invoices and expenses is quite easy. What makes things easiest of all, though, is that we have a firm of accountants based in Sheffield, UK, that handles the end-of-year accounts and makes sure we pay our VAT bill. They cost a little money each year, but we figure it's well worth it.

How do you go about attracting work today? Do you rely entirely on people seeing your work in magazines and books, or do you have other techniques?

KE: We certainly do rely a great deal on word of mouth and that can be a very powerful tool, especially as these days it seems to be more 'word of blog'. Design gossip, and therefore a designer's reputation, can spread very quickly right around the globe and, although it's probably true that the majority of blogs aren't read by anyone but

14/15/16/ Covers from *Varoom: The Journal of Illustration and Made Images*. Client: Association of Illustrators. Cover Illustrators: Brad Holland (14), Jasper Goodall (15), Thomas Hicks (16). Art direction and design: Non-Format. 17/18/19/ Project: Typographic Photo/ Illustration for Danish lifestyle publication *S* magazine. Client: *S* magazine. Imagery: Non-Format/Jake Walters. Typography and design: Non-Format.

their respective authors, when blogs, design forums, regular design publications – not to mention our own website and monograph – are taken into account, it can add up to some very effective publicity. Of course, being a two-man team means that while we're taking care of replying to magazine interviews, or submitting work for books or design competitions, or updating our website or, for that matter, writing answers to the questions in this very book you're reading, we're not getting on with any work that earns us any money. We have to regard the time it takes to do all these tasks as PR time for our business.

You're not the only interviewees to complain about the demands of interviews for books and magazines [see Marian Bantjes, page 122]. I know it can be a drain on time and energy, so let's end this interview by asking, if you could start all over again, what would you do differently?

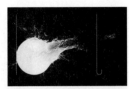

KE: Nothing really – I'm enjoying every aspect of Non-Format on a professional level, and as both Jon and myself have met our wives more or less directly as a result of different Non-Format projects, I see no reason to dwell on what we could have done differently. Where we are is the result of all the small and large decisions we've made over the past decade and if there is anything we feel needs to change then it's just a matter of doing so. I'm all for being analytical and learning from the past, but seeing the potential in what we can do next is a far more complex and interesting task.

OK, this really is the last question: how would you define your studio's culture today?

JF: We try to offer a service that's not unlike a bespoke tailor. Although we have a very clear idea about the way we like to cut our cloth, so to speak, and a recognition that our work isn't going to suit everyone, we offer a very personal service and devote our time to each project very carefully. We spend a lot of time exploring new creative avenues because we know it's the experimental work of today that has the best chance of becoming the most sought-after work for our clients of tomorrow.

1 M/M Paris, art and design partnership consisting of Mathias Augustyniak and Michael Amzalag. Established in Paris in 1992.

2 Graphic Thought Facility (GTF). London-based design consultancy formed in 1990 by Paul Neale and Andy Stevens.

3 The Designers Republic (1986–2009), uniquely influential and pioneering design studio formed by Ian Anderson in Sheffield, England. Best known for anti-consumerist sloganeering, radical digital typography and ground-breaking album cover art for the Warp label.

Pentagram
Joined 1991
Personnel: 7 (Paula Scher's team),
60 (Pentagram New York office)
Location: New York, US
www.pentagram.com

Paula Scher is a luminary of contemporary
American graphic design. She began her
working life at Atlantic and CBS Records
designing album covers. Much of her work
from this period has passed into pop culture
cosmology. Later she ran her own studio in
partnership with the designer Terry Koppel.
But it is her work as a Pentagram partner
that forms her most enduring legacy.

Scher is not only known for her distinctive
and readily identifiable design work. She also
works as an artist, although an artist whose
work is imbued with the spirit and techniques
of a graphic designer. Admirers collect
her typographic maps of the US and other
countries around the world zealously.

Scher is a sharp-brained observer of the
contemporary design scene. Her book – *Make
it Bigger*, published in 2005 – is a compendium
of her best graphic design work, and also her
wit and New York savvy.

The interview was conducted via email.
–

You've worked variously as an in-house
designer (at CBS Records in the 1970s) and
as one half of a two-person partnership
(Koppel/Scher in the 1980s). What were the
key differences – good and bad – between
each type of studio?

Paula Scher: At CBS Records in the 1970s
there was a lot of work (I designed over
100 album covers a year) and a lot of money.
The art department was very atelier-like.
We experimented when we could. We had the
freedom to make mistakes. Recording artists
had cover approval, but you could make
anything you wanted as long they were in
agreement. Sometimes the recording artists
wanted silly ideas and you were forced into
designing something sub-standard, but that
was offset by other cover projects. Classical
and jazz albums were less political than pop
and rock music, so that's where most of the
exploration occurred. The CBS Records art
department was filled with very talented
designers and we collaborated and competed
with each other. Some of them became lifelong
friends. All of this was financed by CBS. It
was the best of all worlds, and something I've
tried to duplicate ever since without success.
But in the early 1980s there was a recession,
cutbacks, fear, and a very ugly atmosphere
prevailed. Then it was the worst of all worlds.
I quit in 1982.

After freelancing on my own for a year and
half, I founded Koppel and Scher with Terry

Koppel in 1984. I hated being on my own and wanted to duplicate the best years of CBS. Terry and I also developed a very atelier-like environment. Unfortunately, experimentation was less easy unless we accomplished the experimentation on free jobs. We were very concerned with supporting our overhead and constantly had cashflow worries. The environment was creative, but there was no room for failure, an important component of growth.

Then you joined Pentagram – was that a big change?

I joined in 1991. The power, size and structure of the organization has afforded me the ability to be more secure financially, though I still continually worry about overhead. Having more partners, some in different disciplines, have expanded my own design opportunities and allowed me to stretch my own range. I wish I felt more comfortable with experimentation. The high profile of many of my clients sometimes forces me to discard the 'experimental' in favour of the 'established'. That's bad for my own personal growth. I try to experiment more on pro-bono projects.

With your experience you are extremely well placed to answer this question – what makes a good graphic design studio?

I think the best graphic design studio provides time for R&D. A designer should be able to experiment and produce professional work at the same time in a pleasant and reasonably secure environment.

Design history is written from the perspective of the individual designer – but it's a rare designer who works alone. Why do you think studios are neglected by historians and commentators in favour of the individual?

A succinct graphic point of view generally comes from an individual, not a collective. Sometimes it's two partners, like Milton Glaser[1] and Seymour Chwast[2] forming Push Pin[3]. They may influence a broad group of people who pass through a studio, but in the end the vision of the individual is what is definable.

Can you describe Pentagram's unique structure?

Pentagram is a cooperative. It is essentially a bunch of small design firms, some with different disciplines, that share space, services and good fellowship. Each partner manages his or her own team, maintains their own client base, bills their clients and puts all the money in the middle. The partners draw the same salary and share profit. The partners are kept honest by the fact that no one wants to be the poorest performer, so they all work hard not to be. That peer pressure is considerable.

01 |
02 |
03 |

01/ Project: Selected design for the Charm Bracelet Project, Pittsburgh. Date: 2006–2007. Client: The Charm Bracelet Project. Designers: Paula Scher, Andrew Freeman, Nikola Gottschick. 02/03/ Project: Proposals for the Charm Bracelet Project, Pittsburgh. Date: 2006–2007. Client: The Charm Bracelet Project. Designers: Paula Scher, Andrew Freeman, Nikola Gottschick. 04/05/ Project: Identity redesign for The Public Theater. Date: 2008. Client: The Public Theater. Designers: Paula Scher, Lisa Kitschenberg.

When you were invited to join Pentagram in 1991, why did you feel it was the right move for you?

After seven years running my own business, it became apparent to me that as a woman in business my design opportunities would be limited to things I had already done, that I would start to repeat myself, and ultimately stop growing as a designer. Pentagram afforded me an opportunity for growth. It was a bigger, more powerful playing field.

Like all Pentagram partners you have your own dedicated design team. What do you want from your designers – slavish, unquestioning devotion, or do you want them to have opinions and ideas?

I want the designers who work for me to have opinions, ideas, a sense of humour. I want them to inspire me, to have good judgement and excellent craft skills. And then I want them to accept the fact that I am the final word on everything.

What happens if a team member rebels and fails to toe the line?

I've always told my team that working for me is like being in a band. My team is my band. When you play on my team you get to learn, you get exposure, and you can grow, but in the end, it's my band. Ultimately, if you want to play your own tunes, you have to form your own band.

Do you see it as part of your job to educate and develop the designers who work for you?

I have tried to be a mentor to most of the designers who have worked for me. I have done this for 35 years. It's part of my working life. I am proud of almost everyone who has worked for me, and that's a lot of designers.

How do you find talent?

For many years, I taught at the School of Visual Arts in New York and I hired my students. Sometimes I hire my friend Carin Goldberg's[4] students because I like how she teaches them. Often, I'll be working with an intern who was hired temporarily by someone at Pentagram, and I will find them to be talented and productive, so I will hire them. I don't think I have ever interviewed a total stranger and hired them based on their portfolio.

Do you expect them to stay for a long time, or are you happy with a regular turnover of staff?

I expect my staff to stay with me for as long as they are still learning from me. They are usually hired directly out of school. Sometimes, I promote them to positions of greater responsibility, so they stay longer.

06/07/08/09/10/11/12/13/ Project: Identity for The Criterion Collection. Date: 2006.
Client: The Criterion Collection. Designers: Paula Scher, Julia Hoffmann.
14/ Project: Environmental graphics for Bloomberg L.P. corporate headquarters.
Date: 2005. Client: Bloomberg.L.P. Designers: Paula Scher, Lisa Strausfeld (Dynamic
Media), Rion Byrd, Jiae Kim, Andrew Freeman. Photographer: Peter Mauss/Esto.
15/16/ Project: Identity for the Museum of Modern Art (MoMA). Date: 2008.
Client: Museum of Modern Art (MoMA). Designers: Paula Scher, Lisa Kitschenberg, Julia
Hoffmann. 17/18/19/ Project: Environmental graphics for the Children's Museum of
Pittsburgh. Date: 2006. Client: Children's Museum of Pittsburgh. Designers: Paula Scher,
Rion Byrd, Andrew Freeman. Photographer: Peter Mauss/Esto.
20/21/ Project: The Numbers poster series. Date: 2005–2007. Client: Grafx.
Designers: Paula Scher, Andrew Freeman.

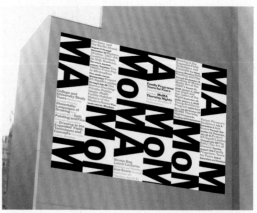

The average entry-level designer stays about two and a half years without a promotion. The longest anyone has stayed was nine years, when I made them an associate. But, the turnover is usually good for both me and the designer.

What would you say to someone who wanted to know what the benefits are from working in Paula Scher's team at Pentagram?

If you work for me, you get to know what I know. That may be limited, but I find it catapults my staff into some very good situations after they leave.

How do you deal with administration at Pentagram?

Administration at Pentagram is shared among the partners. Each partner in a local office is responsible for a given shared area of responsibility, such as PR, accounting, tech, etc. Every partner has a project coordinator who helps manage budgets, collects timesheets, and compiles billing information from each individual team. The coordinator serves as a conduit between the individual team and the local Pentagram office.

Can you tell me how studio space is organized in Pentagram?

All of the partners in the New York office sit in a row in open space on a mezzanine level at Pentagram. Our teams can sit near us. My team is a half level up from me, in open space where I can see them all. Other teams may be located on a different floor (we are in a small, vertical building) and in those cases, the partner retains an extra desk within the team.

How important is the physical space you work in?

I've become accustomed to working in open space, but really no physical space at all, and in utter disorganization. I can't see my own work over a course of a year (it gets put away) and don't remember a job after it's finished. I have absolutely nothing special in the way of tools, unlike my architect partner Jim Biber, who has really nice pens. If I had nice pens I'd just lose them.

I'm curious to know how working in a busy studio at Pentagram contrasts and compares with working in your home studio in the country where you paint and make personal artworks?

My painting studio in Salisbury, Connecticut, is the opposite of my workspace at Pentagram. I have real space, a view and I don't share it with anyone. I often paint all day without talking to anyone, even my husband. My paintings take a long time.

22 |
23 |
24 |

22/23/24/ Project: Book design for the School of Visual Arts Senior Library. Date: 2005. Client: School of Visual Arts. Designers: Paula Scher, Lenny Naar. 25/26/ Project: Identity for the New York City Ballet. Date: 2008. Client: New York City Ballet. Designers: Paula Scher, Lisa Kitschenberg. Photographer: Jim Brown, Andrew Bordwin.

At Pentagram I'm with people every minute, I have no space and I work very quickly. I need both extremes. Maybe one day I'll strike a happy medium.

You have written and spoken eloquently about the value to be found in rejection and failure. You stated that: 'You have to fail in order to make the next discovery. It's through mistakes that you actually can grow.' I agree with this strongly, and I can see how it works in a personal context. But how does it work in a group setting? When the Paula Scher team fails at something, how do you stop the group imploding?

Group failure is not the same as my individual failure because in my team the designers in the end are not responsible for the failure, I am. I think the failures can be more demoralizing for the team because they have less control. I am the only one who can really stop a client from screwing up work. I am the only one who can change the direction of a project gone wrong. I am the only one who can push the design, or the projects we take on, in a new direction.

My team serves as advisors. They warn me about problematic clients or sticky political situations that arise while they are working. They find vendors like printers or software developers, or signage manufacturers and often introduce me to new materials. The young designers on my team can make design mistakes that are corrected by me, or my senior designer, but these are craft issues, and part of any young designer's early experience. They are not major failures. When we fail big time, I'm at the heart of it.

1 Milton Glaser, seminal figure in modern graphic design. See page 130.

2 Seymour Chwast, American graphic designer, illustrator, and type designer. Formed Push Pin with Milton Glaser.

3 Push Pin Studios, formed in 1954 in New York by Milton Glaser, Seymour Chwast, Reynold Ruffins and Edward Sorel. Under Glaser and Chwast's leadership, Push Pin became one of the most important graphic design studios in the world. Published the *Push Pin Graphic*.

4 Carin Goldberg, New York-based graphic designer. Worked at CBS Television, CBS Records and Atlantic Records before establishing her own firm, Carin Goldberg Design in 1982. Best known for her distinctive book jacket designs.

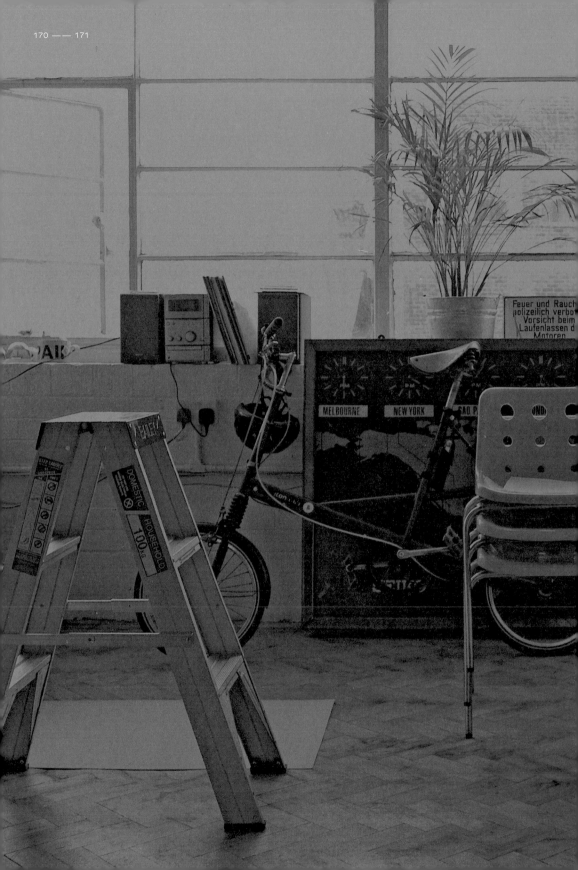

Practise
Founded: 1999
Personnel: 1, plus assistants and interns
Location: London, UK
www.practise.co.uk

James Goggin is a member of the new wave of intelligent, typographically sophisticated and conceptually minded British graphic designers that emerged in the last years of the old millennium. Shy, bookish and modest, but with an air of internal rigour and self-belief, Goggin has run his one-man studio – Practise – since he graduated from the graphic design course at the Royal College of Art in London in 1999. He had previously studied at Ravensbourne, a college near London, famous for its typography. Today he works on mainly arts-related projects and boasts Tate as one of his clients. He runs his studio from his north London home, which he shares with his wife – a fashion designer – and his two young daughters. Energetically independent, he survives with help from occasional interns, usually from European countries.

The interview took place at Goggin's studio.
–

You set up Practise as soon as you graduated from the Royal College of Art in London. Normally people get a job and work for three years, but you didn't. Why?

James Goggin: I was interested in the idea of getting a job, but I assumed that the people I wanted to work for – people like Fuel[1] and Graphic Thought Facility[2], who I still admire – were too small to employ new designers. I was a bit shy, and I didn't go to see many studios. I thought that if I wanted to do the kind of work that the studios I admired were doing then I'd have to start up on my own.

I remember being impressed with your graduation show and asking you to come and see me at my old studio. But I remember thinking that you had already made up your mind to go it alone.

You were one of the few people I ended up seeing when I left the RCA, and I still remember your advice. You strongly advised that I should work somewhere first. I had a bit of arrogance, I think, and I didn't want to start as a junior designer.

Well, you've proved me wrong.

Maybe I have, but I could probably have condensed my first two or three years of studio practice into a much shorter period of time if I hadn't had to learn everything from scratch. What do you do when you go on press? How do you make a pitch? How do you quote? How do you invoice? All the basic stuff I had to learn the hard way.

Do you think you would have started your studio if you hadn't gone to the RCA as a postgraduate student?

I did a lot of reading at the RCA and started doing commissions and a bit of teaching. I was going up to Cambridge one day a week, and it really helped me form my own idea of what I wanted to do. There's a tradition of students going to the RCA, meeting a group of people, getting on with them, and setting up a studio together. I'd always assumed that would happen to me as well. I got on with everyone in my year and had a fantastic time, but there wasn't anyone I could really picture myself working with. I still had the plan that I wanted to start a studio like Fuel or GTF, but it ended up with me on my own.

What about the practical stuff involved in setting up a studio – finding premises, buying equipment, and so on? Where did you turn to for help with that?

I pretty much discovered everything by trial and error. I think I could have applied for grants and gone to see a lot more designers to ask for advice, but I felt like I couldn't go and ask people for help because they had obviously struggled and fought their own way through to get to where they were.

That's a slightly odd view to have taken, because designers are actually usually willing to pass on their knowledge.

Yes, in hindsight I realize this. And I now get lots of students asking me questions, and I give them what I think is quite useful advice. I wish I'd done that myself, but at the time I felt like I really had to try and make this happen by myself. I worked out of a small apartment. My wife was starting up a fashion label and I was working with her as well. I had a rule that I wouldn't send work to magazines. My work had to be seen in the real context – if I designed a book, it was seen in a bookshop and someone liked it and wanted to commission me, I felt like that was the right way for things to work. It was all very slow. I bought a laptop – it was just at the time when you could pretty much run a studio off a laptop and a laser printer.

Where does the name Practise come from?

I felt that I should have a proper studio name rather than just run under my own name. I guess coming out of the 1990s there were a lot of one-name studios – Tomato[3], Fuel, etc. – which I wanted to avoid. But I was also reading linguistics and anthropology, and I liked the word 'practise', the verb form spelt with an 's', which is only used in British English. In American English they spell both the verb and the noun practice with a 'c'. Practise with an 's' means you're repeating something to try and get better, which I liked. I wanted to retain the spirit I had at

01 |
02 |

01/02/ Project: Book design and editing, Peter McDonald 'Teaching Airport Hair Salon Bakery Snooker'. Date: 2007. Client: Kate MacGarry/Veenman Publishers. Designers: James Goggin, Annette Lux. 03/04/05/ Project: Art direction/design, The Wire. Date: 2006–2008. Client: The Wire. Designer: James Goggin. Photographers: Körner Union (03), Ivan Jones (04), Daniëlle Van Ark (05).

college where I was always trying to learn.
I thought Practise was a good name, it
sounded bookish. And if you're a small studio
with some kind of company name, it can make
you look a bit bigger than you really are,
which is useful on occasion.

Did you put together a portfolio of work?

I had a box of books that I'd made at
college. I didn't like leaving my folio with
clients because it was full of one-offs. I'd
call up publishers and they'd ask me to
drop off my book. As I didn't want to just
leave it there, I made a little A5 inkjet work
book, which I still make today sometimes,
handbound and perforated. So that's all I
had really, and I would just send it to places
I admired. Of course, I had the Catch 22
problem when I left college, which I suspect
that students don't have so much anymore.
I would go to places like the Hayward Gallery
and they would look through my books from
college and say, 'This is all very interesting,
but come back when you've done a few real
projects.' Everyone was telling me the same
thing, so I didn't see how I could actually
ever get a 'real project'.

What were the early days like? Were you
sharing space?

In 2003, I met the designer Sara de Bondt[4]
who was working at Foundation 33[5] at the
time. She was interested in leaving, and was
looking to set up on her own, but she also
wanted to assist me. I had been living in New
Zealand for two years, and I thought I'd
have to start all over again as if I'd just left
college. It's still a mystery to me, but somehow
when I got back, more people knew about
me and within the first few weeks I got a
project from the British Council, and the Tate
commissions came along. We found a space in
Bethnal Green, East London, and that was my
first official studio.

Did you manage to deal with things like making
sure you got paid and invoices got sent out?

I was very bad at that, but I was lucky that
I had my wife Shan working with me. We worked
together on her fashion label and she still
helps me out with running the studio. She's
much more business-minded than me, and
reminds me that I should be invoicing people.
I think if it was just me, I'd be in trouble.

You've now set up a studio at home — why
did you do this?

Family was a big factor. I have two young
daughters and I wanted to spend more time
with them. We were squashed into a tiny flat
and wanted a bigger place. We did the maths
and worked out that if we transferred the
money we were spending on the studio then
we could just about afford a house. When
I had my studio I'd get home at 5.00pm to

06 | 07 | 08 |
09 | 10 |

06/ Project: 'Again for Tomorrow', Catalogue for MA Curating Contemporary Art.
Date: 2006. Client: Royal College of Art, MA Curating Contemporary Art.
Designers: James Goggin, Sara De Bondt. 07/ Project: Untitled Gallery, Modular signage
system, programmed flipdot dot matrix sign. Date: 2004. Client: Tate Modern.
Designer: James Goggin. 08/ Project: Dominique Gonzalez-Foerster: TH.2058. Exhibition
graphic design: reflective typographic signage, Turbine Hall, Tate Modern. Date: 2008.
Client: Tate Modern. Designers: James Goggin, Régis Tosetti. 09/ Project: Air Mobile
prototype. Date: 2004. Client: Practise. Designers: James Goggin, Shan Connell,
prototype made with Mark Owens. 10/ Project: Olafur Eliasson: The Weather Project,
Poster design. Date: 2003. Client: Tate Modern. Designers: James Goggin,
Laurenz Brunner.

47% OF PEOPLE
BELIEVE THE IDEA OF
WEATHER IN OUR
SOCIETY IS BASED
ON CULTURE

53% BELIEVE IT IS
BASED ON NATURE

The Unilever Series:
OLAFUR ELIASSON

16 October 2003 – 21 March 2004

Free Admission
Open Daily 10.00 – 18.00
Late nights Friday and Saturday until 22.00

Visit www.tate.org.uk
⊖ Southwark/Blackfriars

The Unilever Series:
an annual art commission sponsored by

Unilever

MODERN
TATE

11/ Project: Momus 'Ocky Milk', Album cover art direction, design and photography.
Date: 2006. Client: Analog Baroque. Designer: James Goggin. Design Assistant: Julie Kim.
Model: Kajsa Ståhl. Photographer/Illustrator: James Goggin. 12/ Project: 'Critical Notice:
New Work by British Composers', CD-book packaging. Date: 2007. Client: Unknown Public/
British Music Information Centre. Designer: James Goggin. Design Assistant: Johanna
Kallin. 13/ Project: David Kohn Architects, identity, stationery. Date: 2008. Client: David
Kohn Architects. Designer: James Goggin. 14/ Project: Ground Zero Zero, A1 poster
imposed as 32pp booklet investigating colour and voids as architectural gestures.
Date: 2007. Client: Architectural Association. Designer: James Goggin.
Photographer: Cover photography courtesy The New York Times.

spend time with my daughters, and then
work half the night at home. I would find
myself cycling back to the studio in Dalston
in the middle of the night to get a particular
book I needed. I was sad to give up my studio,
but it feels like a luxury to have a good
space at home – everything in one place.

Are there any negative aspects about
working from home?

It can be too easy to keep working
on something after you've had dinner,
whereas you'd think twice about going
back to an outside studio. Because it's
just me – I'm the one answering the phone,
I'm the one managing print jobs – I'm doing
everything. I can go for several days in a row
with the daytime solely taken up by answering
phone calls, calling printers, getting quotes,
seeing something on the press, meeting
students, giving a lecture. So night-time is
often the only time I get things done – when
it's quiet. On the other hand, I've always
worked well at night, so perhaps it's not
entirely bad that I can just go upstairs
to my studio and work on things.

The situation you've just described –
dealing with phone calls, printers, etc –
could be done by a project manager. Have you
thought about getting someone for this role?

A friend of mine asked me why I was looking
for a design assistant when what I really
need is a studio manager. It's a good point.
It's only recently that I've started working
with assistants, and because I've had so
many years working on my own, I still find it
very difficult to delegate. I'm sure it's quite
frustrating for people working for me –
someone will do something perfectly well and
I'll find myself staying up all night going over
what they've done. Because of that I don't
think I'm the kind of person who's ever going
to run a studio with ten people working under
me, and just dictate what's done.

Do you find that you are missing out on work
by staying small?

I do on occasions. I have several long-term
clients. Tate Modern are fairly big and I
handle a steady stream of large projects
for them – exhibition signage, dealing with
spaces in Tate Modern, as well as all the 20
or 30 press ads, posters, invites – often the
catalogue as well, and I seem to run them
fairly well. So a lot of people see that I'm
not daunted by large projects.

You've obviously reached a point where work
comes to you and you don't need to go out
and find it.

That's been happening for quite a few
years now, which I've always been amazed
by. There is that situation where you've just
left college and you're sitting either at home

15 |
16 |

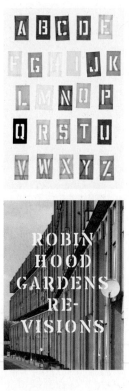

15/ Project: ABC for A & B. Date: 2006.
Client: Letraset/GFSmith/Grafik.
Designer: James Goggin.
Illustrator: Beatrix Goggin.
16/ Project: Robin Hood Gardens
Re-Visions, exhibition graphic design.
Date: 2009. Client: The Twentieth Century
Society/Royal Institute of British
Architects. Designer: James Goggin.
Photographer: Ioana Marinescu.

or in your first studio looking at the phone and wondering how on earth it's going to ring with nice work? I couldn't imagine how that worked when I left college. Now I get a constant stream of interesting projects coming in, always seemingly at the right time. But because I'm so busy with my clients I never send out work or promote myself in any way. I don't even have business cards at the moment, I've never felt the need for that kind of thing.

But you've got a website?

Yes, but because I've been so busy, it's four years out of date, apart from the homepage.

Can you see a time that the workflow is such that you've got to bring people in, or are you happy to stay the way you are?

Over the last two years I've been thinking 'what's next?' I work too hard, and have a family who I need to spend time with, and I think my balance of clients is probably not the best for a small design studio – it's pretty much 100% cultural and I probably could work a lot less if I had a better mix of clients. I really miss the luxury of focusing on one project for two months. I'm always multi-tasking and having to work on a lot of different things. I still have the right balance at the moment where I can spend enough time and detail on projects, but it's hard and I can't see myself working like this forever. At the moment I haven't figured out what the answer is.

How are you going to break away from just doing cultural projects?

I might have to do something I've never been good at: self-promotion. I might have to contact companies who don't know about me. I think I need to diversify and get bigger clients, but on the other hand I often think about maybe getting even smaller – going back to being just myself, no assistants, and moving into academia and concentrating on teaching. I'd like to do more writing and spend more time on neglected areas of my work, like making typefaces.

You've designed a very successful typeface – Courier Sans – do you want to do more?

Yes. A lot of my projects use my own typefaces, but I never have enough time to complete them. Lineto's[6] been waiting three or four years for my latest typeface to be finished. I have at least four or five that could have been released but I just never have the time. I often think about whether we should go back to New Zealand and lie low for a few years – it's tempting, but I'm not sure that is the answer. It's a difficult point, but I do feel fortunate to be in the position I'm in and that I get a good stream of work – but I do work too hard.

How would you sum up Practise?

The only time I find myself attempting to sum up what I do is when I'm giving lectures, and it seems to be the one time where I actually find a space to think about what I'm doing. I guess a lot of it comes down to purely objective description – I work for these kinds of clients and I do this kind of work. My self-initiated work operates on an equal level to commissioned work and I attempt to use my teaching and writing activities as a way of connecting the two. How any of this work actually looks is completely dependent on a given project's context. Therefore I've gradually arrived at a position where I think that my work always looks different. I have no particular dogmatic rules about doing things in a certain way or always using a certain typeface.

One of the things I love most about graphic design is the content I deal with as a designer: working in cultural, contemporary art or architecture fields and often designing books, one spends a lot of time reading. I like the idea of learning new things from each project. Which is kind of the literal definition of 'practise': repeatedly performing an activity and learning from it.

1 Fuel, English design duo. See page 98.

2 Graphic Thought Facility (GTF), London-based design consultancy formed in 1990 by Huw Morgan, Paul Neale and Andy Stevens.

3 Tomato, launched in London in 1991 as art and design collective by John Warwicker, Steve Baker, Dirk Van Dooren, Karl Hyde, Richard Smith, Simon Taylor and Graham Wood. Work includes television and print advertising, corporate identity, art installations, clothing, and design for Underworld (Smith and Hyde were founding members of Underworld). James Goggin spent time at Tomato working with Graham Wood and Dirk Van Dooren during summer 1997 between graduation from Ravensbourne and starting at the Royal College of Art.

4 Sara de Bondt, London-based Belgian graphic designer who has been running her studio since 2003.

5 Foundation 33, design studio formed in 2000 by graphic designer Daniel Eatock and architect Sam Solhaug. Later merged with the creative agency boymeetsgirl. In 2003 Daniel Eatock began work as Eatock Ltd.

6 Lineto, font house founded by Cornel Windlin and Stephan Müller in 1993. Lineto.com distributes digital typefaces via the internet. The name comes from PostScript™ page description language.

R2
Founded: 1995
Personnel: 6
Location: Porto, Portugal
www.r2design.pt

Lizá Ramalho and Artur Rebelo founded
R2, a graphic design studio, while studying
at Porto Fine Arts University. The
studio works for a wide range of cultural
organizations, curators, artists and
architects. Projects include identity work,
poster design, book design and exhibition
design. They have won numerous international
awards and regularly act as jurors for
design competitions.

Their work is informed by a strong European
sensibility. Often using illustrative elements
to make compelling visual communication,
R2's work is undeniably contemporary in
flavour, yet at the same time linked to the
great tradition of European humanism.
Their striking typographic mural for The
Hermitage of Nossa Senhora da Conceição,
a small chapel built in 1707, located in an
alleyway in Lisbon, is a striking example of
their contemporary sensibilities at work in
a traditional setting. Ramalho and Rebelo
teach in various Portuguese colleges. They
have been members of AGI (Alliance Graphic
International) since 2007.

This interview was conducted via email.
—

Tell me how you came to form R2.

Lizá Ramalho: We met at the Faculty of Fine
Arts in Porto and started working together
on school projects. In doing so, we realized
the advantages of working as a team,
discussing ideas and experiences, sharing
and capitalizing on our joint resources.

Forming a studio straight from school is a
brave thing to do. Do you think you might
have benefited by working for a few studios
before starting R2?

Of course we would. The organization and
managing model we have now is based on our
own experience; we made a lot of mistakes
during that process. More importantly, we
never saw how other designers developed
and presented their projects to clients.
Finding the right producers and controlling
production was also another thing that we
had to figure out ourselves.

Were there any studios you admired?

Many. One of them was Alan Fletcher's[1].
The Portuguese Youth foundation had a grant
program that included visits to European
cities to meet professionals working in your
field of study. We applied and got a grant to
travel to London to meet him. It was
very inspiring.

Tell me about the practical side of starting
your studio – did you have to borrow money?
How did you find premises? What professional
advice did you get?

Our studio developed very slowly, step by
step. We started working in my room [Lizá]
while we were still students, with one Quadra
450 and one A4 inkjet printer. From my room
we moved to a small place in Porto's industrial
area. The money from our first projects was
used to pay the rent on our studio and to
buy a scanner. The building was so scary at
night that some clients were afraid to visit us.
Later on we found a nice space in a business
building. But then we got tired of the Xerox
machine sellers. Recently we moved to this
small house in a quiet neighbourhood.

We started without taking any professional
advice. As we hadn't worked for other
studios, the organization and running of our
studio was a real challenge. We were always
asking friends, office neighbours – mainly a
photographer and a jewellery designer – and
some suppliers. Now we have professional
management and accountancy advice.

Did you have a vision of how you wanted your
studio to be?

We wanted to be involved in interesting and
challenging projects. Invest a lot in research
and experimentation. Take risks. Be very
critical of our own work, never be satisfied,
and always push it further. Also, to have
fun while working.

Graphic designers often imagine that they
have to move to their country's capital city
to be successful. You are in Porto, Portugal's
second city; did you contemplate moving
to Lisbon?

In the past yes, we thought about moving
to Lisbon or abroad… now we manage to
organize things from Porto. We travel often
to Lisbon, since we have a lot of clients there.
It is a three-hour journey. We use this time
to work; it can be very productive. If we
travel together, we mainly use the time to
discuss projects.

What are the advantages of being in Porto?

It's a good place to live; we have the ocean
and the river. The city is changing. It's
growing. There is a lot to be done and people
are aware (of what needs to be done) and
are working on it. You can easily focus on
work. There is also the financial aspect; it is
cheaper to live in Porto than in Lisbon, we
could not afford our house if it was in Lisbon.
Our studio is not far from the contemporary
art museum, which has great exhibitions. A
little bit further away is the main concert hall
and the biggest city park links our studio to
the ocean. Finally, our house is next to the
studio, so we do not lose any time getting

01 |
02 |

01/02/ Project: Espaço de Encontro-
Lugar de todos os virtuais (Meeting Point),
Poster/Leaflet. Date: Sep 2005.
Client: Festival Internacional de
Marionetas. Designers: Lizá Ramalho,
Artur Rebelo. 03/04/ Project: BES
Revelação, Art Book. Date: Nov 2008.
Client: Serralves Museum. Designers: Lizá
Ramalho, Artur Rebelo.
Assistant Design: Liliana Pinto.

stuck in traffic. It is also our town; we have
our roots and emotional links here, so, for
the moment, we will stay put and, if possible,
contribute to its development.

Any disadvantages?

The normal disadvantages that you have
in small cities, fewer cultural opportunities,
fewer job opportunities, lack of flights.

The name R2 is an amalgamation of both your
names – was it hard to choose a name?

It was difficult; we tried several names, made
lots of lists. Then we turned to the obvious,
we have a common letter in our names. Now
it feels right.

How did you attract work in your early days?

Well, work came to us before we were even
thinking about it. We were on our third year
of a five-year diploma when we started
working on some illustrations for a friend
who was starting a business. That project
was seen by a small theatre company, and
they asked us to do some design work for
them. It was a great job; it gave us room for
experimentation and provided visibility for our
work, mainly via street posters. By the time
we had finished the degree course, we had
already established a reasonable portfolio of
clients – which led us to believe that we would
be able to set up our own studio. We therefore
decided to take the plunge.

Do you both have clearly defined roles within
the studio?

No, we both do design, art direction and
everything else.

How do you deal with the everyday aspects of
studio life – invoicing, bookkeeping, software
updates, soap in the washroom?

This year we started training a person to
take care of all of that, except the invoicing,
which we still do ourselves. Recently we hired
a firm that controls the client's payments
and costs.

Is this what is called a factoring service –
where a company pays all your invoices on
time, and then recovers the money from the
client, taking a percentage of the amount for
this service? How has it benefited you?

No, it's just a company that does our financial
control. We pay a fixed fee per month and they
do everything.

Tell me about the R2 studio – is it just you two
or do you employ designers?

At the moment we have three designers
working with us.

05 | 06 |
07 | 08 |
09 | 10 |

05/07/09/ Project: 6=0 Homeostética, Art Book. Date: Apr 2004. Client: Serralves Museum. Designers: Lizá Ramalho, Artur Rebelo. Technical Design: Nuno Bastos. 06/08/10/ Project: Unfinished Trajectories, book and installation. Date: Nov 2007. Client: Casa da Música. Designers: Lizá Ramalho, Artur Rebelo. Technical Design: Liliana Pinto, Nuno Bastos, Yannik Kohanna. 11/ Project: Em torno/ Surround, poster 170x120cm. Date: June 2006. Client: NEC. Design and art direction: Lizá Ramalho, Artur Rebelo. Date: Jun 2006. 12/ Project: Reunião de obra (Site Meeting), poster 170x120cm. Date: Dec 2005. Client: OASRN Order of Architects/ Northern Chapter. Designers: Lizá Ramalho, Artur Rebelo. 13/ Project: Stop, Poster. Date: Feb 2009. Client: Good 50x70. Designers: Lizá Ramalho, Artur Rebelo. 14/ Project: Hospitalidade, Poster. Date: Feb 2009. Client: Hospital S. João (Porto). Curator: Miguel Von Hafe Pérez. Designers: Lizá Ramalho, Artur Rebelo. 15/ Project: 20th International Poster and Graphic Arts Festival of Chaumont, Poster 70x100cm. Date: Feb 2009. Client: Festival Affiche de Chaumont. Designers: Lizá Ramalho, Artur Rebelo. 16/ Project: I love Távora, Poster 170x120cm. Date: Nov 2005. Client: OASRN Order of Architects/Northern Chapter. Designers: Lizá Ramalho, Artur Rebelo.

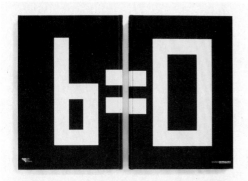

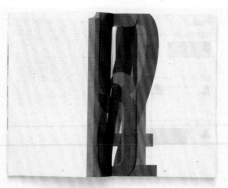

What is your attitude towards the designers you employ – do you want them to follow your art direction, or do you want them to contribute their own views?

We worked for a long time as just the two of us. We built R2 based on our dialogue and our own perspective. We do a lot of projects that take a significant amount of time with corrections and other implementations, but to give an appropriate response, we needed more people. We looked for designers who would feel comfortable being assistants. Actually, we have really good ones that enjoy doing that part of the design process, which is very important. We actually have a lot of fun working and we like our team very much.

What about interns?

We usually receive one or two interns each year. Mostly from abroad, as we like to have this cultural exchange. We've had students from several different countries (Germany, France, Canada, Lebanon, Czech Republic). Most of them were really good experiences.

What do you ask your interns to do? Do they fetch coffee from the coffee shop or are they given projects to work on?

They participate in the current projects of the studio. We try to make them participate in development, presentation, implementation and production.

How does your teaching and lecturing inform your professional practice?

We learn a lot. It is stimulating, and provides an opportunity to do research on different kinds of projects. Lecturing makes you look at your own work as a whole. You select, organize and explain. It's a great exercise. More importantly, you get a chance to receive feedback from the other designers or students, which is very good.

What about your physical environment – is your studio an immaculate designer space?

No, it's superficially messy. We often work away from the computer. We experiment with objects, with photography, and we use different materials. We keep too much stuff, too many found objects, too many mock-ups...

What are the essentials for a good studio – effective interior space planning? Storage space? Natural light?

We are located in a 1950s house with lots of small rooms. We are divided across two floors. We have one or two people in each room, all of them with natural light and big tables. We have a small garden, which is very good in the summer; sometimes we lunch together there. This space works well for us, we get a home-like atmosphere.

17 |
18 |

17/18/ Project: Museu Coleçcào Berardo, Sign system. Date: Jun 2007. Client: Museu Coleçcào Berardo. Design and art direction: Lizá Ramalho, Artur Rebelo. Technical design: Nuno Bastos, Liliana Pinto, Ana Fárinha.
19/20/21/ Project: Vai com Deus (Go with God), typographic installation. Date: Sep 2008. Client: Ermida Nossa Senhora da Conceição. Designers: Lizá Ramalho, Artur Rebelo.

You enter a lot of design competitions and take part in design events. Is this an important part of your business, or do you do it because you like doing it?

The visibility that every work gets is in relation to its own context. We wanted to show our work outside Portugal, not in a business perspective but a way of showing it to designers from other countries. Participating in design events gives a chance to travel, to meet designers from other countries, to exchange ideas. It gave us incredible moments and it is an opportunity to meet fantastic people. We've made many great friends.

How do you think your election to AGI affects your business? Does it help attract clients?

We have been AGI members only since 2007. We never saw it as way to get clients but rather as recognition from people we admire. Hopefully this will also mean more interesting projects.

What about a potfolio, website... are these things important? Or does finding new clients just happen?

We were always aware of the importance of both, but we just had the website, maybe because the clients just show up. Most of them did not come because of the website but because they had seen the actual work. That is one of the reasons that we never invested in a portfolio, but now we are working on it.

What about the future – do you envisage R2 growing? Will there be a time when you have an office in Lisbon as well as the Porto office? Or will it always just be you two and a few assistants?

We don't know what the future will be, but we are quite happy with the actual size. Anyway, if we feel this formula is not the best for a different context, we will change; we are always questioning and redirecting the goals and process inside the studio.

Last question... if you were starting again what, if anything, would you do differently?

Back then, knowing what we know today, we would have done lots of things differently. In some aspects we chose the longest way... but in the end we've managed to get where we wanted, plus it made us value what we have achieved and we learned a lot from our mistakes and the choices we made.

1 Alan Fletcher (1931–2006), British graphic designer described by the *Daily Telegraph* as 'the most highly regarded graphic designer of his generation, and probably one of the most prolific.'

Research Studios
Founded: 1994
Personnel: 10
Location: London, UK
www.researchstudios.com

Neville Brody achieved a level of international fame that no British graphic designer has experienced before or since. Yet he remains a tangential figure within contemporary design. Unusually for someone of his status, he's still actively designing. He refuses to join the design establishment, and retains the radical political convictions of his youth.

Brody's sensibilities were forged in the anti-authoritarian climate of the years following former British Prime Minister Margaret Thatcher's rise to power. Despite an early interest in fine art, he went to the London College of Printing because it offered an orthodox and disciplined graphics course. He left without a degree, but shot to recognition with his pioneering work for the influential style magazine *The Face*. Books and exhibitions followed, but so did setbacks and financial collapse.

After various incarnations of the Neville Brody studio, he abandoned the use of his name and set up Research Studios, with satellite offices in London, Berlin, Paris, Barcelona and New York. The interview was conducted at Brody's London studio.
—

Let's start with the early days. Was there a moment when you realized there was something called a design studio, and you wanted to have one?

Neville Brody: I have been freelance since leaving college, and my only experience of a studio since then was working for Al McDowell[1] at Rocking Russian[2], and although it wasn't the most professionally run outfit, it was exciting. The work and the dynamic attitude towards creativity meant that I learnt a lot from Al. Business-wise I didn't learn anything, probably I learnt how not to run a studio. But in terms of energy, and in terms of potential, and what you could do with graphic design, I learned a great deal. Al was from a fine art background, so I learnt a different kind of exploratory route, a lateral way of dealing with graphic design. It wasn't strategic but somehow in everything he did there was a strategy. It was fantastic.

At what point did you realize 'I have to do this on my own, I have to set up my own studio'?

I left Rocking Russian and then worked on the other side of the fence at Stiff Records[3] until I got fired for being late. But I used to hide in the darkroom (with the PMT camera on because that was the only way I could get light in there), and do my freelance work. I'd come out of this sauna at 4.00pm and do the

01 |
02 |

Stiff work. But I was starting to pick up a lot of record cover work – Fetish Records[4], 23 Skidoo[5] – and very quickly I realized I needed to leave Stiff and set up a small studio. I was the worst employee ever.

Did you find premises?

I was working for a film company and they gave me a little room at the back of their office. I had an assistant at that point, Simon Halfon[6], who started working with me right at the end of Stiff. This was the point at which I could say 'here's my studio'. It was basically me with an assistant and the PMT camera. The camera was in the same room so that if we needed to make a print we had to black out the whole room.

Did you have any knowledge of other design studios?

No. I knew about Malcolm Garrett[7] at Assorted Images[8], of course, Peter Saville[9], and Vaughan Oliver[10] had 23 Envelope[11]. I was more aware of other record sleeve designers than 'proper' studios.

Do you think you would have benefited if you'd done the traditional thing and worked for one of the big English design groups of the time?

I never would have done that. I knew what it meant to work at one of those companies, and that situation could not have existed on this planet. It's not something I would ever have done, despite having four years of abject poverty after college.

I can see how spiritually and emotionally you would not have taken a job in a big design group, but do you think in retrospect you might have learnt something by doing this? After all, even Barney Bubbles[12] worked for Conran[13]!

Well, I might have learnt something about business, but I always figured that stuff would come. My decision was to never compromise, and if I had compromised at any point we wouldn't be talking today. You and I come out of a revolutionary generation where we believed in culture being for the benefit of society and that we could help make things better. I didn't go into design for business reasons. I went into design because it was creative, challenging, thoughtful and could move people's minds. And actually the business idea was anathema to me at that point. At some point during my four years of poverty my father said to me: 'Go and get a job in an ad agency', and I said 'Absolutely not'. It was a defining moment. It became clear that I would never do that, and I felt that if I believed in what I was doing and didn't compromise, it would bring its own success. And it did.

It certainly did, because you got your first major client – *The Face* – and that was to propel you to become the most famous British graphic designer of any era.

I'd already met Nick Logan, the founder and editor of *The Face*, when he was editor of *Smash Hits*. At the time I was sharing the same tiny studio with Ian Wright[14]. It was 24-hour days, seven days a week. The film company I was renting from wanted to move out and I didn't want to move. So I went to Nick and persuaded him to move in and take over the lease. That became *The Face*'s first proper office. I was constantly on hand doing art direction and commissioning, and at the same time I was paying rent to him. Slowly we were getting more work, and I met Fwa Richards who then became my business partner. She took over managing the studio. At this point it was called Neville Brody Studios. We moved to a tiny studio where the Sainsbury's is today on Tottenham Court Road.

How many designers have you got working for you at this point?

We'd grown to four or five people. Our work was getting broader, yet none of it was corporate work. It was cultural and music industry. Towards the end of the 1980s, we started getting work from Japan. And then we published the book and suddenly there were eight people in this tiny space.

The book was a pivotal moment. You also had a major exhibition at the V&A. This had never happened to a graphic designer before. This must have been a real test for you?

It was very difficult, actually. The clients expected me to do every project and to be at every meeting. We were doing *Arena* magazine[15], and working on *Lei* and *Per Lui*[16], so I was travelling a lot. It was exhausting. Managing client expectations is a huge part of what you do, and it was a very hard thing.

How was the studio's work credited at this time?

We shared credits. Work would always be credited to whoever had done the work. It would read: Neville Brody Studios, plus the name of the individual. I felt that this was very important.

It's unusual to credit co-workers.

From early on my understanding of art direction was that it wasn't vertical, it was horizontal and democratic. A good idea could come from anywhere. And that what a good art director did was choose the right team, and if you chose the right team you shouldn't then tell them what to do. So photography in *The Face* and at *Arena* was never commissioned, it was always invited.

It was always shared, it was always – 'here's six pages, go away and make the most of this opportunity'. You get the best work that way. I've never, or very rarely, told people what to do. I don't come up with a design, put it on the table and say to someone 'OK, that's it. You go away and do it. You complete this.'

Is nurturing talent part of running a studio?

Yes. I think that's one of the biggest areas of responsibility. You have a responsibility to mentor people.

Yet many studio heads, often the ones with their names over the door, are not interested in mentoring and development. They want their designers to adhere to their vision. But that's not your model, is it?

No, nothing like that. But it's a difficult balance because if someone in the studio has produced an idea that I don't like, what do I do? Do I say 'you can't continue with this'? If I go in and you say 'it's wrong, you can't do that, you have to change it, here's what you should be doing,' then I'm not nurturing. But if something's really wrong then of course I have to say so. Managing creative staff is so difficult because by the same token, they could have the same point of view about your work. This happened recently. The studio produced a bunch of work for a client – a website – and they produced a lot of work that I thought wasn't good. We'd written a full strategy, which is usually what happens. I will sit with a client and develop a solid strategy, an understanding of where they're coming from, where they want to go, and how they need to manage that through a design structure. I will then take that and give it to the studio, they'll read it, absorb it, and then develop ideas. But in this case, most of what was produced was not, in my opinion, on-strategy. So I said, 'you can't show this'. I did some other stuff that I thought was on-strategy, and they then edited my stuff out. So in the end you had this kind of unhappy compromise and the client picked the thing that wasn't on-strategy, even though the client had signed up for the strategy. It caused quite a difficult situation. Sometimes those situations are explosive, they're not easy.

Let's go back to the middle period of your career. You'd published your book and had a major exhibition, and in doing so you'd become famous, with the consequence that you frightened off nearly all your British clients. As a result your business collapsed. Can you talk about this?

Just trying to think about that period is difficult. It was a watershed for us because we went from 95% UK work to 5% UK work overnight. Within six months we'd lost every single client we had and no one would open their doors to us any more. Yet all we were

03 | 04 | 05 | 06 |
07 | 08 |

03/04/05/06/07/08/ Project: D&AD Annual 2008. Client: D&AD.
09/10/11/12/ Project: *Public Enemies*, title design. Client: Universal Pictures.
13/14/ Project: Art and Sex, Seduced: Art and Sex from Antiquity to Now.
Client: Barbican Gallery.

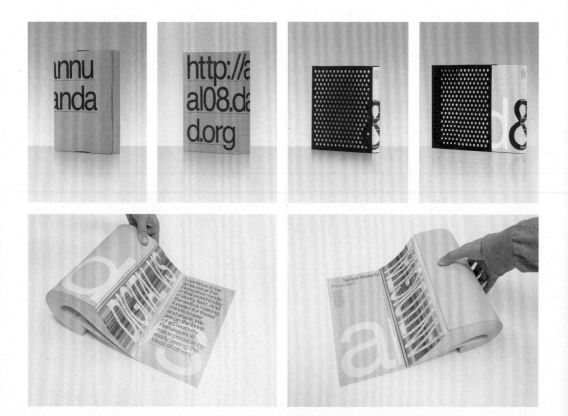

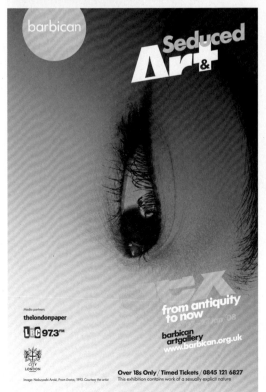

seeing around us was people copying our work. And that was extraordinarily painful. Psychologically for me it was one of the hardest things in my life. Just to see a poster opposite your studio where someone had ripped off your font and been paid for it. But my best friend from school, a guy called Grant Gilbert, had come to me with the idea of going out to Japan and trying to get work from there. This happened just before we were doing the V&A exhibition. He went to Tokyo and started finding work. So at least we had a bit of non-UK work.

What lessons did you learn from this period?

The dangers of print handling! For two major projects we took on the print handling, which means paying the printers and charging the client a percentage for managing it. But two clients refused to pay for the printing and we got landed with several thousand pounds worth of printing costs, and that's what nearly tipped us over the edge. We've never done it since. With print buying, you have to look at the risk to your income if a client doesn't pay.

But at this point you had a business manager. Wasn't it part of their remit to look after that sort of project?

Yeah, but we had no experience. We just saw £20–30,000 worth of print, with a management-handling fee. We didn't put the proper guarantees in place, we had no protection, so when the client pulled away, the printer came after us. It was down to lack of experience. Earlier we talked about whether it would have been better if I'd spent some time in a big studio – yes, I would have learnt certain things, but I think I would have unlearnt other more important things.

You then seemed to disappear from view...

As far as the UK was concerned we disappeared. We stayed in London but went deep underground, we avoided interviews, press, everything. I avoided any exposure whatsoever.

You emerged as Research Studios. Why the change of name?

Changing the name from Neville Brody Studios to Research Studios was another watershed moment. As Neville Brody Studios, the client's expectations were difficult to manage. They expected me to be on every project. I'd go to a meeting, I'd take a designer with me, but the client just wanted me. So there was no possibility of a handover, and I was spending more and more time doing business, and when this happens, you end up just managing projects and client liaising, which is an impossible situation if you're a designer and you want to be creative. So what do you do? Do you reduce your ambition and say OK, I'm going to boil it back down to me, a business person and two assistants? Or, do you say, well actually, there are possibilities here. So we felt the only way forward was to have a name that was more inclusive.

The name Research Studios has a dry, almost industrial tone. Was this intentional?

Originally it was Research & Design. We were going to be called R&D because we really like the idea that projects would be credited Design by R&D, and then we realized that actually we weren't strong enough in the development area so we just kept the research bit. That's how the name arrived.

You seem to have a settled team now?

Yes. I'm getting back into creative work again and that means it's going to become a new mix of vertical and horizontal. I was talking to the architect David Adjaye[17] about this. I said we've been a horizontal studio, which means that the solution can come from anywhere. I'm not walking in the room saying 'here's the next idea, make it happen.' David Adjaye said it's his name on the door, he decides everything and if people don't agree then they shouldn't be there. And there are enough people that want to work for him. I've deliberately tried this mentoring, nurturing, and it doesn't always work. You don't always get the best quality. You don't always manage to further your own creative ambitions, so now I'm trying to look at a mix of the two strategies. Quality control is really hard.

There's a dilemma here that lots of studios have to face up to. You take on talented people, but they're almost certainly going to leave, and many will set up their own studios in competition. This has happened to you, hasn't it?

We've had a history of that. Designers would be trained up, we'd invest a lot in people, and then they'd leave and we'd have to start all over again.

But there's a good side to this, too – lots of designers have emerged from under your wing and gone on to do interesting things. Surely this makes you proud?

Yes. Recently Ben Reece[18] has left and I think is headed for very great things. Swifty[19] [Ian Swift] of course. Cornel [Windlin][20] has done amazingly. Robert Wilkinson did some absolutely stunning work with us and is now on a volunteer program in Nigeria using his skills to inform about HIV. He's one of the most amazing designers I've ever come across. And then there's the bit that you haven't mentioned, which is that our designers have gone on to open studios in other countries that are part of the Research network.

Yes, I want to talk to you about this. You have branches of Research Studios in London, New York, Paris, Berlin and Barcelona...

I'm the majority shareholder so these studios are not owned by Research Studios. They are owned by me with a local manager who runs things. The studios use the reputation of Research, plus me, as a gate-opener to get work. But what we didn't put in place properly was the business relationship. We'd opened a Paris office originally because we were getting a lot of work in France and we thought, let's open a local office and then that'll be a way of channelling work to London and managing it locally. And then after a little while Ian Lionel thought, hang on, why am I giving the work to London? I'll just do it here. So in the space of a year we had a 40% drop in work and income. But we didn't have the mechanism in place to say OK, well you need to be paying a flat percentage, or paying franchise fees, we didn't do any of that.

Berlin's the same, but Berlin has never made any money because we opened in Berlin at the point when Germany was going bankrupt. Daniel Borck and Jason Bailey who set up Berlin had both been with me for a long time in London. Then Pablo Ravalo who had worked here for a long time, too, set up the Barcelona studio. He's worked for us for two long stints. We've ended up with this incredible family of Friends of Research. It's really amazing.

The only link is that you're the majority shareholder in all cases?

Yes. I've always said that if you're too big to have lunch together, then you're too big. So in London we're still nine or ten people. I never wanted a big, big studio. I didn't want 30 people. But what we decided to do was become a big studio by network. We did a big brainstorming project for MSN and for that we connected all the studios as one studio. And we do it from time to time on major projects. We've ended up with this incredible scaleable situation, where everyone is working locally, but if it's a massive project we just combine. And we're still growing. We're talking about India, and about Africa.

You always use the collective pronoun. You always talk about 'we'.

I've always seen it as 'we'. I'm not sailing out to sea by myself, I'm part of a crew. Jeff [Knowles] has been here for 12 years, which is extraordinary.

Tell me about the team you have now?

Six designers, plus Phil Rodgers who does new business and special projects. Right now, we are appointing a new manager to do studio management and all my admin. There's Emma Brocklesby on support, and that's it. And that's comfortable.

15/ Project: *The Times*, newspaper design and font design. Client: News International.
16/ Project: Dom Perignon packaging and branding evolution.
Client: Dom Perignon.

17 |
18 |
19 |

17/18/19/ Project: This is War, exhibition graphics. Client: Barbican Gallery.

Do you have a profit-sharing scheme?

Not strictly speaking. But Jeff and Nick are junior shareholders so they'll be on dividends if we're in profit. And if one of the designers brings in a major client then we pay a small finder's fee.

We're sitting in your elegant building in Islington – a chic part of London – do you own it?

It's a Georgian building, dated 1740. I bought it with Fwa [Richards] and it's the best thing we ever did. Milton Glaser said he never made any money from his studio, but he made money from having bought the studio building. It's one of Stefan Sagmeister's best quotes.

So you'd recommend buying premises?

Employees tend to be far more protected, but as principal you're quite often either sole trader or you're on a director's salary and have to take dividends, which creates a vulnerable situation. I'm 52 now, and thinking, well, in 20 years' time am I going to be chasing clients? What do you do in 20 years' time? Wise investment is the only way forward. My accountant urged me to start a pensions scheme when I was in my 20s. Whether that's worth anything still, I have no idea. But every month, no matter what, I've been putting money into it. You have to, because as principals we're incredibly exposed. We take the full risk. We stand to make the most benefit, but we also take the full risk.

Have your business skills improved over the years?

2004 was the worst year I ever experienced. My business partner, Fwa Richards, had to leave the studio suddenly for personal reasons, and I was left having to run the business on top of managing projects and trying to bring new work in, and I'd had no experience of that. It was an extraordinarily difficult learning curve, as well as the fact that the creative industries were going through a very barren patch due to the war in Iraq and post 9-11 fears. The studio at that point was down to just myself and Jeff. We were one week away from bankruptcy for the whole year, and I very nearly had a breakdown as a result. The following year we had the opposite experience, one of overload, having to say yes to everything that came in without the budget to pay for a large team. And I was still struggling with learning about the business.

Let me ask you about your physical environment. Do you need to work in a certain sort of environment, or could you work anywhere?

You can work anywhere, there's no doubt. I mean especially with computers. You can have a creative idea on a plane or in a hotel room or in the middle of your office. But to work anywhere and to be seen to work anywhere are two different things. Space is important for image, as you know.

So you're talking about the impression clients have when they come visit?

Yes, and you can play with it ironically, we could be in a modern office building but we'd have to be able to be ironic with that. The design industry still has a level of artisan and workshop and craft attached to it, and we want to maintain that as part of our image. Even though nearly everything's done on a computer.

You're separated from the actual studio. They are in the basement and you are on the first floor. Do you ever sit down there?

Not that often. But again, we're changing that, we're readdressing the horizontal to vertical mix. I needed this separate space for me.

You have client meetings here in your office, but you've also got a workstation, so I'm guessing you work here too?

I like having a meeting table on one side of the room, and a work table on the other. It means I can just go from one side of the room to the other.

1 Alex McDowell, English record sleeve designer, now working as leading production designer in Hollywood. Films include *Fight Club*, *Minority Report* and *Watchmen*.

2 Rocking Russian Design, studio founded 1978 by Alex McDowell working mainly on record sleeves and design for the music industry.

3 Stiff Records, influential British record label formed in 1976 by music business entrepreneurs Dave Robinson and Jake Riviera. Artists included Elvis Costello, The Damned, Ian Dury and the Blockheads, Lene Lovich, Nick Lowe and Madness.

4 Fetish Records, pioneering industrial and electro record label with acts that included 23 Skidoo, Bush Tetras and Stephen Mallinder.

5 23 Skidoo, formed 1979 in London. They were prominent figures on Britain's experimental/industrial music scene.

6 Simon Halfon, English graphic designer who has designed record sleeves for The Style Council, George Michael and Oasis. Worked with Sir Peter Blake on Paul Weller's *Stanley Road* album cover.

7 Malcolm Garrett, English graphic designer and digital design pioneer. Designed record covers for Buzzcocks, Duran Duran, Culture Club, Simple Minds and Peter Gabriel.

8 Assorted Images, multidisciplinary design group formed in 1983 by Malcolm Garrett and Kasper de Graaf.

9 Peter Saville, English graphic designer best known for his iconoclastic work for Factory Records' recording artists Joy Division and New Order.

10 Vaughan Oliver, English graphic designer celebrated for his dark and mysterious work for UK record label 4AD.

11 23 Envelope was a collaboration between graphic designer Vaughan Oliver and photographer Nigel Grierson.

12 Barney Bubbles (1942–1983), radical English graphic artist who often refused to sign his work. Designed sleeves for Hawkwind, Elvis Costello and Ian Dury and the Blockheads. Suffered from bipolar disorder and committed suicide in 1983.

13 The Conran Group was formed by English designer and retailer Terence Conran. Barney Bubbles worked at the studio as a designer in the 1960s.

14 Ian Wright, English illustrator. www.mrianwright.co.uk.

15 *Arena* magazine, British monthly men's magazine, created in 1986 by Nick Logan, who had started *The Face*. Neville Brody was Arena's first designer. The magazine closed in 2009.

16 *Per Lui* and *Lei* were two fashion magazines published by Condé Nast in the 1980s and 90s. Produced in Milan, they were targeted respectively at young men and women.

17 David Adjaye, rising star of British architecture. Trained with David Chipperfield Architects. Won the RIBA First Prize Bronze Medal and started Adjaye Architects in 1994.

18 Ben Reece, British designer now based in Paris.

19 Swifty (Ian Swift), influential British graphic designer and typeface designer, self-styled 'Godfather of the Sampling Generation'.

20 Cornel Windlin, Swiss type and graphic designer. Worked for Neville Brody in London before returning to Zurich.

ShaughnessyWorks
Founded: 2004
Personnel: 1, plus assistants
Location: London, UK
www.shaughnessyworks.com

Adrian Shaughnessy co-founded the
design studio Intro. In 2003 he left to
pursue a career as an independent art
director, consultant and writer. For three
years he was consultant creative director
for This is Real Art, a studio that operated
with a roster of design talent rather than
salaried designers. Since 2007 he has run
ShaughnessyWorks, offering consultancy,
art direction and editorial skills to a range
of clients.

Shaughnessy has written, edited and
designed numerous books, including *How
to be a Graphic Designer Without Losing
Your Soul*, which has sold over 70,000
copies. Between 2006 and 2009 he edited
the magazine *Varoom*. He writes for Design
Observer, the world's most widely read design
blog. He has a monthly column in *Design Week*,
and hosts a radio show called *Graphic Design
on the Radio*. He is a frequent lecturer, and
has been interviewed on radio and TV on
numerous occasions. In 2008, he
co-founded Unit Editions.

The interview was conducted via email.
—

You have been involved in several studio
incarnations, but for our purposes let's
talk about Intro. What prompted you to
start Intro?

Adrian Shaughnessy: In the late 1980s, I was
working with my future business partner –
Katy Richardson[1], a non-designer – at a
design company. It was a business-focused
company with the emphasis on profitability.
Everything had to be sacrificed for the
sake of preserving profit margins. We were
expected to do every job quickly, and we
mainly worked for clients who didn't give
a hoot about quality. It taught me that
you couldn't run a design business if your
primary focus was making money. In fact, the
opposite is true. To make money, you have to
concentrate on the work.

But this apprenticeship served us both
well when we came to set up Intro. We always
asked ourselves – what would our former
employer have done? And then we'd do the
opposite. You learn as much from working for
bad studios as you do from good ones. There
is no such thing as a bad job when you're
starting out.

So you went into partnership at the outset?

Yes. Katy, my business partner, was a very
smart person. She had all the talents and
skills I lacked. Her background was film

production. She was financially astute.
She was an organizer. And she liked doing
the stuff that I hated: business planning,
accounting, administration. She left me free
to do what I liked doing, which was running
a creative team and dealing with clients. But
the crucial point in all this was that we both
respected what each other did. Katy loved
to see good creative work being done, and
I slept soundly at night knowing the studio
was organized along rock-solid lines. We also
got on well, although we both had separate
lives outside of work.

Did you employ designers from the off?

We started with one designer. But I made
a terrible mistake. I was so appalled by the
way that designers had been treated in my
old company that I went out of my way to
treat our sole employee with velvet gloves.
I treated him so well, in fact, that he started
to behave like someone who had been let out
of prison, and he went on an orgy of self-
indulgence and produced introverted and
selfish work. It was a lesson in how not to
treat designers. Designers actually don't
want limitless freedom. In fact, they respond
best to clear guidelines of what is expected
of them, and then to be given the respect,
support and encouragement that enables
them to produce good work. So one of my
first jobs was to dismiss our only designer.
It hurt me more than it hurt him. I felt a
sense of failure.

Did this cause you to rethink the way you
went about hiring and managing designers?

Definitely. But about the same time,
someone gave me a piece of advice that really
opened my eyes: always employ people who are
better than you. This was a revelation to me.
I thought I had to be the best. But yet again,
the opposite was true. Studios grow by hiring
and developing talent. I also discovered
that we needed to employ people who were
self-motivated. If you constantly have to tell
designers what to do, they get pissed off,
and so do you. So I learned to spot self-
motivated people who wanted a supportive
and fertile environment where they could
produce good work.

Did you have a vision of how you wanted your
studio to be?

I had the usual romantic notions of doing
great work and making lots of money. But
of course, it wasn't like that. It was about
long hours, working for lousy budgets and
always over-delivering. But eventually, after
four or five years, a vision emerged. I wanted
us to produce work that was unclichéd and
unpredictable. I wanted to produce work in
different media (a rare thing in the early
90s). I wanted a studio where everyone was
happy to turn up for work. I wanted a studio
that clients liked coming to. I wanted a studio

01 |
02 |
03 |

01/02/03/ Project: front cover and
spreads from *Graphic Design: A User's
Manual*. Date: 2009. Client: Laurence King
Publishing. Designer: Adrian Shaughnessy.

that earned the respect of other designers. And finally, I wanted to make a decent living. I wanted us to earn fees that reflected the value we gave to our clients, and I wanted financial stability. I'm not a financial risk – taker and I can't function if I'm worried about money. All this might not add up to a very sophisticated or enlightened 'vision', but it was one we all shared, and one that we could achieve collectively.

Which studios and designers influenced you?

Funnily enough, it was the bad ones. I looked around and saw so many badly run studios where everyone was miserable that I vowed to make our studio different. I liked – and envied – many of the new wave of young British studios that grew up in the 1980s. 8vo[2], Cartlidge Levine[3], Designers Republic[4], Why Not Associates[5]. Some of the greats also inspired me – Total[6], Pentagram[7], Studio Dumbar[8]. But I quickly realized that we had to find our own identity.

Where did you go for help and advice?

We had an independent accountant. He didn't know anything about design, which used to drive me mad, but which later I came to see was a good thing. He thought that some of my ideas, such as taking on low-paid jobs because they allowed the designers to work on interesting projects, were potty. He also thought I was daft to do a job (design) that I loved. He reckoned it warped my judgement. Much better, he said, to do something that you don't have a personal investment in. But he gave us good solid business advice, and although I sometimes resented it, I knew it was usually correct.

The one thing I didn't do was talk to other designers. Because I hadn't gone to design school – and because Katy wasn't a designer – we hardly knew any other designers we could turn to for help. In the end we worked it out for ourselves.

Did you have to borrow money?

Katy negotiated an overdraft facility with our bank. This was readily offered by the men in grey suits because they could see that her business plan was realistic. Also, we had paid work from the outset, so they were happy to support us. In the end we hardly used the overdraft.

How did you find clients when you started out?

Finding clients was my job, and I both loved and hated doing it. If someone called me and asked for a meeting, I was Mr Invincible. Yet when I had to call people to try and hustle work, I was Mr Wimp. But I forced myself to do cold calling, and even had some success at it. However, I soon realized that the best way to

win new clients was to get them to call you. So my driving ambition was to always do the sort of work that attracted attention.

Did you have a portfolio?

The great conundrum with new studios is that you don't have a body of work and therefore putting together a portfolio is difficult. In the early days, I was so embarrassed by the thinness of our portfolio that I developed ways of talking about our work without the need to show it. But eventually we developed a portfolio that we could show with confidence.

Intro was well known for its record sleeve design. What prompted your expansion into motion graphics, corporate work and new media?

Even back then – the mid-1990s – we could see that the music business was headed for trouble. Budgets were falling and it was becoming harder to do good work due to the rise of marketing departments staffed by people who had worked at Unilever and Coca Cola. Plus, we could see that if we were to grow creatively (and financially) we needed to do other sorts of work. Thanks to Katy's background as a film and animation producer, moving image work had always been part of what we did at Intro.

The corporate work actually grew out of the music work. I'd go and see really dull companies and show them what we did for bands like Primal Scream[9] and Stereolab[10], and amazingly, lots of them really liked this approach. We got into new media early because it fitted with my idea of what a modern progressive studio should be doing. Plus our artworker came to me one day in the mid-1990s and said – look at this, I've designed and programmed an Intro website.

How were things structured at that point?

We were growing rapidly. In the dotcom boom we grew to around 40 people and we realized that we needed to manage this expansion carefully. We spent long hours planning our growth, and decided on a team-based system. We formed three teams – moving image, corporate design and music/cultural design. A designer led each team, with a project manager/producer as support. Katy and I were not in a team. We went to whoever needed us – Katy for finance and production: me for creative and new business. The teams were financially and creatively accountable – they had to be profitable and maintain a high standard of work – but otherwise they were autonomous.

How did it affect Intro creatively?

If anything, creativity got better. I can't say there weren't teething problems, but we had good people who relished the responsibility of

04 | 05 |
06 | 07 |
08 |

04/06/08/ Project: Front cover and spreads from *Cover Art By:*. Date: 2008.
Client: Laurence King Publishing. Designer: Adrian Shaughnessy. 05/ Project: Front
cover, Images 33. Date: 2009. Client: AOI. Art direction: Adrian Shaughnessy. Design
and artwork: Simon Sharville. 07/ Project: Art cards for Depeche Mode's *Sounds of the
Universe* box set. Date: 2009. Client: Paul A Taylor at Mute Records. Art Direction: Adrian
Shaughnessy. Original symbol designed by Anton Corbin. Individual remixes by (L/R)
James Brooks, Adrian Shaughnessy, Tom Browning, Spin, Kate Dawkins, Bibliothèque,
Karlssonwilker, Zip, Kim Hiorthoy. 09/11/13/ Project: box set, booklet cover and spread
for Mute Audio Documents. Date: 2007. Client: Mute Records.
Design and art direction: Adrian Shaughnessy. Additional design: Sam Renwick, This is
Real Art. 10/12/14/17/ Project: Memory and Autopsy, unpublished book. Date: 2007.
Client: Self-initiated. Art direction, design, photography and text: Adrian Shaughnessy.
15/16/ Project: Poster. Date: 2007. Client: Long Lunch. Designer: Adrian Shaughnessy.
Photographer: Angus Muir.

autonomy, and who rose to the occasion and became better designers and better people.

Did you have a profit-sharing policy?

Yes. We had a system where everyone benefited if the company did well. We believed in the idea of everyone sharing in the success of the studio, and we were careful to avoid the 1980s and 90s disease of bosses earning much more than their staff. There were no directors' Porsches at Intro.

How would you define your role as creative director?

I was like a doctor doing a tour of his surgical ward. Each morning I spent time with everyone going over problems and reviewing work – especially with the younger ones. I also tried to do as many client meetings as possible and spend time each day on new business activity.

Did you ever socialize together?

We had regular company outings. But we all spent so much time in the studio that we were happy to go our separate ways outside of work. I'd say that like all good studios there was a genuine family feeling: we certainly worked hard to build one. There was always a cake for birthdays – that sort of thing.

Did you have formal rules about things like timekeeping and so on?

Yes, we had formal employee contacts that stated the basic rules. But I always considered it a failure when we had to enforce them. I only wanted to employ people who didn't need to be told that if we were busy they had to get in early and only leave when the job was done. If someone had to be told this, they probably weren't right for us. But it's a great mistake to think that this formal stuff doesn't matter. Employment law is a minefield and as soon as there is a problem you realize how important it is to be properly set up with everything in writing.

How did you maintain the balance between creativity and profitability?

By always putting the work first. If you do that, profitability takes care of itself. We also invested in project managers who ensured good financial control and reporting. But we did this to improve our service to clients and not to increase our profitability. My motto has always been – get the service right and the profitability will follow.

What was your attitude to interns?

We took them very seriously. We always paid them, and I always spent time with them. We had some great interns and many stayed on to become valued team members. Others have gone on to be successful designers.

18 |
19 |
20 |

18/19/20/ Project: Book covers, Sampler series, Volumes 1, 2 and 3.
Date: 1999/2000/2003. Client: Laurence King Publishing. Design: Intro.

I occasionally meet former interns and none of them have punched me yet. Of course, we had our share of misfits. Young designers who mistook the sense of freedom as a signal to be casual and undisciplined.

If you could start all over again, what would you do differently?

The only thing I regret is that I didn't work in some other design studios before starting Intro. I wish I'd done an apprenticeship at Wolff Olins[11], or somewhere like that. Instead I worked in a succession of dreadful places – but as I've said, there was a good side to that, too.

You started to author books at Intro; how did this come about?

I discovered something interesting about how to promote the studio around this time. I noticed that if you bleated about yourself no one noticed. But if you talked about things other than yourself, people sometimes listened. We put together the first of three books devoted to radical music graphics [see 18/19/20]. We included some of our own work, but we mainly featured the work of other designers. The book was a success and it was written about in the national press and in the sorts of publications that wouldn't be interested if we just said – hey, look at us, we're a cool design studio. I also developed an interest in writing about design and I was asked to write for *Eye*, *Creative Review* and other design journals. It became a bit of a passion.

What made you want to leave Intro?

In the end it happened very suddenly. I always thought I'd have to be carried out in a box, but I'd done 15 years almost to the day, and I found that I'd reached the end of a cycle in my life and I needed to change everything. Besides, I didn't feel I could take Intro any further, and my interest in writing needed more time than I could devote to it as creative director of a 25-strong design company. We had directors' agreements in place, which made it possible for one of us to leave. You don't think directors' agreements are important when you are starting out, but you need them because no one knows what might happen. So, I jumped ship. My departure was managed amicably, and because of the team system it was possible to extract myself without damaging the studio. Intro continues to do well, and we are all still friends.

How would you define your studio's culture today?

ShaughnessyWorks is just me. And it's a great relief. I wouldn't have missed a day of my time at Intro, but in the end, running a studio ceased to be of interest to me. Also, it's my belief that to be the creative head of a design company, you have to put yourself last. By this I mean that you have to make sacrifices that you wouldn't ask your staff to make; you have to submerge your own ego in favour of individuals and the group. Inevitably – if you are a creative person – this becomes a bit wearing after a while, and I wanted to be a bit more selfish. I now earn less money than I did when I was a director of a successful design company. I spend my time writing and designing books, doing consultancy work, lecturing and hosting my occasional radio show. And of course, co-running Unit Editions.

1 Katy Richardson, MD and co-founder of London - based design group, Intro. Business partner of Adrian Shaughnessy (1989–2003).

2 8vo (Octavo), London-based graphic design firm formed in 1985 by Simon Johnston, Mark Holt and Hamish Muir. Closed in 2001.

3 Cartlidge Levine, formed 1987, by Ian Cartlidge and Adam Levene. British design group with strong typographic ethos.

4 The Designers Republic (1986–2009), uniquely influential and pioneering design studio formed by Ian Anderson in Sheffield, England. Best known for anti-consumerist sloganeering, radical digital typography and ground-breaking album cover art for the Warp label.

5 Why Not Associates, British design group run by co-founders Andy Altmann and David Ellis, graduates of the Royal College of Art.

6 Total Design, highly influential Amsterdam design group formed by Wim Crouwel, Benno Wissing and industrial designer Friso Kramer in 1963.

7 Pentagram, eminent design group formed in 1972 in London by Alan Fletcher, Theo Crosby, Colin Forbes, Kenneth Grange and Mervyn Kurlansky. See page 162.

8 Studio Dumbar, esteemed Dutch studio established in 1977 by Gert Dumbar.

9 Primal Scream, Scottish rock band best known for album *Screamadelica*, released in 1991 at the height of the Acid House/Rave movement.

10 Stereolab, Anglo-French band formed in 1990 by Tim Gane (guitar/keyboards) and Lætitia Sadier (vocals/keyboards/guitar).

11 Wolff Olins, design group founded in London in 1965 by Michael Wolff and Wally Olins. Wolff left in 1983, and Olins in 2001. Today it is a brand consultancy, based in London, New York City and Dubai. Subjected to international media attention when it launched the controversial London 2012 Olympic logo.

Spin
Founded: 1992
Personnel: 8 plus interns
Location: London, UK
www.spin.co.uk

Tony Brook works at the coalface of modern visual communication, producing sharp, highly disciplined, zeitgeisty work in print and electronic media. Yet Brook is firmly rooted in the grand tradition of graphic design, with a profound respect for and knowledge of graphic design's history.

In partnership with his wife Patricia Finegan, Brook began Spin in the spare room of the couple's flat. The studio grew rapidly, employing 32 people in the late 1990s. Today, Brook and Finegan run a studio that produces distinctive and ground-breaking work for a rich mix of clients, while at the same time producing ambitious self-initiated publishing projects that define the studio's culture of excellence and its respect for the art and tradition of graphic design. Working with a broad range of clients, Spin is now one of the most respected studios in Europe.

The interview was conducted via email.
—

What prompted you to start your own studio?

Tony Brook: I was working at a studio that had no real design pedigree. I'd gone there for the money, which was a big mistake and I was very unhappy. I started thinking about what my next move might be. I was bringing in a lot of new business for the studio, a very different situation to working on existing clients, and this was really the deciding factor. It's not a big leap from 'I got you clients' to 'I can get my own clients'. Even though this was happening in the middle of a recession, it felt right. Another motivating factor was that after ten years working almost solely for the record industry, I was ready for a new challenge. Once my partner Patricia and I made the decision to set up a studio, I couldn't wait to get on with it. I remember being quite excited and unafraid.

It's interesting that you were winning clients even while a studio employee. Most people don't get this experience until they set up on their own. Was this a good grounding for the future?

Definitely, it helped enormously. Most employers are delighted to hear that one of their staff has ideas about new clients or contacts that might lead to new work. Making business is a buzz whether you are working for someone or not, and setting up is certainly an easier step to make if you have had a taste of it.

Did you have a vision of how you wanted your studio to be?

I wanted a highly motivated, dynamic, creative studio that made challenging, intelligent and engaging work, a studio that would experiment and try new things. This is how we got into interactive design and motion graphics; there is a feeling in the studio that if we put our minds to it we can do anything. This probably came from working solely on record sleeves for a long time. I also had an atmosphere or an attitude in mind. It sounds peculiar, but I wanted a kind of relaxed intensity.

Which studios and designers influenced you?

My early influences were Peter Saville[1], Malcolm Garrett[2], 8vo[3], 23 Envelope[4], Barney Bubbles[5], David Gentleman[6], Grapus[7], Studio Dumbar[8].

Are they the same people who inspire you now, or have you found others?

I'd certainly add Wim Crouwel[9], Ben Bos[10], Mary Vieira[11], Jan Van Toorn[12], Benno Wissing[13], Dieter Roth[14], Karl Gerstner[15] and Wolfgang Weingart[16] to my list . I also love a lot of what's going on now; there is so much inspiring and exciting work being made. I enjoy designers who have strong, well-thought-out positions, with a singular vision. It's something I envy and aspire to.

Where did you go for help and advice?

We did a fair bit of research ourselves, preparing a business plan and reading up about how to run a business. Tricia's father, Cartan, gave us a huge lift with desperately needed money and advice. I remember my last boss, after telling me I was insane for setting up, saying: 'Try and earn something each day, it doesn't matter how little, it all adds up'.

Where did the name Spin come from?

Coming up with a name was like water torture. I fixed on Spin because I love the game of cricket and have always admired spin bowlers for their nerve and skill, brains over brawn, and I'm a failed 'tweaker'[17] myself. It seems to work – a short, sharp, multifaceted word that you can say without blushing when answering the phone. I have to confess that some of the names we toyed with were absolutely diabolical; I still get a hot flush when I think of them.

Did you have to borrow money?

Yes. The bank wouldn't give us a loan to set up the studio, but they said they would give us the money if we 'bought a car'. So we agreed to 'buy a car'. Although it is better not to have to borrow money, we picked up one or two clients quite quickly, so financially we were soon self-sufficient.

01 |
02 |

01/ Project: Spin/3, Action Time Vision poster. Date: 2008. Client: Self-initiated. 02/ Project: How Very Tokyo poster. Date: 2008. Client: StudioKanna, Tokyo.

Can you describe the process you went through to get started? How did you find clients, for example?

Once the decision was made, I gave up my job straight away. Trish stayed at her job for another month and then we were Spin. I remember lots of meetings with banks and showing them our business plan. Even though they pretty much ignored it, the business plan really helped us. Then we started calling people, making meetings, showing the portfolio. We basically tried to contact anyone we thought were interesting. It was quite surprising how open people were to seeing us.

Was it just you and Trish at this time or did you have any staff?

We realized pretty early on that it's tough to go out to meetings with any regularity and not have someone back at the ranch moving projects along and taking calls, so we had a junior designer almost from day one.

Spin went through a phenomenal growth spurt – you grew to 32 people in the late 1990s. How did you deal with this?

Not very well, I'm afraid. I had only experienced small studios and was totally unprepared for all the issues size threw up. There were problems with staff, with taking on projects that I didn't want to do but had to in order to pay the wages, and with having to make compromises in our work as a result of taking on those jobs. I think it takes a certain kind of person to control a studio of that size; I must admit it made me miserable. It was a huge relief to get back down to a size that I was comfortable with.

Coming up to date, can you define your role, and that of Trish?

Besides my role as a designer, my primary responsibility is to keep Spin in the right place creatively. I have a very strong idea of what I want Spin to be, and of the standards required. This part of my job is easy right now; I am surrounded by designers who have incredibly high expectations and who push me. Trish is the managing director and runs all the non-creative aspects of the business, including finance, billing, client relationships, new business and all organizational requirements. Basically the stuff that allows us to exist!

Could you talk about how you find new clients – have you reached the point where they come to you?

We are very lucky that clients often come to us now. But we do approach clients where we see a good fit. It has to go both ways.

Is there a type of client you look for?

Definitely, clients are as responsible for good design as designers are. I'm excited to learn about different sectors and to respond to new challenges, but at the core of each project is the relationship between us and our client. A good relationship with a client is something to treasure.

Can you talk about how you present Spin to new clients? You've got a very cool-looking website, do you have a printed portfolio?

Our website is designed to give people a quick taste of what we are about. We see our printed portfolio slightly differently; it gives us an opportunity to talk in depth about projects.

Let's talk about employing people. It's often the most difficult aspect of running a studio. You have to start worrying about the welfare of others, and keeping them motivated and inspired. How do you go about this?

Employing people can certainly have its issues, but the benefits outweigh the problems. Generally I have been very lucky; I work, and have worked, with talented designers throughout my career. As far as motivation is concerned, our process of engagement doesn't really allow for complacency. I think we are all aware of being in a privileged position and in no sense do we take it for granted. I'm grateful for the ability and hard work that have made Spin what it is, and I hope the designers who have worked here feel that Spin has given them something too. As an employer you have to treat people with respect, and be honest and open. As far as inspiration is concerned, it is a collective responsibility; we help each other and we talk about things a lot (design, politics, anything).

What qualities do you look for in a designer?

The first thing is the right personality; you need the correct chemistry. This is something I have been guilty of ignoring in the past, but it is fundamental. Only after that do you get on to ability, intelligence, mindset and so on. Our process requires an ability to share thoughts and ideas, to stick those ideas up on the wall, be prepared to talk about them, defend them, rip them to shreds, maybe start again. We want to make the best work we can, and that requires a degree of collaboration, which many designers find difficult.

How do you handle ambitious designers who want a sense of personal authorship?

We are a small company, we have designers who are more experienced than others, but ultimately everyone is at the coalface. There is no great hierarchical structure in terms of titles. The more experienced designers mostly run their own jobs, but everyone

03/ Project: Whitechapel Gallery identity. Date: 2009. Client: Whitechapel Gallery.
04/ Project: Proa Foundation identity, poster. Date: 2008. Client: Proa Foundation.
05/ Project: Mythologies catalogue. Date: 2009. Client: Haunch of Venison.
06/ Project: Spin Long Lunch poster. Date: 2007. Client: Long Lunch, Scotland.
07/ Project: Caruso St John book. Date: 2008. Client: Caruso St John Architects.
08/ Project: Dispatches identity. Date: 2008. Client: Channel 4. 09/ Project: More4
identity. Date: 2008. Client: Channel 4. 10/ Project: Mayfly poster. Date: 2004.
Client: Nike. 11/ Project: 25x4: Channel 4 at 25. Date: 2008. Client: Channel 4.
12/ Project: Zhang Huan catalogue. Date: 2008. Client: Haunch of Venison.
13/ Project: Visuell 5. Date: 2007. Client: Deutsche Bank. 14/ Project: D&AD Annual.
Date: 2005. Client: D&AD. 15/ Project: Logo book. Date: 2007. Client: Laurence King.

16 |
17 |
18 |

16/ Project: Guy Tillim advert. Date: 2008.
Client: Haunch of Venison.
17/ Project: Adam Pendleton advert.
Date: 2009. Client: Haunch of Venison.
18/ Project: Al Taylor advert. Date: 2006.
Client: Haunch of Venison.
19/20/21/ Project: D&AD Presidents
Lectures. Date: 2006. Client: D&AD.

has to take responsibility. Spin works as a collective entity; everyone who works or has worked at Spin has every reason to feel a sense of connection and ownership with the successes that have made it what it is. Every job we undertake is a Spin job and is credited as such, it is pretty fundamental to the way we work. Spin projects always have a number of fingerprints on them. Designers here do occasional lectures and talk to the design press, but in the end we all have to put our ego and our effort into the collective Spin pot. It is a team effort.

Do you have a profit-sharing policy?

We give bonuses when we make a profit. It has always been important that we share any success we have.

Do you ever socialize together?

Yes, everyone gets on well. We have tea and cake at 4.00pm every day, and we have our regular Friday Thai curry. The table football and pool table are in use every day. We don't go out as often as I'd like, but when we do it's always a good laugh.

Do you have formal rules about things like timekeeping and so on?

We start at 9.30am and finish at 6.00pm with an hour for lunch. I like the idea of having to focus during the working day. I used to have problems about never being able to switch off and always being in work mode – it just makes you very tired and less effective. We try to do as much of our work as we can in the day and make an effort not to work late or at weekends if we can possibly help it. I like the thought that we can all have a life.

How do you maintain the balance between creativity and profitability?

It's a tough one. If you make choices based on creative opportunity, and we do, your profit margins tend to suffer. So we aren't ever going to be wealthy. But as long as we keep relatively busy we tend to be OK at the end of the year.

What is your attitude towards interns?

We have interns all year round. They are usually here for two to three months at a time. They come to experience a working studio, to feel a sense of responsibility, and to get a sense of what is required from them when they leave college. We do our best to make sure that we give them that. They are introduced into projects and are encouraged to contribute. There is no mollycoddling; they're seen as members of the team from the off. The response to this approach has been great; I think people respond to high expectations. Our interns come from all over the world. So far we have had designers from

Germany, Switzerland, Portugal, Sweden, the US and of course the UK.

How do they go about getting an internship at Spin?

The process is simple: students send in their work on PDF or send us a link to their website, and we invite the best ones in.

Spin has an admirable track record in self-initiated publishing. You produce a 'newsprint' journal that is widely read and sold in shops. Is this an outlet for your well-known interest in design's heritage, or does it have a business rationale as well?

We have always enjoyed personal projects, it's great to have something going on in the background. At one time or another we've done short films, photo essays, interactive pieces and exhibitions. Some of them have resulted in business, although they haven't ever been conceived with that in mind. The paper [see 22/23/24] came out of a discussion we had about how we could make our personal projects less self-indulgent and a bit more meaningful. It has been really well received and has been really enjoyable to work on. The paper is not for profit.

If you could start all over again, what would you do differently?

We've made pretty much every mistake it's possible to make at one time or another, but I think the biggest howler and the one I would wholeheartedly not make again was getting too big. I think there is an optimum size for a design company to function effectively at; it's anywhere between one and, perhaps, 12. After that it all gets a bit weird.

Why do you think big studios are problematical?

Because individuals can feel excluded, and indifference starts to spread. Cliques start to form, which is poison in a creative company. Large numbers are all too often the road to mediocrity. People can hide for years at a place and not contribute anything. The bottom line and the killer blow against size is that the work is not as good. I feel quite strongly about this.

How important is the physical environment you work in?

The layout and style of your studio supports the tone and attitude you have to your work, and the way it is made. It also puts you in the right frame of mind. So, yes, I think it is very important. At one point I had a desk away from everyone, in a desire for a bit of personal space. It didn't work for me at all. I need to be at the centre of things, and I found I missed so much.

22 |
23 |
24 |

Does this mean a pristine environment with designer furniture?

Eames[18], Vitsoe[19], Apple – designer clichés – but they work functionally and tonally. I waited a long time before I succumbed to my Eames chair; I don't see it so much as feel it. What can I say, it makes me very happy. These things form a background atmosphere, a sense of order. I'm fairly chaotic and untidy, my desk is usually a blizzard of paper and Post-it notes, so the possibility of underlying order is a nice thought.

You have an open-plan studio?

Yes, our process involves a lot of chat and impromptu meetings so our main working space has to be open-plan really. That said, I find a change of environment really useful, so we have quieter spaces for research or reading and meeting. I also like sitting at home poring over books and sketching things out. I'm a great believer in physical spaces acting as a stimulus for ideas. Our current studio has a nice feel to it that is much more personal and intense than the aircraft hanger we were in previously and that has made a big difference to our work, I'm sure. Your environment can be a great creative trigger.

Do you have a music policy?

I love music playing when I work, it helps me to focus, and I can listen to pretty much anything. The only thing I struggle with is a DJ talking, or Jonathan from Spotify[20], I can't see how you can listen to someone spouting rubbish and work at the same time (although I'm sure some people can). The only rule is that if the level of sound or style of music is intrusive to anyone they can turn it down or change it.

How would you define your studio's culture today?

Friendly, open, enthusiastic. Everyone is included and everyone contributes. We share influences, both new and old, and aren't scared to try things that are outside our comfort zone. The studio is a living thing; it feels as if it is growing, developing, changing. Which is good because I get very itchy if things get too comfortable or predictable.

Do you have any advice to give to someone thinking of setting up?

It is the most basic, obvious, straightforward and unavoidable fact, but the difference between survival and demise is money. Survival is the first thing. You can't just steal your old firm's clients, or at least you shouldn't if you live by any reasonable moral standards. So you have to get out there and make your own business. Starting to make money from your own clients with your own work is the single most exciting thing about setting up. The next, and much less exciting part, is collecting the money. If at all possible, don't be the designer and the one who chases the money. It's very difficult not to get emotional if some bastard isn't paying on time for the beautiful job you have made. And it's going to happen. It is much better, if possible, to have a dispassionate voice chasing your hard-earned dough.

This might be stating the bleeding obvious, but the reason you set up business is to be in control of your own destiny. To do the work you want to do in the way you want to do it. You may be lucky, and the most wonderful commissions from the most compliant and supportive clients may fall out of the clear blue sky into your lap. But if your journey resembles a salmon swimming against the tide, you may be forced to compromise to some degree. If this happens, try not to get too downhearted; be as true to yourself and your vision as you can, and hold your nerve.

1 Peter Saville, English graphic designer best known for his iconoclastic work for Factory Records' recording artists Joy Division and New Order.

2 Malcolm Garrett, English graphic designer and digital design pioneer. Designed record covers for Buzzcocks, Duran Duran, Culture Club, Simple Minds and Peter Gabriel.

3 8vo (Octavo), London-based graphic design firm formed in 1985 by Simon Johnston, Mark Holt and Hamish Muir. Closed in 2001.

4 23 Envelope, collaboration between graphic designer Vaughan Oliver and photographer Nigel Grierson.

5 Barney Bubbles (1942–1983), radical English graphic artist who often refused to sign his work. Designed sleeves for Hawkwind, Elvis Costello and Ian Dury and the Blockheads. Suffered from bipolar disorder and committed suicide in 1983.

6 David Gentleman, English artist, illustrator and designer, studied at the Royal College of Art under Edward Bawden.

7 Grapus, radical French collective of graphic artists working between 1970 and 1991. Founded by Pierre Bernard, François Miehe and Gérard Paris-Clavel, they met during the student movement of May 1968 and were influenced by the Situationist International.

8 Studio Dumbar, highly regarded Dutch studio established in 1977 by Gert Dumbar.

9 Wim Crouwel, Dutch graphic designer and typographer. Best known for his posters and exhibition design for the Stedelijk Museum in Amsterdam and for his font design. Founder member of Total Design.

10 Ben Bos, Dutch designer and first employee of Total Design. Wrote the foreword to this book (see page 8).

11 Mary Vieira (1927–2001), Brazilian graphic designer and educator.

12 Jan van Toorn, Dutch graphic designer. Since 1957, van Toorn's work has been informed by his interest in visual meaning and the social role of the designer.

13 Benno Wissing (1923–2008), painter, graphic designer, architect, industrial designer and one of the founders of Total Design.

14 Dieter Roth (1930–1998), Swiss-German artist known for his artist's books, sculptures and pictures made with rotting food.

15 Karl Gerstner, Swiss graphic designer, studied under Emil Ruder and Armin Hofmann. Formed Gerstner, Gredinger and Kutter (GGK). Currently works solo in Switzerland.

16 Wolfgang Weingart, German-born graphic designer and typographer, widely credited as 'the father' of New Wave typography. Published My Way to Typography in 2000.

17 Tweaking, cricketing term meaning to give extra spin to the ball.

18 Eames, famous US product design studio formed by Charles Eames (1907–1978) and his wife, Ray (1912–1988). They designed furniture, toys, films, exhibitions and buildings.

19 Vitsoe, celebrated furniture design company founded in 1959 to realize the furniture designs of Dieter Rams. The proposition was to create long-lasting, down-to-earth furniture. Vitsoe shelving is famous the world over.

20 www.spotify.com.

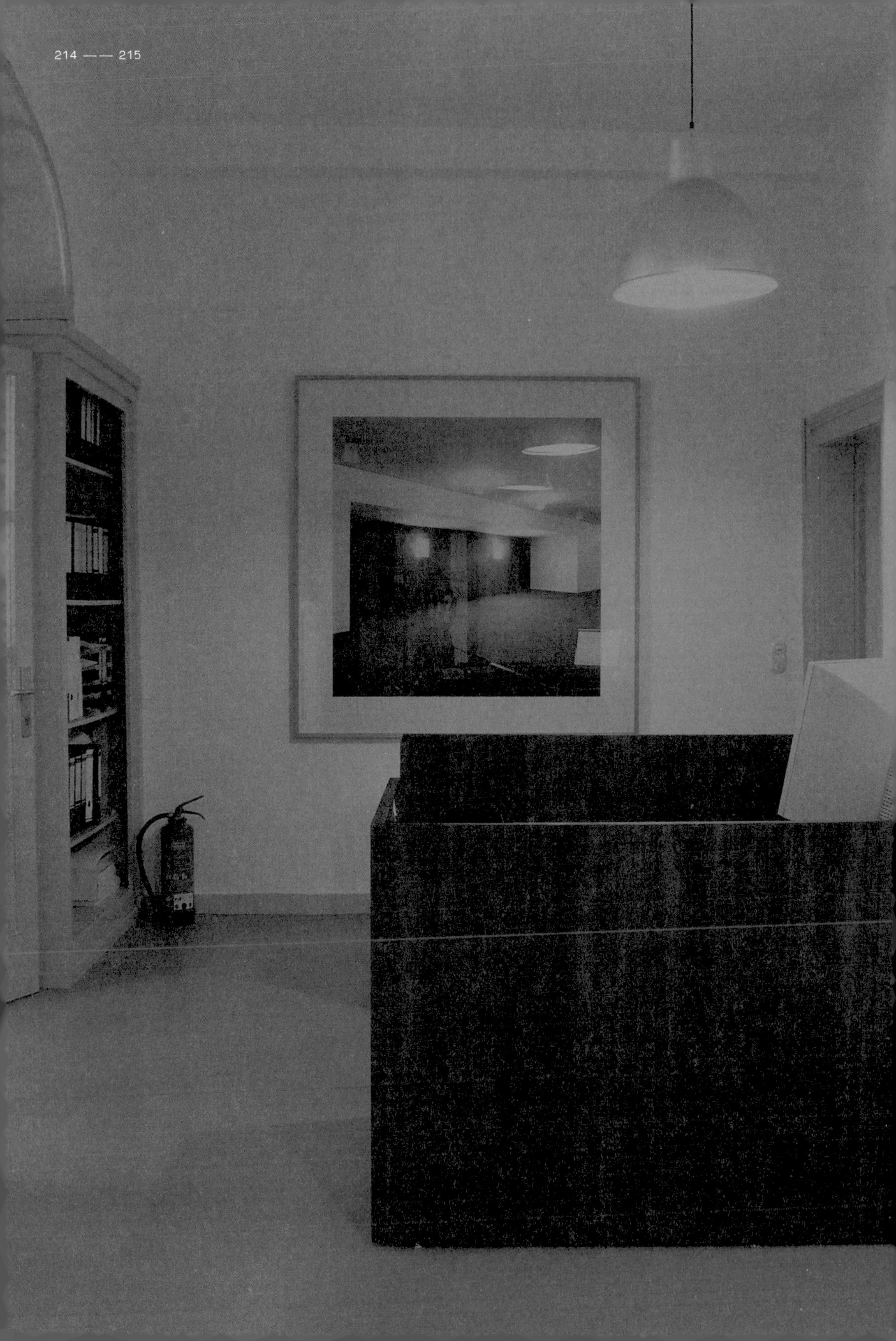

Surface
Founded: 1997
Personnel: 10
Location: Frankfurt and Berlin, Germany
www.surface.de

Markus Weisbeck runs Surface. The company
has two locations: Frankfurt (where it does
mainly publishing-based work) and its main
office in Berlin (where it works for both
cultural and commercial clients).

Since its inception in 1997, Surface has
worked almost principally in contemporary
art, the performing arts, architecture and
music. The studio defines its conceptual
approach as 'without exception, dependent
on the content of the inquiries and subjects
are developed accordingly, in order to avoid
style arbitrariness.' This avoidance of style
arbitrariness can be seen in the group's
measured and carefully modulated work.
Everything they do is hallmarked by the
attention lavished on the smallest details.

Clients who appreciate Surface's
trademark thoroughness include the
Serpentine Gallery, London; Zumtobel AG;
Hugo Boss; BMW; Sternberg Press; Jewish
Museum Berlin; DuMont Press; Manifesa;
Siemens Art Program; Documenta; Jewish
Museum and Frankfurt Historical Museum.

The interview was conducted via email.
—

How would you characterize German graphic
design studios?

Markus Weisbeck: In German graphic design
there is the history of the Hochschule
für Gestaltung in Ulm (1953–1968), where
you can find Otl Aicher[1] and his students,
and later, Rolf Müller[2], co-designer for the
Olympic games in Munich 1972. More or
less at the same time we had the Kasseler
Schule (Kassel School) running in parallel
to the first Documenta exhibitions, with
Hans Leistikow[3] as their first teacher, and
educated designers like Hans Hillmann[4],
Gunter Rambow[5] or Jan Lenica[6]. In the former
GDR (German Democratic Republic), there was
the HGB Leipzig (Academie of Visual Arts) with
Albert Kapr[7] and in Berlin Weissensee Klaus
Wittkugel[8]. Most of these graphic artists ran
independent design studios, some throughout
the late 1970s, and some that have lasted
until the present day. 'Ulm-Thinking' is still
alive in many schools and studios, especially
in music and its visual culture over the last
years. But also because of the popularity
of German contemporary art, small design
studios have designed exhibition catalogues,
websites and posters.

Can you describe your early history and what
led you to start your studio?

During my studies in Offenbach (near

Frankfurt), I started to design flyers and record sleeves for clubs, warehouse parties and DJs. At this time, in the early days of the worldwide web (Mosaic/Netscape), two friends and I bid for the design of the website of a huge chemical company and they actually gave us the job. At that time no one had any idea how much to charge for this type of work, so they paid us something and I founded Surface.

Were there studios you admired and wanted to emulate?

Before I started my studies, I was in art school in Stuttgart. My colleague and best friend at the time had this famous Luxemburg graphic design dad, Dieter Wagner, who gave us 1960s Graphis Yearbooks from Switzerland. They contained works from Massimo Vignelli[9], Paul Rand[10], Josef Müller-Brockmann[11], Ladislav Sutnar[12] and Alvin Lustig[13]. Later, I tried to make an exchange with the Academy of Art in Warsaw, Poland, where I tried to find the roots of the Polish Poster School like Roman Cieslewicz[14] or Henryk Tomaszewski[15]. But even in the early 1990s, I was ten years too late.

Can you talk about the early days of Surface – did you have to borrow money?

Our first studio was a former garage for newspaper trucks. The photographer who had redesigned the space as a photography studio had forgotten to allow for the circulation of air. Every morning we had to exchange the air in our 'garage-room' by using a huge perpendicular ventilator so that we could breathe – so before that, everyone had to lock down every single piece of paper on their desks. During this time we realized several campaigns for the Deutsche Guggenheim in Berlin for artists such as Dan Flavin[16], Rachel Whiteread[17] and Gerhard Richter[18], and some artworks for Sven Väth[19] releases.

Surface is not an obviously German name. Why did you choose it?

In the beginning, a lot of jobs had to do with interface design, the surface of the web.

You run Surface without any business partners. Did you consider using your own name as the studio's name?

In the beginning we worked with teams on websites and other new media products with programmers etc, so I thought it's more elegant with an artificial studio name.

There are advantages in not having partners. For example, you don't have to agree everything with someone else. Yet sometimes having another person to share problems with can be helpful. Does being the sole person in charge ever become a strain?

01 |
02 |
03 |

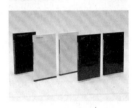

01/ Project: Pocket Book Series.
Date: 2007. Client: Johnen + Schöttle.
Designer: Markus Weisbeck.
02/ Project: März–Wir sind hier.
Date: 2006. Client: Karaoke Kalk.
Designers: Indra Häussler, Markus Weisbeck. Photographer/
Illustrator: Markus Weisbeck.
03/ Project: Pocket Book Series.
Date: 2001. Client: SternbergPress.
Designer: Markus Weisbeck.
04/ Project: Johann König–Advertisement.
Date: 2006. Client: Johann König.
Designer: Markus Weisbeck.
05/ Project: Anniversary Poster.
Date: 2007. Client: raster-noton.
Designer: Markus Weisbeck.

There is a lot of discussion in our studio and also criticism about wrong design decisions during our testing of how a specific idea should work. This also includes my work.

Tell me about the designers you employ. Do they stay with you for long periods or do you have a high turnover of staff?

We have designers who've been with Surface from nearly the beginning, and other who have been here for only two or three years. Often this has to do with moving to another city or country.

What is the secret of being a good employer of creative talent?

Playing a fair ping-pong game of ideas and giving credit of authorship to the individual designers in the studio.

Designers are often ambitious. They want to be credited for the work they do and many of them want to start their own studios. How do you deal with ambition among the Surface designers?

We credit the individual designers in larger productions like books or campaigns.

If I were to ask the Surface designers what they thought about working life at Surface, what do you hope they would say?

A kind of family sentiment with the daily discussion of which radio station we should tune into.

You have offices in Frankfurt and Berlin. Does having two locations cause any problems? What are the benefits?

Frankfurt is our head office. Berlin works in close contact and collaboration with the publisher SternbergPress, which moved from New York City to Berlin some years ago. In Berlin we work mainly on contemporary art projects.

Do you spend time in both studios?

Sure, up to four days a month, especially after I return from Weimar where I have a temporary teaching job.

Tell me how the studios are structured. Do you have account handlers and administration staff as well as designers?

Myself and a colleague do these jobs mostly.

Many studios – often highly creative ones – neglect administration and financial control in favour of creativity. Where do you stand on this?

It also took us a while to understand these facts. Now, we are working with a very simple

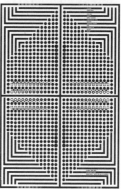

06 | 07 |

08 | 09 |
10 | 11 |

06/ Project: Liam Gillick, German Pavilion, Venice Biennale 2009. Date: 2009.
Client: Institute for Foreign Cultural Relations. Designers: Markus Weisbeck, Liam Gillick.
Photographer: Jörg Baumann. 07/ Project: The Forsythe Company, Campaign 2007/2008.
Date: 2007–2008. Client: The Forsythe Company. Designers: Katrin Tüffers, Markus
Weisbeck. Photographer: Dominik Mentzos. Illustrator: Katrin Tüffers, Markus Weisbeck.
08/ Project: Manifesta 7. Date: 2008. Client: Manifesta–International Foundation.
Designers: Oliver Kuntsche, Pascal Kress, Max Nestor, Markus Weisbeck.
09/ Project: The Forsythe Company, Campaign 2007/2008. Date: 2008–2009.
Client: The Forsythe Company. Designers: Finn Sienknecht, Katrin Tüffers, Markus
Weisbeck. Photographer: Dominik Mentzos. 10/ Project: Isa Genzken–Oil, German Pavilion,
Venice Biennale 2007. Date: 2007. Client: Institute for Foreign Cultural Relations.
Designer: Markus Weisbeck. Photographer: Jörg Baumann. 11/ Project: Public Lecture
Series 2008–2009. Date: 2008. Client: Städelschule Architecture Class. Designers: Max
Nestor, Markus Weisbeck. Photographer: Filippo Lodi.

Deutscher Pavillon
53. Esposizione Internazionale d'Arte
La Biennale di Venezia 2009

MANIFESTA7

LA BIENNALE EUROPEA
DI ARTE CONTEMPORANEA
DIE EUROPÄISCHE BIENNALE
FÜR ZEITGENÖSSISCHE KUNST
TRENTINO-ALTO ADIGE/SÜDTIROL
19.07.–02.11.2008

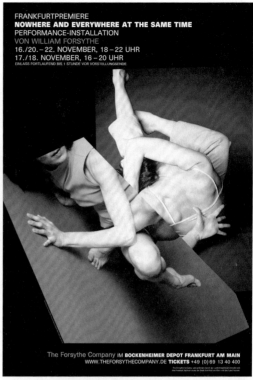

FRANKFURTPREMIERE
NOWHERE AND EVERYWHERE AT THE SAME TIME
PERFORMANCE-INSTALLATION
VON WILLIAM FORSYTHE
16./20.–22. NOVEMBER, 18–22 UHR
17./18. NOVEMBER, 16–20 UHR
EINLASS FORTLAUFEND BIS 1 STUNDE VOR VORSTELLUNGSENDE

The Forsythe Company IM **BOCKENHEIMER DEPOT FRANKFURT AM MAIN**
WWW.THEFORSYTHECOMPANY.DE **TICKETS** +49 (0) 69 13 40 400

Isa Genzken
Oil
German Pavilion
Venice Biennale 2007

but effective in-house control system to deal with hours of individual work and general project management.

Do you foresee a time when you will employ project managers and account handlers?

Maybe when we've grown substantially in the future.

A lot of your work is for cultural institutions — do you also have commercial clients? If so, what is the difference between the two?

Communication should be much more abstract with commercial clients. Every argument should be vague rather than exact. This way there's enough space for their own 'ideas', and then they can sell it much better to the next-level decider. When you work with artists it's the opposite, as they allow you to work on your own ideas.

How do you balance commercial demands with the need to maintain high creative standards? Or, to put it another way, is creativity ever compromised by the need to make money?

I really work at getting the job done without any antagonism. Maybe we are too naive to distress ourselves with our design transfers and our specific formal and conceptional methods of communication.

Is your physical environment important to you? Did you have any help with space planning and interior design?

We realized the studio with a young interior designer (Johannes Fuchs) who is also a close friend of the studio.

Otl Aicher has written that a communal workspace is essential for a design studio. Do you have an open-plan studio or are there places for private work?

Exactly, Mr. Aicher. We need these open spaces.

Tell me how you promote the studio.

Mostly with the graphic designs as reference, and at the end of 2009 a new book will be released.

Can you talk about the book? Will it be self-published or will it have a commercial publisher? Is its aim to promote the studio?

The book will be part of the Lukas&Sternberg pocket series, which we designed nine years ago. It will be a documentation of a dozen different art projects with short statements from the originators about the individual performance of the designs.

If I was a potential client looking at Surface, how would you describe the company?

We have a conceptual design approach, which is without exception, dependent on the content of the inquiries, and subjects are developed accordingly in order to avoid style arbitrariness.

Your website offers an English-language version — why is this?

We also work on projects in Italy, the UK, and the US.

Is this unusual for German design groups to work abroad?

Absolutely, several studios I know do it in a similar way.

Do you enter design competitions and awards schemes?

We've never had the money to spend on something like a 'steel nail in a plexicube' trophy, where you must communicate this benefit to your client, who is hopefully interested in this information. When we have money left over we spend it on the production of a new release for our in-house record label Whatness.

Can you tell me about your record label?

Whatness is an audio gallery founded in 2000 with the aim of combining structures of the visual and musical arts. Internationally renowned artists such as Liam Gillick[20], Joseph Suchy[21], Frank Bretschneider[22], Stephen Galloway[23], Markus Schmickler[24], Ekkehard Ehlers[25], William Forsythe[26], Olafur Eliasson[27] and Peter Röhr[28] present their own works as entirely autonomous artistic positions. The fusion of these positions into a project especially created for Whatness generates an expansion of the original media and explores the possibilities of an exchange between art and music by various means, such as graphic notation, instrument-making and vocal art. The respective collaborations are then published as a CD.

What are your long-term aims for Surface?

a.) Combining specific art forms as geared elements into corporate design projects (a bit like a vague translation of the John Stezaker[29] way of transforming library image-material into new images).
b.) Editing a revolved version of 'Vision in Motion', the exposition masterpiece of movement and velocity from László Moholy-Nagy[30], Chicago 1947.
c.) A typeface.

1 Otl Aicher (1922–1991), leading German graphic designer. Co-founded the Hochschule für Gestaltung in Ulm (Ulm School of Design) in 1953. Best known for work as head designer for the 1972 Munich Olympics and creating the first Olympic mascot.

2 Rolf Müller, studied at the Hochschule für Gestaltung in Ulm. He went to Munich in 1967 to work on the design of the 1972 Olympic Games with Otl Aicher.

3 Hans Leistikow (1892–1962), German graphic designer during the Bauhaus period. Known for his cover designs for the periodical *Das neue Frankfurt*.

4 Hans Hillmann, German designer of movie posters.

5 Gunter Rambow, German designer with the Rambow & Lienemeyer graphic design studio. Pupil of Hillmann.

6 Jan Lenica (1928–2001), Polish designer and animator.

7 Albert Kapr (1918–1995), German calligrapher, book and type designer.

8 Klaus Wittkugel (1910–1985) German graphic designer and poster artist.

9 Massimo Vignelli, Italian-born designer, founded Vignelli Associates, working for clients such as IBM and American Airlines.

10 Paul Rand (1914–1996), American graphic designer, best known for his corporate logo designs.

11 Josef Müller-Brockmann (1914–1996), highly influential Swiss graphic designer. Founding editor of *Neue Grafik* (*New Graphic Design*).

12 Ladislav Sutnar (1897–1976), Czech-born designer. First to design what has since been called 'information design'.

13 Alvin Lustig (1915–1955), American graphic designer and typeface designer. He went blind from diabetes in 1954.

14 Roman Cieslewicz (1930–1996), celebrated Polish poster artist. Studied at the Academy of Fine Arts in Cracow.

15 Henryk Tomaszewski (1914–2005), Polish poster artist. Studied and later became professor at Warsaw Academy of Fine Arts.

16 Dan Flavin (1933–1996), American minimalist artist. Noted for his installation works using fluorescent lights.

17 Rachel Whiteread, British artist. First woman to win the Turner Prize. Best known for her works *Ghost* and *House*.

18 Gerhard Richter, German artist credited with rejuvenating painting as a medium at a time when many artists chose performance and ready-made media.

19 Sven Vath, German DJ. Trance music pioneer.

20 Liam Gillick, British artist, critic, curator, designer, and writer. Works include public projects, critical and theoretical writings, design objects and graphic materials, films and musical scores.

21 Joseph Suchy, Cologne-based experimental guitarist. Worked with Ekkehard Ehlers, among others.

22 Frank Bretschneider, German electronic musician. Founded the Rastermusic record label in 1995, eventually merging to become Raster-Noton.

23 Stephen Galloway, American choreographer and artist.

24 Markus Schmickler, German electronic musician.

25 Ekkehard Ehlers, electronic musician. In 2001 began producing singles in honour of his heroes including John Cassavetes and Cornelius Cardew.

26 William Forsythe, American dancer and choreographer.

27 Olafur Eliasson, Danish-Icelandic artist. Created a number of projects in public areas.

28 Peter Röhr (1944–1968), one of the first German minimal artists.

29 John Stezaker, British artist working with images found in books, magazines, postcards and encyclopaedias.

30 László Moholy-Nagy (1895–1946), celebrated Hungarian photographer and painter. Professor at the Bauhaus school.

Tassinari/Vetta
Founded: 2003 (current formation)
Personnel: 10 plus interns
Location: Trieste, Italy
www.sonnoli.com

Leonardo Sonnoli's work is remarkable for its
graphic precision and visual dexterity. Born
in Trieste, Italy, in 1962, he founded CODEsign
with Paolo Tassinari and Pierpaolo Vetta in
2002. He is currently a partner in Tassinari/
Vetta, where he works on the visual identity of
private and public companies. He specializes
in cultural events, book design, signage
and exhibitions graphics. His work has been
exhibited in numerous exhibitions, and his
posters – for which he is widely acknowledged
as a modern master – are collected in several
public and private collections.

Sonnoli has always combined professional
practice with teaching. He lectures at the
Faculty of Design and Arts of the IUAV
University of Venice and at the ISIA (High
Institute of Industrial Arts), Urbino. He lives
in Rimini and works at the Tassinari/Vetta
studio in Trieste.

Sonnoli is a member of AGI (Alliance
Graphique Internationale.) He is the body's
Italian president.

The interview was conducted via email.
—

Tell me about your background?

Leonardo Sonnoli: I started to study graphic
design when I was 20. The reason I started
late was that in Italy there was only one
school teaching graphic design. It was in Isia
in Urbino, in the middle of Italy, and difficult
to get to. I was really poor, and shared my
bedroom with rats, rain and cockroaches. But
I wanted to continue to study, so for about
two years I studied history of art at my local
university in Trieste in the north of Italy. To
get money I worked as a bartender, theatre
usher and delivering flowers for a shop. Then
I sat the exam for Isia in Urbino and was
accepted for a four-year course in graphic
design. After two years I was called up into
the army. But I refused to go, so I did civilian
service instead at a place close to Trieste.
In this period I knew Paolo Tassinari and
Pierpaolo Vetta (both seven years older than
me), who were working as graphic designers
in Trieste. Their studio was called Tassinari/
Vetta and they offered me an internship.
Working for them for a few months I learnt
more about graphic design than I did during
two years at school.

What happened when you finally graduated?

When I finished my studies at the school,
I continued to work with Paolo and Pierpaolo.
As well as learning from them, I developed an
interest in design history and criticism. We

also became good friends. After two years
I needed another experience so I accepted
an offer from the studio of Massimo Dolcini[1],
a well-known Italian designer, based in
Pesaro, in central Italy. His way of thinking
about design was different from mine. But he
offered me a job as art director of a 10–12-
people design studio. For me, this was an
opportunity to concentrate only on design
matters, and not to get involved in managing
the studio and the clients.

How long were you there?

I worked with Massimo Dolcini for 11 years.
Over time it became more and more difficult,
and in 2002 I was fired, mainly because of the
economic crisis at the time. I was immediately
asked to join the Tassinari/Vetta office. In
2003 my mentor and closest friend Pierpaolo
Vetta died, and I decided to buy a little part
of his shareholding. So I became a partner
in the Tassinari/Vetta studio.

Independent-minded graphic designers
can often benefit from working in large,
professional, business-focused studios.
It gives them a good grounding for when they
want to branch out on their own. Do you think
your 11 years with Massimo Dolcini prepared
you well for becoming a partner in
Tassinari/Vetta?

The fact that I mainly concentrated on design
in the Dolcini office helped me grow as a
designer and taught me, as an art director,
how to manage lots of people working on
several projects at the same time. On
the other hand I didn't learn much about
managing an office. When I became a partner
I was probably better known as a designer
than Tassinari and Vetta, but not so well
prepared for the task of managing a studio.

The studio name is Tassinari/Vetta, but you
also use the names CODEsign, COdesign and
codeSIGN. Can you explain this?

Tassinari/Vetta are the names of the two
founders. The company has never changed
its name. When I joined we decided to sign our
work with another name (codesign), but from a
legal point of view the company doing the work
was Tassinari/Vetta.

Have you ever thought about incorporating
your own name into the studio name?

I wanted to change the studio's name to
indicate my presence in it, but my proposal
was not accepted.

Why do you think there was a reluctance to
change the name? Was it because any sort
of name change is commercially risky?

I think there were a number of reasons. I
proposed different solutions but none were
accepted. It was clear that Paolo Tassinari

01 |
02 |
03 |

01/02/03/ Project: Poster series.
Date: 2003–2005. Client: Conservatorio
Giuseppe Tartini, Trieste.

wanted to maintain the status quo even if the studio changed radically. I think this was more emotional than rational. It was not a commercial decision, because often my name is better known than the founders. But I was forced to accept the decision. Because of this I often add my name to the office signature.

How is your studio organized?

Besides Paolo Tassinari and me, we have two people doing organization, archiving and administration, and we have six designers and usually two or three interns.

You don't live near the studio, though, do you?

I live 400 kilometers from the studio, so I'm there more or less two days a week. I'm usually working in a tiny office in Rimini connected with the studio in Trieste via Skype or mobile.

Are there times when it is frustrating to work remotely, or do you like the sense of being one step removed?

It's not easy to manage it. First, to work with the studio mainly through phone calls is different from speaking with people and looking into their eyes. Second, a long drive is very tiring.

Well, I've got to ask you, why don't you live closer to the studio?

I often ask myself this question. The true reason is probably deeply personal and would need psychoanalysis. But more practically, my wife has her own office in Rimini and looking after my two children is easier in Rimini, where we have a good quality of life.

Can you describe your studio – its layout, its furniture, its features?

The office is located in the centre of the city, along a small canal, 200 meters from the waterfront. The building is in neoclassical style, being built in the nineteenth century in the period when Trieste was an Austro-Hungarian city. The apartment is quite large. The main space is devoted to the designers working on several tables arranged as a big island. In the same room there is a glassed-off area hosting the administration department. Another room is used for me and my partner, and also as a meeting room. There is a kitchen and a space used for archiving and as a workshop.

Did you have any professional help with the interior space?

The office has been designed in collaboration with an architect. The tables, the closets and the doors are made in dark red MDF; tables are made in white Corian. The floor is partly in wood and partly in black slate. Most of the table lamps are the Artemide De Lucchi's Tolomeo.

How important is the physical environment you work in?

Really important. But what I see out of the window is equally important.

Do you own the studio, or rent it?

We have a mortgage, mainly to buy the place and to pay for its restoration.

Can you define your role within Tassinari/Vetta

Paolo and I manage the clients, and we take the key design decisions. We decide which designers work on which projects, and who among the assistants gets to follow the work through. Often we work together on one project. For example, I might design the typographic part, and Paolo its applications.

Does your work as a teacher affect the running of the studio?

I try to manage my role as a teacher in Venice and Urbino as part of my studio work. In fact, it forms part of my income. Of course, the lectures and workshops I do around the world (mainly for free, only with travel reimbursement) affect my work in terms of the time I'm able to dedicate to design. On the other hand, it's a way to be stimulated and to learn something new.

Could you tell me about the type of clients you have?

They are publishing houses, public institutions, museums, art galleries, theatre and music festivals.

Could you talk about how you find new clients?

Usually clients knock on the door.

Clients knocking on the door! That's what every designer dreams of. But is it really that simple? Surely you must do some promotional work: do you send new work to magazines? Do you enter design competitions? Do you have a portfolio? How much care and attention do you put into your website?

Yes, it should be a dream, but it can also be a nightmare. Usually clients arrive because they know your work. So, for example, if you work for furniture companies, you are less likely to be asked to do an identity for a museum or to design an exhibition. In a way you get labelled. As regards promotion, I submit work to competitions and sometimes magazines ask me to send them some work. But this is done more

04 | 05 | 06 |
07 | 08 |
09 | 10 |

04/ Project: Bunker book. Date: 2006. Client: Guido Guidi, Photographer.
05/ Project: Essays book series. Date: 2007. Client: Mondadori Electa, Milano, with Igor Bevilacqua. 06/ Project: Pesci Rossi book series. Date: 2006. Client: Mondadori Electa, Milano. 07/ Project: Fiori Blu book series. Date: 2008. Client: Mondadori Electa, Milano.
08/ Project: Identity/communication material. Richard Long installation. Date: 2008. Client: Palazzo Riso Museo d'Arte Contemporanea della Sicilia, Palermo (Sicily).
09/ Project: Catalogues, Eliseo Mattiacci/Annamaria e Marzio Sala. Date: 2006. Client: Museo d'Arte Moderna of Rovereto, Rovereto. 10/ Project: Freedom and Order poster. Date: 2008. Client: Tassinari/Vetta Studio. 11/ Project: Berlin Poster. Date: 2005. Client: AGI. 12/14/ Project: Book, Luciano Baldessarri, la Breda e la Fiera di Milano. Date: 2009. Client: Mondadori Electa, Milano, with Paolo Tassinari.
13/ Project: Identity/communication material. Date: 2008. Client: Palazzo Riso Museo d'Arte Contemporanea della Sicilia, Palermo (Sicily), with Lucia Pasqualin.

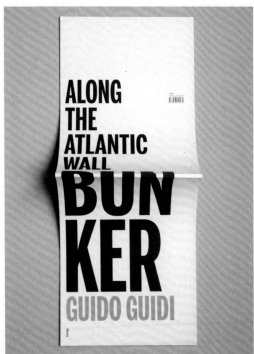

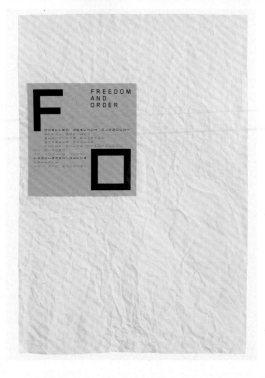

as an individual, and not as a studio (even if the name of the studio is always quoted). Of course, competitions and magazines increase your popularity with other designers and not among new clients. We don't have a portfolio and we don't have a website. I have my personal website used mainly to share files with my students.

Let's talk about employing people. It's often the most difficult aspect of running a studio. You have to constantly look after the welfare of others, and you have to keep them motivated and inspired. How do you go about this?

I think it's important that people see you as a model, as a point of reference. They have to really want to work with you. It's a matter of esteem. Unfortunately I'm not in the office often, but I speak with everyone by phone and not only about work, but about the lectures I give, and the ones that I attend, and about the international designers I know. We also organize exhibitions and lectures in the studio.

What qualities do you look for when employing a designer?

I need people who are very passionate about design, and who are interested in graphic design culture. It's not important whether a designer is talented or not. It's more important that he or she is interested in working together and in learning continuously. Another important thing is the reliability of people, and their ability to organize the work and to have relationships with the clients and suppliers.

OK – this is a big question. Are you saying that you are only interested in employing designers who will comply with your vision?

If by the word 'vision' you mean having the same ideas of work as relating to history, and designing with the goal of timelessness and appropriateness, then I'd answer yes. Everyone should have their own knowledge, but I'm not interested in developing our work in a fashionable way.

What is your approach to designers who want a sense of personal authorship?

I ask them more to follow my ideas, even if in a free way. I love my work and I like to direct the creativity.

Do you have a profit-sharing policy?

No, usually we don't. We sometimes reward those who have worked harder than usual.

15 |
16 |
17 |
18 |

15/16/ Project: Identity/exhibition graphics/signage, Eros, The Love God. Colosseo, Rome, with Francesco Nicoletti. Date: 2007. Client: Archeological Office of Rome.
17/18/ Project: Typographic installation, Grassitypographicalassemblage, Palazzo Grassi, Venice. Date: 2007. Client: Palazzo Grassi, with Francesco Nicoletti

Do you socialize together?

I'm not in the office very often, as I've said. But when I stay there I'll have dinner with some of them. In the summer it's easier, because we go for a drink or have dinner outside.

Do you have formal rules about things like timekeeping and so on?

We usually start at 9.00am. We have a lunch break at 1.00–1.30pm and half the people eat in the studio in our kitchen (especially in the winter). We stop around 7.00pm, but often two or three people remain till late. To keep the kitchen clean we use a dishwasher and throw out the garbage.

How do you maintain the balance between creativity and profitability?

In the majority of the works the two things are not connected.

Perhaps I need to rephrase the question. Is the studio's work ever compromised by the need to make a profit? By this I mean, do you have projects that don't turn out the way you want them to and result in you doing work that is purely for the money? Or are you saying this never happens?

Any recrimination on bad clients is useless. But to go back to your question, sometimes we understand immediately that some work will not result in a good design, but we accept it for the budget. But also these are works made in the correct way. I mean that they are designed in an anonymous way instead of being badly designed.

What about the opposite scenario – are there times when you do work that is not profitable, but you do it because it is the sort of work you enjoy doing?

Yes, it happens. I include in this kind of work all the lectures/workshops/juries I do abroad. And the time I spend with my students away from the school. Often they come to my home, to visit my library and to discuss things with me. All these activities are completely not profitable in term of money, but are greatly profitable in term of professional and personal development.

How does a young designer go about getting an internship at Tassinari/Vetta?

While teaching I often receive requests for internships from my students and I'm lucky to be able to take on designers who I know. Usually we take three interns a year. Sometimes we receive requests from other schools and from abroad. We look at all the portfolios sent to us, and in some cases we offer internships. Because interns usually come from other cities and other countries, we give them a small fee, around half the salary of a designer. For a few years I paid interns in the equivalent value in books, because an internship is not for profit but to learn more.

If you could start all over again, what would you do differently?

Maybe I'd try to have an experience abroad.

How would you define your studio's culture today?

The studio's culture corresponds mainly to me and my partner's professional culture and knowledge. We have worked in the field of traditional graphic design, often for cultural clients. In my case I think my knowledge of the international scene influences our studio's culture.

1 Massimo Dolcini (1945–2005), Italian graphic designer and founder of Dolcini Associati.

Thirst
Founded: 1988
Personnel: 4, plus interns
Location: Chicago, US
www.3st.com

Rick Valicenti's work fizzes with a uniquely American energy. His work – and the work of his studio – is as American as the Chicago skyscrapers that distinguish the city where Valicenti is based. He says that his studio is dedicated to 'art, with function and real human presence'. He is the recipient of countless awards including the American Institute of Graphic Artists (AIGA) Medal in 2006 – the highest honour in the American graphic design profession.

Valicenti is a member of AGI (Alliance Graphique Internationale). His work is included in the permanent collections of the Art Institute of Chicago, the Cooper-Hewitt National Design Museum and the Denver Art Museum. He is also a teacher. For the past two decades he has given his time and energies to college and high school students in the form of lectures, workshops and personal critiques on the design industry. In 2004, a 356-page monograph on Thirst work was published by the Monacelli Press, entitled *Emotion as Promotion*.

The interview was conducted via email.
–

At what stage in your career did the urge to have a studio hit you? Was it there from the start?

Rick Valicenti: Twenty years ago, Thirst was founded on the desire to pursue 'art with function'. When I went on my own in 1981, I was a relatively fresh designer, president of the STA (Society of Typographic Arts) and a new father with a desire to be certain that a paycheck was regular. It took roughly six years for me to discover and come to understand that there is a thin line and a big difference between being a designer who is a preferred vendor and a designer who has a consultant's seat at the table. In 1988 I no longer wanted to be the preferred vendor. It was this motivation and clear image of the creative life I wanted to design that Thirst came to be.

You are well known under your own name, but your studio is called Thirst, which suggests a collective rather than solo approach. Outsiders might imagine that Thirst works to your agenda, but you refer to Thirst as a 'design collaborative'. What does this mean?

The output of Thirst is a reflection of those with whom I share my life's work. While I am the reason opportunities arrive, I share the process with those who have exemplary and unique talents.

There are three names on the website –
Rick Valicenti, John Pobojewski and
Bud Rodecker – can you explain the
relationship here?

These are the individuals with whom I share
studio time with. John and I have been working
together for over four years, and Bud, our
intern two years ago, was invited to stay.

Is a shared vision essential or are
divergences useful among studio personnel?

Individuals are just that. Everyone sees
the world through their own filter(s), and
when they enter the studio I encourage
each member to share their perspectives.
The ideation of Thirst work originates
conceptually with me, and because presence
is catalytic, the process and artefact of our
thinking and making has evidence of
my curation.

Can you tell me about the internal structure
of Thirst? Number of designers? Number of
support staff and so on?

In addition to the three of us, who
work very closely together in a campfire
arrangement, we are blessed by my sister
Barbara's presence. She is our business
manager and gatekeeper. We bring into the
studio programmers, industrial designers,
architects, printers, artists, and of course
clients.

What qualities do you look for in the designers
you hire?

Reasonable talent, a manageable ego, and
good character – period. I suppose good
hygiene too!

You teach and lecture extensively – do you
see it as part of your job to nurture and
develop the talent you employ/work with/hire?

That is a good question, as I am forever the
mentor of design. It happens with the clients
I collaborate with as much as it does with
those whose path braids with mine. While I am
a gentle and supportive pedant, I am always
conscious of my role.

I recently spoke to someone who runs a
successful studio and he told me that he
likes employing designers who ultimately want
to run their own studios. He knows they will
leave him at some point, but while they are
with him, he benefits from their drive. Where
do you stand on the question of ambitious
designers?

I too am ambitious… ambition, however, is not
the secret to being a successful employee
or employer. I would say for me one needs to
be ready to practise (seduction), represent
presence, indulge knowingly, serve happiness,
and master humility.

01 |
02 |

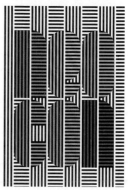

01/ Project: Richard Marx Event Poster.
Date: 2008. Client: Zacharias Sexual
Abuse Center. Art Director: Rick Valicenti.
Designer: Bud Rodecker.
02/ NeoCon 2009. Date: 2009.
Client: Merchandise Mart Properties, Inc.
Designers: Rick Valicenti, Bud Rodecker.
03/04/05/06/ Project: UV/TV/RV.
Date: 2008. Client: Classic-Color.
Designer: Rick Valicenti.
Photographer: Tom Vack.

Is there room within Thirst for someone to follow their own vision, even if this runs against your instincts and tastes, or do you insist on adherence to your design vision?

At any given time, I am the one to initiate the (personal) professional curiosities that become the filter through which all Thirst design passes. There was a time when it was expressive typography, but since 1999 I have been consciously curious about design underscored and emboldened with 'real human presence'. Today that filter is evolving into an awareness of how we are crafting and shaping narratives in this post-medium time we live in. We are calling it storytelling and our experiments are in this realm.

How do you keep everyone motivated – or is that not an issue at Thirst?

Thirst is a campfire and if everyone does not contribute some wood to the fire, we will all soon be breathing and coughing in smoke. Simply by painting this picture and reminding everyone of our braided path, the privilege to sit by this fire is shared.

Do you have clearly defined rules about timekeeping and lunch breaks?

No...

What is your recruitment policy?

We do our share of due diligence and realize Thirst is not suited for every designer because we are either too small or too whatever. A designer's character is exhibited through their work. If the timing is right and our needs match their desire to enter the profession or to change their workplace, we will invite them to join us for three months before offering full-time employment.

Do you have a policy on interns?

We have had at least one intern every semester and often work closely with their school to ensure curriculum lessons and often ensure up to 12 credit hours. In addition, we pay a modest monthly stipend.

Can you talk about how you deal with the business side of the studio? How much of your time is spent overseeing balance sheets, sales projections, and the mundane stuff like rent and salary reviews?

Having a trusted business manager is heaven-sent and liberating. I closely review the status of business weekly and often multiple times during the week. We track and invoice time in 0.25-hour increments when we are not billing by value.

07 | 08 |

09 |

07/08/ Project: 2007/2008 and 2008/09 LOEB Fellowship Poster. Date: 2007 and 2008.
Client: Harvard University. Designers: John Pobojewski, Rick Valicenti. 09/ Project: AGI
Student Conference Poster. Date: 2008. Client: AGI. Designer: Rick Valicenti.

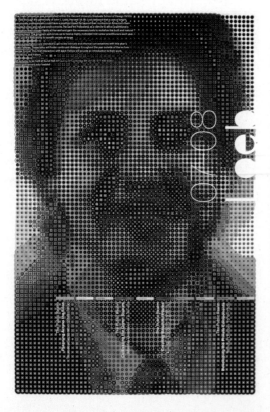

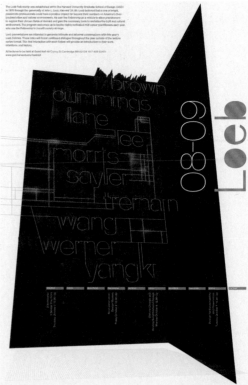

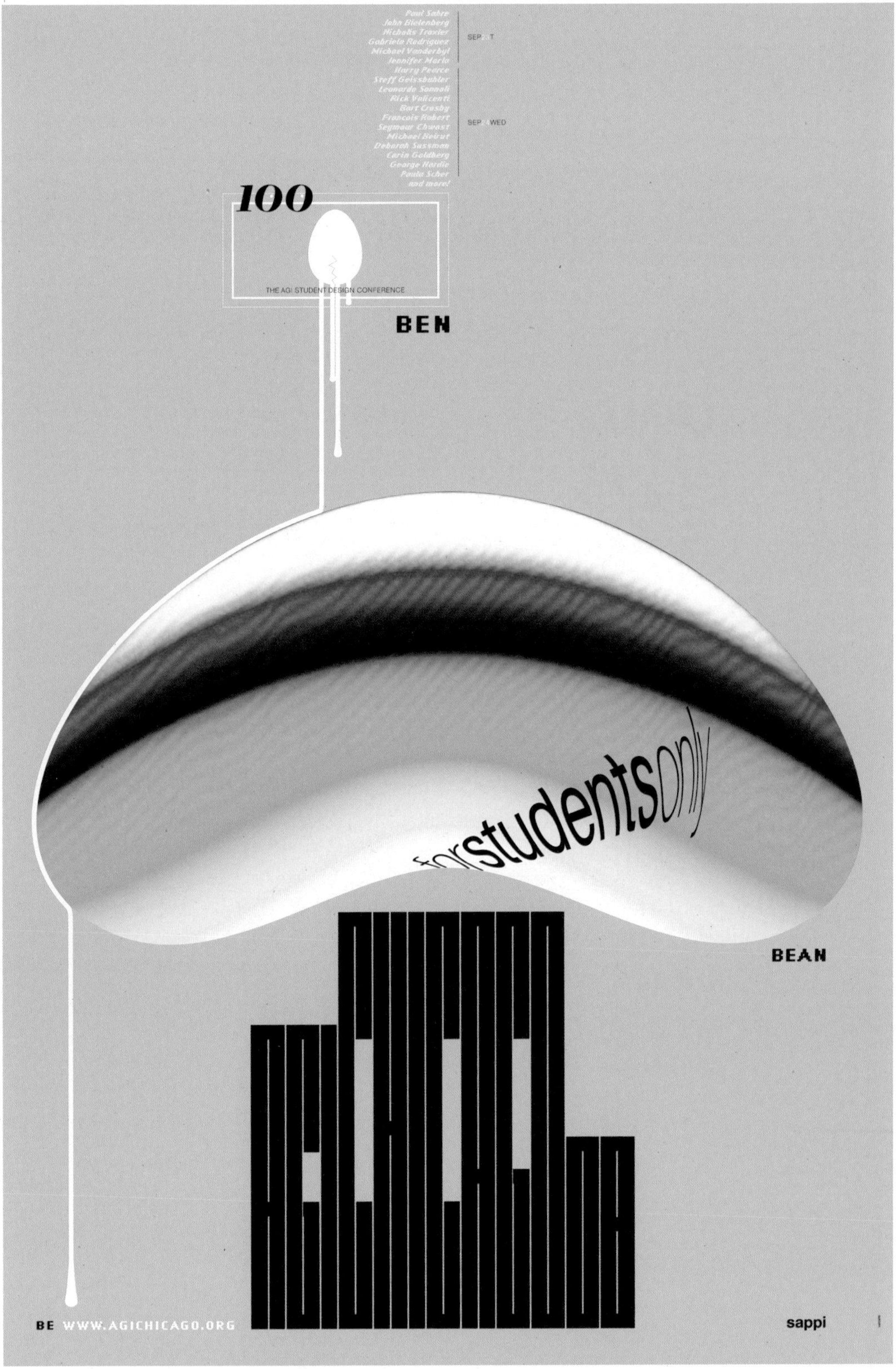
Paul Sahre
John Bielenberg
Nicholas Traxler
Gabriela Rodriguez
Michael Vanderbyl
Jennifer Morla
Harry Pearce
Steff Geissbuhler
Leonardo Sonnoli
Rick Valicenti
Bart Crosby
Francois Robert
Seymour Chwast
Michael Beirut
Deborah Sussman
Carin Goldberg
George Hardie
Paula Scher
and more!
SEP T
SEP WED
100
THE AGI STUDENT DESIGN CONFERENCE
BEN
forstudentsonly
BEAN
AGICHICAGO08
BE WWW.AGICHICAGO.ORG
sappi

10 |
11 |
12 |

10/11/12/ Project: Notes to Self.
Date: 2007–2008. Client: Self-initiated.
Art Director/Artist: Rick Valicenti.
Designer: Bud Rodecker.
Programmer: Robb Irrgang.

Where do you stand on the deep-rooted notion that designers don't make good businesspeople?

As you know, most don't make good businesspeople, only some do. Of those who do, some are exceptional... I have been personally very successful, but my success is not defined by my client list or my gross income. I have, however, put my two children through very expensive universities, and participated in the design of my time in practice.

You are based in Chicago – what impact does geography have on your business? For example, could you function just as well in another location?

There was a time in the late 1980s and early 90s when most of the Thirst work was coming from outside the US (from Japan and Germany) and the majority of the domestic work was from outside Chicago. Today, by design, I am interested in serving clients in Chicago or on other continents. There is a wealth of talent in other US cities, so unless the opportunity is exceptional, I have no desire to pass through airport security simply to go to Cleveland or Los Angeles.

Let's talk about your physical environment. Do you have a pristine white-walled studio, designer furniture, with a swish reception area?

No. When I go to visit other designers I like to imagine their overhead!

Thirst is located in the warehouse galleries of Wright Auctions, where each and every day we pass loading docks and open spaces littered with twentieth and twenty-first-century important furniture design and art. Our space is 2200 square feet with two large walls covered with design from living and dead master designers. The dense salon hanging is a reminder to us all that we practise in a continuum of design and designers. We have Lustig[1] next to Bass[2], Rand[3], Weingart[4], Gehry[5], Mau[6], Massey[7], Greiman[8], Sahre[9], Sagmeister[10], Bantjes[11], Fella[12], Victore[13], Pickleman[14], Glaser[15], Fairey[16] and Kalman[17]. All are signed originals, and many are one of a kind or of very limited editions.

Do you encourage clients to visit your studio?

Yes, both to work and socialize.

Is your studio open-plan? Do you have your own private area? Is an area for quiet study and thought necessary?

We work within a very open environment so when the music is on mute, the thinking goes deep... in fact right now it is very quiet but for the click of the Apple keyboards.

What about studio communal life – do you socialize? Do you do studio activities?

We have some socializing... among my younger collaborators, they enjoy each other's time outside of work. I discovered recently that as I got older, my collaborators have remained the same age as they were in 1981. Fortunately, I am young at heart and in spirit so I can sleep at night knowing I go to work in some surreal reverse Peter Pan world.

In 2004 you published a monograph – *Emotion as Promotion*. What effect did this have on your business? Did clients come flocking?

For the record, we did not receive one new business call as a result.

The same is true when I received the AIGA Chicago Fellow and the AIGA national medal. The same was true when I was inducted into the AGI. These successes and publications do more to stay within design's discourse than attract new business. I must say, however, to hear my existing clients boast that they are working with a published and recognized designer is heartwarming.

How do you attract new clients?

By being present and making certain that we are responsive to those we have served over time and to those who come for the first time pre-qualified and interested in growing a relationship. Most of all I am always keeping a balance of work initiated by curiosity and work funded by commission.

If you had to describe your studio culture – how would you phrase it?

Magical, fertile, and personally rewarding.

1 Alvin Lustig (1915–1955), American graphic designer and typeface designer. He went blind from diabetes in 1954.

2 Saul Bass (1920–1996), American graphic designer and Academy Award-winning filmmaker, best known for his design of movie title sequences, including *The Man with the Golden Arm*, *Vertigo*, *Psycho*, *Goodfellas* and *Casino*.

3 Paul Rand (1914–1996), American graphic designer, best known for his corporate logo designs.

4 Wolfgang Weingart, internationally known German-born graphic designer and typographer, widely credited as 'the father' of New Wave typography. Published *My Way to Typography* in 2000.

5 Frank Gehry, Pritzker Prize-winning architect based in Los Angeles. Best-known works include Guggenheim Museum at Bilbao, Walt Disney Concert Hall at Los Angeles and Experience Music Project at Seattle.

6 Bruce Mau, Canadian designer and creative director of Bruce Mau Design. Author of *S,M,L,XL*, with Rem Koolhaas.

7 John Massey, American designer. Started his design consultancy, John Massey Inc, after working for the Container Corporation of America.

8 April Greiman, American graphic designer and pioneer of digital technology in design.

9 Paul Sahre, New York graphic designer and teacher.

10 Stefan Sagmeister, Austrian graphic designer and typographer. Runs design company Sagmeister Inc. based in New York. Designed album covers for the Rolling Stones, Lou Reed and David Byrne.

11 Marian Bantjes, Canadian designer/illustrator. See page 122.

12 Ed Fella, artist, educator and graphic designer. He practised as a commercial artist in Detroit for 30 years before receiving an MFA in Design from the Cranbrook Academy of Art in 1987. Teaches at the California Institute of the Arts and produces his own self-published work.

13 James Victore runs a design studio working on projects from book and web to product design. He teaches at the School of Visual Arts in New York City.

14 Jason Pickleman, member of Chicago design team JNL.

15 Milton Glaser, seminal figure in modern graphic design. See page 130.

16. Shepard Fairey, contemporary artist, graphic designer and illustrator. Achieved worldwide fame with his Barack Obama HOPE poster.

17 Tibor Kalman (1949–1999), influential American graphic designer of Hungarian origin. In 1979 he co-founded design firm M&Co. Best known for his work as editor-in-chief of *Colors* magazine.

Universal Everything
Founded: 2004
Personnel: 2, plus roster of collaborators
Location: Sheffield, UK
www.universaleverything.com

Matt Pyke is an example of a new breed
of designer who works for major global
corporations – as well as other smaller
entities – yet has none of the trappings of
a large studio with a smart metropolitan
address. Instead he produces a fizzing
cocktail of commercial and art-based work
from his custom-made studio in his garden in
Sheffield, in the north of England. He does
this with the assistance of a project manger
(his sole employee) and a roster of designers,
animators, coders and musicians from around
the world. Pyke's network of talent – with him
at its centre – is living proof that the design
studio no longer needs to conform to the old
rigid formula.

Pyke is a frank and willing interviewee with a
keen interest in debunking many of the myths
that surround studios and contemporary
professional practice. He is an iconoclast in
more ways than one. 'I hope you are going to
ask everyone how much they charge?' was
his first question when approached about
this interview.*
–

You worked for eight years for one of the
most famous graphic design studios in the
world – the Designers Republic. Was it there
that you got the itch to start your own
studio, or did you have the desire from
the start?

Matt Pyke: I grew an itch over the eight
years I was at DR. In the first three years
it was the best art school education I could
have had – learning from my peers, insane
deadlines, talking about music and not design,
being given autonomy on entire projects
from brief to delivery. The next three years
was spent outgrowing square music sleeves,
and I explored Flash, interactive and motion
design. In my naivety I found unusual ways
of achieving things. The final two years I felt
constrained by the stylistic legacy of the
studio, and what the public had begun to
expect, but this gave me the impetus to
build my own universe-sized blank canvas.

Ian Anderson who ran DR is an individualist –
a strong personality. What do you take from
him that you've used in your own studio?

That the best can be bettered, to
always push things beyond a 'nice' design,
to embody artworks with provocation and a
voice. To reach further than a pure designer/
maker, and to explore publishing, DJing,
broadcasting, teaching, sharing, writing,
and avoiding the threat of boredom with
my day job.

Your studio has evolved into an unusual global collaborative entity. Was this your vision from the start, or did the vision evolve?

At the start I had a desire to explore everything – a dangerous vice, as it's so easy to spread yourself too thinly. I wanted to resist becoming a manager, and was desperate to avoid becoming pigeon-holed. Projects came in that were beyond my skill-set, and I began bringing in the amazing talent I had met over the years to assist me in the conception. This network began to grow in new fields with each diverse commission, and has now become a global roster of over 50 experts in everything from code and structural engineering to stop-motion and woodcarving. Now we have a core of regular members, and a full-time studio/project manager to ensure a well-managed creative environment for us and the clients.

So you've employed a studio/project manager. That's a big step after working solo for so long, isn't it?

As the projects became bigger, the production and management responsibilities grew in parallel. An increasing amount of energy was going into managing clients, collaborators, schedules and budgets – potentially at the expense of the creative focus. I learnt a huge amount from this hands-on experience, but I knew that a professional could do the job far better. So I hired a superb studio/project manager, whose job is to ensure I am 100% focused on what I do best.

OK, here's the nuts and bolts question – the one that no one asks: how did you fund your studio?

Great question; we should all be more open on these issues. I'd been advised that you needed three months' wages as a cushion when starting as a designer. Towards the end of working at DR I'd be developing new client relationships and projects until it was eight hours doing that job, and then eight hours when I got home working on my own tasks. Then a project came in from a contact in the US motion graphics industry to design a site for an LA production company. They had a $20K budget, which bought me at least six months of income in which I could grow the studio.

In the early days, where did you go for help and advice?

I spoke to Business Link[1] for the objective viewpoint, I wrote a business plan, I met with other studios to see their culture, I talked to agents and production companies, I had peers share their address books, but most helpful of all was my family, who brought all my procrastination into focus.

01 |
02 |
03 |

01/02/ Project: Toonami Channel idents. Date: 2005. Client: Toonami. Designer: Matt Pyke. CGI: Zeitguised. Audio: Freefarm.
03/ Project: London 2012 Olympics brand launch. Date: 2007. Client: London 2012 Olympics. Designer: Matt Pyke. Audio: Freefarm.

How much money did you need to get going?

Laptop: £1500. Smartphone: £300. Programming of www.universaleverything.com: £1500. I've always insisted on keeping the overheads low. The core studio was my laptop and a mobile phone. No office, no commute, no staff. This allowed me to take risks, such as unpaid in-house projects and gallery exhibitions. It also granted me the freedom of turning down unsuitable projects, even if they paid well.

Are there financial complications involved in working with an external roster of creative collaborators?

I bring a particular complication on the studio by insisting on paying external people above the usual rates – preferring that they are motivated and can afford to give their all, rather than the traditional producer-freelancer model of squeezing the most for the least out of them. Again with our model, it's a risk we can afford to take. And I hope everyone feels loved and fulfilled by this.

That's very impressive but also good business sense. As you say, the convention is to do the opposite and grind people down on price. Nevertheless, you have to maintain financial discipline – how do you do this?

We use sales forecasts and cashflow reports. Having a solid financial grounding for the studio means that we can afford to retain creative integrity and choose our own direction. We divide time spent on every project according to budget. Some are worth investing more creative time in if they are leading into a new discipline we'd like to explore more, or will gain us exposure to a new audience.

Another thorny question – do you free pitch for business?

We don't work or pitch for free, preferring to use budgets to 'buy' time for us to develop in-house projects, such as www.everyoneforever.com and www.advancedbeauty.org – which in turn lead to wider audiences and new commissions.

You decided to remain near Sheffield. Most of the leading design companies are in London – was it ever a temptation to move to the capital?

It's never been a temptation to live there again, as much as I love London. The cost of living, the Peak District (where I live now) and the two-hour, near-empty train to London once a week kept me up here. 60% of our clients are in London, the rest overseas. Being there once a week, usually running between four meetings and a couple of galleries squeezes the best out of the time.

Does it ever count against you that you are miles away from most of your clients?

Clients have never had a problem with my location. I'm beginning to hear more people wishing they could escape the capital and continue without compromise.

Where did the name Universal Everything come from?

It was formed in reaction to escape the confines of DR. I needed a name to encapsulate the idea of the biggest blank canvas in the world.

Describe the early days – what were the main obstacles?

Having a slim post-DR portfolio. I had to grow it by producing many in-house projects to get the thinking out there. Being asked to pitch for free – making it impossible to put your heart into a gamble. Negotiating budgets – learning how to have pride in your time and value in your work. Bravely accepting projects that were beyond my skills – but hiring amazing people to pull it off. Naughty clients – being brave enough to fire them and move on. Turning work down, even when things were quiet, was crucial in defining our own path for the studio.

How did you find your first clients?

I knew that wordy emails and in-depth websites are inefficient for communicating an overview of a studio; I wanted to hit people with the diversity of my past in an instant. I emailed a one-sheet collage with 50 thumbnails of past work, which was sent to everyone who I could think of who knew interesting people. It was my viral six degrees of separation theory.

Sounds interesting – could you explain your theory?

If they liked the work, and passed it on, eventually it would land in a perfect client's inbox.

When designers leave a studio to set up on their own, there is often the tricky ethical question of what to do about existing clients. Most designers don't approach their former employers' clients, but some newly independent designers are approached by clients of their previous company who want to continue working with them. Where do you stand on this question?

I had developed hands-on relationships with my clients at DR, but equally I wanted to move on and work with new people. I was wary of approaching former clients as I didn't want to burn any bridges – word travels fast in our community and I had a fragile new reputation to forge. I was contacted by some former DR

04 | 05 | 06 | 07 |
08 | 09 | 10 | 11 |
12 | 13 |
14 |

15 | 16 |
17 | 18 |
19 | 20 | 21 | 22 |
23 | 24 |

04/05/ Project: Toonami Channel idents. Date: 2005. Client: Toonami. Designer: Matt Pyke. CGI: Zeitguised. Audio: Freefarm. 06/07/ Project: Nokia Heathrow Terminal 5. Date: 2008. Client: Nokia. Designers: Matt Pyke and Trev Henderson. Photographer: Flickr group. 08/09/10/11/ Project: History of Dance 90s. Date: 2006. Client: MTV. Designer: Matt Pyke. CGI: Renascent. Audio: Freefarm. 12/ Project: Nokia E71 launch. Date: 2009. Client: Nokia/Wieden & Kennedy/Hi-Res. Designer: Matt Pyke. CGI: Maxim Zhestkov. Audio: Freefarm. 13/ Project: Transistor ad. Date: 2005. Client: Transistor. Designer: Matt Pyke. Photographer/Illustrator/Other: Matt Pyke. 14/ Project: Nokia retail stores. Date: 2006. Client: Nokia. Designer: Matt Pyke. CGI: Mateuniverse/Flight 404. Audio: Freefarm. 15/16/17/18/ Project: Audi TT Viral Video. Date: 2007. Client: Audi/The One Centre. Designers: Matt Pyke and Karsten Schmidt. Processing: Karsten Schmidt. CGI: Realise Studio. Audio: Freefarm. 19/20/21/22/ Project: MLC website. Date: 2006. Client: Manhattan Loft corporation. Designers: Matt Pyke. Site build: Kleber. Project management: TiRA. 23/24/ Project: V&A Forever. Date: 2008. Client: Victoria & Albert Museum. Designers: Matt Pyke and Karsten Schmidt. Processing: Karsten Schmidt. Audio design: Simon Pyke. Project management: Philip Ward. Photography: David Barrington. Podcasts: Kleber.

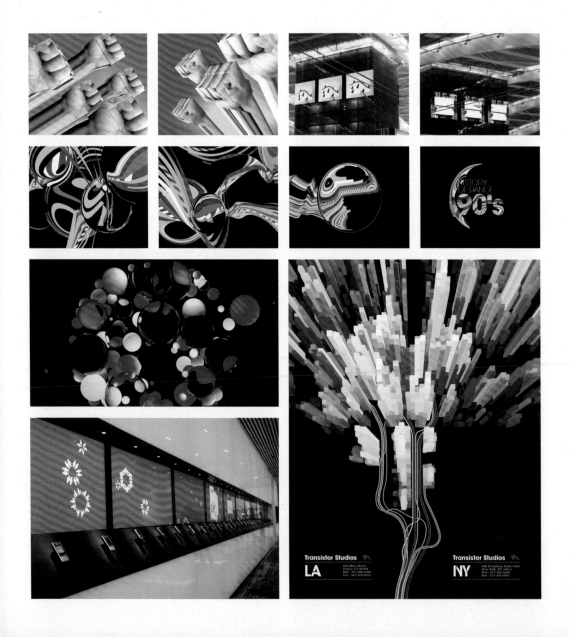

clients after I left, as they were accustomed to working with me. I have outgrown a few, and grown upwards with the remainder.

Now that the tables are turned and you are running a studio, how would you deal with clients who bypassed you and approached someone on your network?

It has happened in the past. Because of the fluid nature of our studio, it's hard to prevent. It has sometimes helped us move on to clients who are more appreciative of our work process. If a client approached a collaborator to continue with an idea we had established, then we would pull them up on this, to protect the ownership of the creative direction. Often other agencies have approached our collaborators asking them to 'recycle' our collaborative work for other projects – it's a grey area between creative ownership and the independence of the collaborator.

Tell me about how you find people for your network of collaborators.

I'm always scouting for new talent, online, at degree shows, at conferences and via recommendations from existing collaborators. I'm attracted to people who have a unique voice and approach, and who constantly push the boundaries of what they do.

What is your attitude to growth? Do you see a time when Universal Everything will have in-house designers?

We were approached by a much larger global agency who wanted to buy into our culture. It was tempting to gain that foundation, but any resistance from us to growth would have been met by the needs of the agency's backers to make their investment grow, so we declined the offer. I'm opposed to the traditional model of expansion, gaining staff and offices and therefore needing clients just to keep it afloat. By keeping the core small and the network growing, we can shift into new directions quickly. I recently read some good advice: 'Only do what only you can do'. This has made me start looking for an all-round senior designer, who can expand upon my initial creative direction and see projects through to completion. In theory this will free me up to focus on development of ideas, research projects, finding talent and finally starting to paint again.

You work from a custom-built studio in your garden – how important is it to separate home from studio?

It's important to have a commute, whether its 25 metres or 30 miles – it's a psychological airlock between home and workplace. It's a very productive place, usually me alone, and time is planned to every half-hour. I'm devoid of any distractions, which helps me stick

to the 9 to 5 regime I impose on myself. It's equally as important to ignore work as it is to obsess about it. Time away gives your mind clarity.

How do you maintain the balance between creativity and profitability?

As with most studios, we take on well-paid commercial projects with less creative freedom. This ranges from internal brand films and advertising campaigns to websites for management and property companies. These sorts of jobs are rarely mentioned but they underpin everyone's creative foundation. These projects buy us time, funding smaller, creative projects that give opportunity to grow in a new direction, or open up another audience to us. The studio is building up cash reserves that give us the confidence to keep taking risks, and having the luxury of choice in which clients to take on.

What is your attitude to interns?

My workdays are so intense and focused I haven't the time to devote to mentoring, but I regularly talk with design students at universities and events.

Regarding your network, are there times when you say, 'I wish we were all in the same room'?

When working with an animator in Siberia, a Japanese programmer in San Francisco, or an opera singer in Brighton – yes, it would be an advantage, if only to overcome cultural and language barriers to keep us all on the same wavelength. The core of us meet often, and know each other inside out – we discuss face to face at the conception of a project to guide us in the same direction. We then return to our own studios to create the first round of production in isolation. We are always surprised and inspired by what comes back. By seeing things fresh we are hit with the impact of the work, without the legacy of witnessing its creation.

You have a very good profile in the design and advertising world. How do you go about building and maintaining this?

When a project is complete, it's essential to get the work out there selling itself – we send updates to press contacts, bloggers and well-connected clients. Our website uses Twitter, YouTube, Vimeo, video podcasts and Flickr to seed our activities to online communities. Once things are out there, they keep the profile buoyant.

You've recently completed an interesting new DVD, Advanced Beauty. Is that part of this process?

Yes, the Advanced Beauty DVD was a method of releasing our collective thinking into the wild. 18 films – one video podcast per

week for 18 weeks – grew our profile as the
project gained momentum. Now the concept
of the project is in the public domain, we are
keeping it alive by inviting new filmmakers
to contribute working within the same
parameters.

How important are external advisors –
accountants and so on?

Accountants – essential for a bird's-eye
view of the studio. Business development
advisors – essential for formulating and
focusing on what we should really be aiming
for. Older, wiser generation of designers –
essential for retaining integrity and vision,
without being seduced by the next big thing.

If you could start all over again, what would
you do differently?

I would hire a studio/project manager
from the start. I had an immense learning
experience being hands-on with everything
from budgets to production to conflicts
to chasing invoices, but it's healthier if
creativity/emotion and business/finance
stay independent.

How would you define your studio's
culture today?

After the effort of encouraging maximum
creativity for commercial clients, we have
now reached a happy medium between the
freedom of art and the realities of design.
We have started generating and self-
publishing our own in-house content, devoid
of brand involvement. This is then often
licensed to brands such as Nokia or Apple.
It's a healthy working method, in which we find
the right homes and audiences for heartfelt
work. Now larger clients trust us on bigger
commissions, through us achieving unproven,
ambitious projects with proven results such
as a recent V&A commission to design and
build a major installation for the museum.
Our next aim is to develop gallery and public
art commissions. The fewer steps between the
creator and the audience, the more fulfilling
it becomes. From a commercial side, we are
now working with brands from the ground
up, being part of their culture, and having
the 360-degree vision for every medium
they communicate in. Most of all, never stop
exploring and evolving.

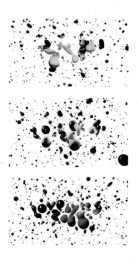

* The editors decided not to ask interviewees how much
they charged. First because the information would soon
be out of date, and second because, although certain
designers might be willing to name figures, it was unlikely
that their clients would be happy to see this information
published.

1 Business Link is a free business advice and support
service, available online in the UK.
(www.businesslink.gov.uk)

25/26/27/ Project: Lovebytes identity
2008. Date: 2008. Client: Lovebytes.
Designer: Matt Pyke. CGI: Trev Henderson.
Audio: Freefarm.

Walker Art Center
Founded: 1940
Personnel: 11
Location: Minneapolis, US
www.walkerart.org

There has been a design studio at the Walker Art Center in Minneapolis for over 60 years. Its work has been exhibited and published worldwide and it has received numerous design awards. Andrew Blauvelt has been the studio's design director since 1998. Prior to his appointment, Blauvelt taught design at several universities including Cranbrook Academy of Art. He has been a visiting professor in the graduate programs of European, American and Mexican universities. In 1995 he was named Educator of the Year by the Graphic Design Education Association, and has served on the national board of directors of the American Center for Design. Blauvelt describes his role as design director as dealing with everything from 'postcards to trashcans'. In addition, he organizes talks, curates exhibitions, and writes and lectures extensively on design.

This interview was conducted via email.
—

There have been many fine in-house studios – the design department at CBS, run by the late Lou Dorfsman[1], for example. Yet the in-house design studio is a somewhat neglected subject among design's commentariat. Why do you think this is?

Andrew Blauvelt: I think that's true and I think it's due to a combination of factors, including the belief that in-house departments are less creative than consultancies. The story is more complicated, especially when a singular name is thought to be necessary to propel a narrative (whether writing history or a profile piece), and that gets difficult when you have many people and processes involved, which is the case of most in-house operations. Perhaps it's structurally suspect too, meaning that in-house design is too bureaucratically managed and organizationally controlled.

As a young designer starting out, what were your ambitions? Did you envisage a time when you would lead a studio?

Before I was in design school I thought I wanted to be an art director of a magazine, but excelled in more traditional academic fare. My intended major was political science and international relations, believe it or not. However, my real interest was in design, so I found the art school. But as I learned more about design I was interested in not only its practice but also its history and theory. So I went to grad school thinking that I would end up teaching. I began my career in academia, so I can't say that I thought I would be

01 |
02 |
03 |

01/ Project: Tetsumi Kudo: Garden of
Metamorphosis. Date: 2008.
Designers: Andrew Blauvelt and
Emmet Byrne. 02/ Project: *Walker*
magazines. Date: Various.
03/ Project: Performing Arts program
postcards. Date: Various.
04/ Project: How Latitudes Become Forms.
Date: 2003. Designers: Andrew Blauvelt
and Chad Kloepfer. 05/ Project: House of
Oracles: A Huang Yong Ping Retrospective.
Date: 2005. Designers: Andrew Blauvelt
and Chad Kloepfer.
06/ Project: D-Crit identity for the School
of Visual Arts. Designers: Andrew Blauvelt
and Emmet Byrne.

leading a studio in the office sense – perhaps
a classroom studio. I've always practised
design, mostly for cultural clients, so the
transition from being a tenured professor
to the Walker wasn't the huge leap it
appeared to be. The leadership skills one
picks up in teaching have worked remarkably
well in the design studio.

Can you define your current role at
the Walker?

I'm the design director, which means I'm
responsible for the design of communications
and public spaces at the Walker, or as I say,
fully aware of the irony, 'from postcards
to trashcans'. The department includes
editorial and publishing, so there is also that
element. I'm also curator of architecture and
design programs at the Walker, which means
planning lecture series, special projects,
and organizing exhibitions on design-related
subjects. Lately, it's more of a strategic role
looking more broadly at how we communicate
to our audiences (and vice versa) and the
experiences visitors can have at the Walker,
both on-site and online. Although definitely
unusual in its combination of duties, my job
at the Walker has been the model for
many decades.

What is the structure of your studio?
How many designers and non-designers
do you have?

Beside myself, there are two senior graphic
designers and two design fellows, who come
to work at the Walker full-time for one year
as graphic designers. The non-designers
include one person who prepares our images
for printing, one studio manager who also
serves as publications director, and two
editors. Since there is an obvious connection
to what happens online, the Walker also has a
separate new media department that handles
web and interpretive technology projects.
I meet regularly with two web-based designers
in that department.

There has been a design studio at the Walker
since the 1940s. Is this heritage a source of
inspiration or a burden?

It is definitely more inspiration than burden.
Few places can boast a tradition that long,
whether a company or a museum. It was a
smart, thoughtful, integrated approach to
handling the museum's communications and
programmatic needs more than 60 years ago
and still is today. When businesses talk about
the value and role of design as a hot topic
today, I have to smile because the Walker has
known this for a long time. When you have
people like Peter Seitz[2], Mildred Friedman[3] and
Laurie Haycock[4] in the position before you, it
can't help but be inspiring. I suppose the only
burden is trying to live up to that legacy.

In this age of outsourcing why does the Walker maintain an in-house studio?

It's a misconception that outsourcing saves time or money. What happens is that you end up with more project management in terms of time and people, and less design. I'd rather employ the designers who actually produce the work and can produce more of it more efficiently – crudely, it's the difference between salary and hourly. The Walker is a multidisciplinary institution, which means we have visual arts exhibitions, performing arts events, film screenings and education programs, so the overall needs for such a complex organization are huge. We produce more than 200 projects a year. In actuality there are only a handful of designers to produce all of this material, on time and on budget, which can only happen when the processes and systems are in place and reliable. This can only happen when everyone knows the project status and their role at any given moment. We also save money on outside fees that can be hundreds of thousands of dollars a year easily, for things like branding and advertising campaigns or book design contracts. All of this is handled internally.

That's interesting, because I see many firms and institutions who employ in-house design staff to do the dull routine work, but give the big-ticket projects to fashionable studios – clearly this is not the case at the Walker.

No, it's not. Each in-house situation is different, of course. Unfortunately, there is a tendency in general to devalue the work of in-house staffs, or simply take it for granted. Of course, how do we know it is less creative when never given the opportunity to disprove it? When it comes to larger-scale projects, we have the talent and expertise to execute the work internally. I'm definitely proud that we routinely produce some of the most interesting and exciting work in the cultural sector, AND we produce all of the other materials as well. For bigger projects we can throw four or five very smart and talented designers at the problem to get the process going. This isn't 'brainstorming', it's actual designing. Sometimes you need specialized skill sets from the outside, like the right illustrator or the right programmer. We try to engage these people as creative collaborators as well.

How do you think your role differs – if at all – from that of someone running an equivalent-sized independent studio?

Well, it is probably similar in a general way, in that I spend a great deal of time in meetings, not with clients but with colleagues. The focus of the meetings is different, I think, in that I'm not meeting about a specific piece usually, but rather about much larger strategies and

07 |

07/ Project: On-site Walker without Walls identity installation. Designers: Andrew Blauvelt and Alex DeArmond. 08/ Project: Film/video program brochures. Date: Various. 09/ Project: Kara Walker: My Complement, My Enemy, My Oppressor, My Love. Date: 2007. Designers: Andrew Blauvelt and Emmet Byrne; Project: The Quick and the Dead. Date: 2009. Designers: Andrew Blauvelt and Chad Kloepfer; Project: Strangely Familiar: Design and Everyday Life. Date: 2003. Designers: Andrew Blauvelt and Alex DeArmond. 10/ Project: Design Fellowship posters. Date: Various. 11/ Project: Walker Expanded identity system. Designers: Andrew Blauvelt and Chad Kloepfer.
12/ Project: Film/video program brochures. Date: Various. 13/ Project: Let's Entertain: Life's Guilty Pleasures. Date: 2000. Designers: Andrew Blauvelt and Santiago Piedrafita; Project: Magnetic North. Date: 2000. Designers: Mevis & Van Deursen with Andrew Blauvelt and Santiago Piedrafita; Project: Painting at the Edge of the World. Date: 2001. Designers: Andrew Blauvelt and Santiago Piedrafita; Project: Worlds Away: New Suburban Landscapes. Date: 2008. Designers: Andrew Blauvelt and Chad Kloepfer.

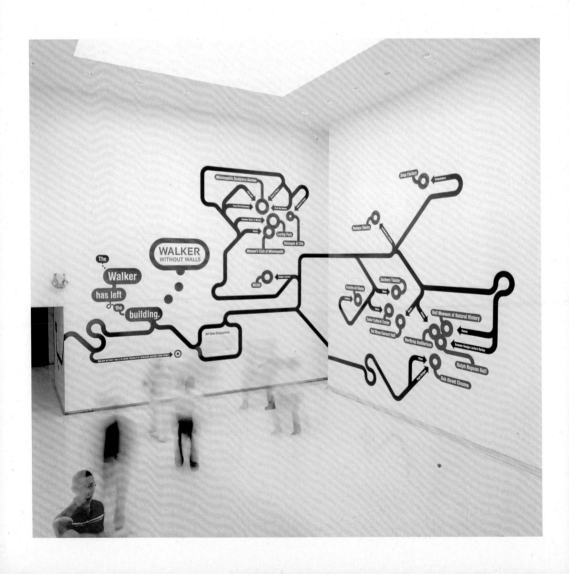

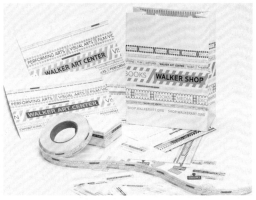

initiatives. Because we are bound together
institutionally, we share more common
interests and of course a mission.
Half of my designers change each year,
the permanent staff constantly adjusts to
this constant churn and change – that might
be different.

Do you feel protected from the realities of
professional life – I'm thinking of things like
monthly sales targets, and the constant
battle to maintain solvency at the same time
as doing creative work – or are you subject
to the normal business metrics?

I believe my answer would be the same
regardless of the situation. We are all
collectively responsible for the overall health
of our particular endeavour or business,
which isn't measured in the same ways as
perhaps the corporate sector is, but there
are still measures and expectations. There
are many factors that can affect the bottom
line, some of which are more in your control
than others. Design is simply one variable
among many in the equation of success
or failure. There is a misconception that
somehow museums or cultural institutions are
more immune to the vagaries of the market,
but that is a fallacy.

Designers who run studios tend to be either
individuals who demand that the designers
who work for them conform to their vision of
what the studio's output should be, or else
they take the view that designers need to
be developed and nurtured to find their own
vision. Where do you stand on this question?

Somewhere in between, I think. By that
I mean that the group of designers as a
whole needs to set the direction and evolution
of the work, not as unquestioning groupthink
but as an organic developmental process. If
one is not hiring randomly, I think one ends
up with a set of people who bring their own
individual tastes and influences with them yet
share some affinity for what already exists.
If so, then the question is what can each
designer contribute to the whole – I don't
mean job duties, but rather aesthetically
and conceptually. How do they see their
contribution reflected? Do they add
breadth to the existing palette or is their
contribution catalytic?

You have written: 'I've always taken pride
and pleasure in operating outside of official
centers – New York City in particular – but
am still struck by people's disbelief that
"interesting work can happen there?"' Is this
an example of the thinking that has led you
to work at the Walker, rather than operating
in the more 'normal' milieu of the independent
design studio?

Definitely, in the sense that the Walker
is the kind of museum that, because of its
programming, one expects to find in New York

14 |
15 |
16 |

14/ Project: Brave New Worlds. Date: 2007.
Designers: Andrew Blauvelt and Emmet
Byrne. 15/ Project: Walker without Walls
identity application to ice cream truck.
16/ Project: Andy Warhol/Supernova:
Stars, Deaths, and Disasters, 1962–1964.
Date: 2005. Designers: Andrew Blauvelt
and Scott Ponik.

or in Europe, but here it is in Minneapolis, of all places. I've lived in the Midwest of the US longer than any other region of the country, and I went to school in the Midwest. I seem to gravitate towards unusual and unexpected places and situations, which appears to be more challenging in that kind of context. A place like the Walker provides a ready and endless stream of problems to solve and issues with which to grapple. To that extent, it's a convenient source of provocation.

You write about design and give frequent lectures. Do you think this would this be possible if you worked in independent practice?

Oh yes. In fact, I've been lapped plenty of times on the speaking circuit by any number of independent designers! One advantage I might have (which is a carry-over from teaching) is that I also work in the realm of ideas and subjects that contribute much to my thinking about design in general. So while I'm happy to talk about the design work produced by the studio, I also lecture about design and culture in general. Of course, I wish I could lecture and write more on these topics, but there are only so many hours in a day.

What is your vision for the Walker studio?

In some ways I hope the design studio continues the way it has for the last 60 years. On the other hand, I wish the design studio could take a leadership role in the realm of research and development, so to speak, with regards to the design field as a whole. I'm not sure what form it would take, or if there is a good analogy, but there is so little R&D in design because it is so defined by traditional practice. In the workaday grind, it is extremely difficult to change gears and instead of reacting to other people's problems that are brought to you, to search out other problems – difficult but not impossible.

You run an internship program at the studio; can you tell me about this?

We used to use the term 'internship', but in the US at least, this can mean anything from fetching coffee or making copies to an assignment that lasts for only a few weeks. Now we use the term 'fellowship', which we changed to match the similar situation for our visual arts program. They work for one year, full-time, and they are paid, although with a modest salary. Fellows design their own projects and handle all aspects, from client meetings through supervising printing. So it gives them access to the full process of design. They often work with the senior designers or me on longer-term or more complex projects. We have had a fellowship program in the design studio since the early 1980s. It was expanded when I arrived in 1998. Basically, we solicit applications from

designers early in their careers – just out of school or in their first job. It's a pretty competitive program and we select about five or six finalists to interview in person, on site. The finalists are always very good and it's very difficult to choose just two – you really want them all.

Where do the applicants come from?

From all sorts of schools, cities and countries, including California Institute of the Arts, Minneapolis College of Art and Design, Rhode Island School of Design, Yale School of Art, etc. We encourage fellows to use the time to also focus on the next step in their career. Some people go to graduate school, open their own business, or become designers at other firms or businesses.

Of all the tasks you have to perform, which gives you the most satisfaction?

I like them all because they provide different experiences. As a designer, I still get excited when a project comes together, when an idea and the form it takes becomes inevitable. As a curator I enjoy seeing an idea grow, change and take shape over years and working with artists and designers, where blind faith is sometimes necessary and the idea of not knowing what will be produced is both daunting and exciting. As an administrator it is developing strategies to solve complex problems. In a way, it's not unlike the Eames film *Powers of Ten*[5], in which the next largest or smallest thing is its own universe but is nevertheless bound together in the entire scheme of things.

1 Lou Dorfsman (1918–2008), pioneering American graphic designer. Ran the design department of the Columbia Broadcasting System (CBS) for over 40 years.

2 Peter Seitz, American graphic designer, trained at Hochschule für Gestaltung Ulm (HfG Ulm) and Yale University. Worked at Walker Art Center before establishing various independent studios in Minneapolis.

3 Mildred Friedman, writer, design curator at the Walker Art Center from 1970 to 1991.

4 Laurie Haycock, American designer, taught at Cranbrook Academy of Art in Detroit. Published *Words and Pictures for Business and Culture* with her late husband, Scott Makela.

5 *Powers of Ten*, documentary film written and directed by Ray and Charles Eames, showing the relative scale of the universe in factors of ten.

4Creative
Founded: 2000
Personnel: 60
Location: London, UK
www.4creative.co.uk

Brett Foraker is one of the foremost creative voices in modern broadcast design. In 2003, he was appointed as the youngest-ever creative director of Channel 4. The channel has always been a byword for innovative visual presentation, and under Foraker's stewardship that tradition has been continued and extended. His mould-breaking station idents have defined a new era in station branding, and his creative strategies to launch the channel offshoots More4, Film4 and E4 have become industry benchmarks.

Foraker is also creative director of 4Creative, a division of Channel 4 that offers creative in-house services for the channel, but that also hires itself out as an independent creative agency. Foraker's work has won numerous awards, including a gold at Creative Circle and the D&AD black pencil in 2005 for his Channel 4 work. In addition to his commercial work, Foraker undertakes personal projects and independent commissions. He is also involved in content creation for Channel 4.

The interview was conducted via email.
—

You have created a rare beast – an award-winning, highly respected in-house creative department. Can you describe the process you went through to shape it?

Brett Foraker: 4Creative was started with the simple idea of creating agency-quality advertisements for television programmes. This has since grown to incorporate moving image, online and print ads. Our client base has diversified accordingly. After we first set up, we soon realized that we were uniquely positioned to build a larger clientele and deliver great creative work at significant savings both to Channel 4 and to external clients. There were several reasons for this. The main one is that we have an internal development system that hot-houses directing and writing talent. In this way, we can get several creatives looking at projects at a very early stage and with an increased emphasis on execution. This carries through to production, where the roles normally occupied by an agency producer and a production company producer are conjoined. At every stage we ask, what will best serve the finished film, website or poster? The end result, rather than the bottom line, is king. We've streamlined our methodology to reflect this and, lo and behold, ended up turning a decent profit.

01 |
02 |

Did you have a vision of how you wanted your role to work?

My role is really that of a player-manager. I started as a writer and then a director, so my involvement could come at any stage of the process. I've written many ads that I didn't direct and vice versa. I encourage all of the other creatives to be similarly collaborative. This generally leads to them taking a healthy interest in one another's work. As we generally hire individuals rather than teams, it's interesting to see. There's a pattern of reciprocity that seems to have developed organically.

Has this vision developed as you have gone on?

Further to the previous question, we often see 'virtual teams' springing up on a project-by-project basis. As the individual creative takes on responsibility for a given job, he or she will look to get the best value out of a script or storyboard and will seek out collaborators within the department that they feel can benefit the work.

Could you explain how things are structured?

We have a central creative director who oversees a team of creative managers who are responsible for individual divisions of the business (Channel 4, E4, More4, external work, etc). They can choose whatever talent they want for a given project (including other creative managers) and are then responsible for bringing the job to fruition. The creative director dips in and out of these projects as needed.

There's an old axiom in design that working 'in house' is less stimulating than working in an independent studio. Do you agree with this?

That depends on where 'in house' is, I suppose. In our case, we are fortunate to have a steady stream of new and quite varied initiatives to work on, not to mention a fairly healthy external client list. Besides, I think the axiom refers to 'variety' more than anything else, so my advice would be to seek variety and opportunity in any work situation and to only commit to a place that can give you both.

Are there different kinds of pressures working internally?

01/ Project: Channel 4 idents – Tokyo.
Director: Brett Foraker. Producer: Gwilym Gwillim. 02/ Project: Channel 4 idents – Dubai. Director: Brett Foraker.
Producer: Gwilym Gwillim.
03/ Project: Desperate Housewives.
Director: David LaChapelle.
Producer: Shananne Lane.
04/ Project: Britain's Forgotten Children.
Art Director: Joseph Ernst.
Photographer: Mark Zibert.
Producers: Gwilym Gwillim, Ed Webster.

The pressure is always to deliver striking work that is as true to the original idea as possible. In each project, corporate politics or market forces can conspire to cloud that idea. This is true both internally and externally, but I suppose over time (on internal jobs at least) you build up enough equity to cut through some of the bureaucracy.

Could you tell me about the scope of your responsibilities?

We are responsible for all of the advertising and branding along the entire network family (C4, E4, More4, Film4, 4Music, etc).

What disciplines are you involved with?

Moving image, online, print, publishing and, increasingly, content creation.

Can you give an example of the sort of content creation you are involved in?

At Channel 4, our public-service remit prohibits us from creating 'traditional' programmes in-house. However, the internet has shifted the goalposts quite a lot in defining what 'traditional' programming actually is. We've been fortunate in that we've been making short-form content for many years. Some of it is fairly straightforward such as the *Self-Portrait* series for Film4. Other projects are more esoteric. For example, we did a 30-minute documentary for Eurostar to commemorate their move from Waterloo to St. Pancras. We are also increasingly making films that try to bridge the gap between a traditional ad and pure content. To this end we've made a three-minute live ad for Honda, a four-minute film for *Big Food Fight*, and a three-minute film for *Disarming Britain*. There are loads more, but the key is to try to make everything as entertaining as possible and to realize that the internet has completely changed viewing habits (not to mention media planning).

Could you describe the creative process that you go through?

It's pretty simple really. The client will come to us with a product or a brand desire. We will then assign several creatives/directors to find the best solution for this particular job. We will take the best two or three routes and present them to the client. After we agree a route, the director begins to develop the project (maintaining maximum transparency at all times). From there it becomes a question of resourcing the director to help them do the best job they can. Because the director was involved early on, they usually have a good understanding of the client's needs and desires.

4Creative works with outside agencies. What do they bring to your creative mix?

Outside agencies have always been an important part of our mix. Not only do we collaborate with numerous designers and photographers, but we ourselves will often work directly with ad agencies to help them solve a particular problem. We seek out talent in all its forms and encourage new collaborations with each job.

05 |
06 | 07 |

05/ Project: More4 – Kubrick Season. Director: Siri Bunford. Producers: Shananne Lane, Louise Oliver. 06/ Project: Disarming Britain. Photographer: Jim Fiscus. Art Directors: Brett Foraker, Alice Tonge. Producer: Shananne Lane. 07/ Project: The Family. Art Director: Alice Tonge. Producer: Ed Webster. 08/ Project: Alan Carr – Chatty Man. Director: Tom Tagholm. Producer: Tabby Harris. 09/ Project: Skins, season 1. Director: Neil Gorringe. Producer: Gwilym Gwillim. 10/ Project: More4 – Pub Quiz. Director: Kjetil Njoten. Producer: Louise Oliver. 11/ Project: Lost. Directors: David LaChapelle, Brett Foraker. Producer: Shananne Lane. 12/ Project: Channel 4 idents – Coastline. Director: Russell Appleford. Producer: Gwilym Gwillim.

What is your recruitment policy? Are you
actively engaged in talent-spotting?

13 |
14 |

Talent-spotting is an ongoing process.
People tend to stay with us for quite a
long time so new spots don't open up all
that often. But since we also use a number
of freelancers we are always looking for new
people to work with. They key is finding people
who are extremely self-motivated, who are
willing to make mistakes then learn from
them and improve.

What qualities do you look for in creative
talent?

Creative talent comes in many forms, but
here are a few of the qualities that are
most attractive to 4Creative: conceptual
confidence, writing ability, wit, visual literacy,
good taste, humour, thick skin, optimism,
auto-didacticism, endurance and selflessness.
Those things will get you in the door. Once in
it comes down to hard work and enthusiasm.

You are responsible for a huge number of
staff, directly and indirectly; how do you
manage this?

As much as possible, we try to hire 'adults'
and give them a limited number of direct
reports to help minimize their stress levels.
We are first and foremost driven by creativity,
so we try to make the path to good work as
easy as possible.

How would you define Channel 4's creative
culture today?

The creative culture is extremely healthy.
Clients seem happy. The work is better than
ever. Outside business is up. The department
routinely wins awards at all of the major
industry ceremonies. Personal projects are
also flourishing. In 2007–2008, department
members produced five short films and won
awards at several international film festivals.
Another department member created a six-
part series for a major UK broadcaster.
Many of the directors are also signed with
outside production companies to shoot ads.
The entrepreneurial spirit is as strong as
ever and feeds back directly to the work made
within the department.

Are there any other in-house broadcasting
design departments that you admire?

Not in England.

What about in-house departments in non-
broadcasting sectors – are there any that
you admire?

Probably some of the fashion houses. I think
that brand-building has to come from a place
where you have an intuitive understanding
of what your business can be and of where it
can go. Fashion at its best does this.

They may outsource some of the production, but the direction and confidence comes from people working inside.

To a young creative person stating out, what would you say are the advantages of working in an in-house environment?

The advantage is that it provides a safe environment in which to learn your craft. Ideas mean little without executional excellence. Once you have both, you can work anywhere in the world.

What are your ambitions for Channel 4's creative development?

Beyond the desire to do good work, my ambition for the department is that we continue to develop the next generation of writing and directing talent in our area.

You encourage your staff to do personal projects – do you find time to do your own? And how does this inform your commercial work?

I write and take photographs every day. I find one must constantly sift through the thousands of linguistic and visual cues that the brain receives on a daily basis. This is how one knows what is good or at least fresh. The commercials benefit from this by having a sense of spectacle that is born from everyday observation and not just other films and media. If you are truly creative, the question you ask yourself each morning is: what can I make today?

15 |
16 |
17 |

13/ Project: E4 idents. Director: Noah Harris. Producer: Jason Delahunty.
14/ Project: Skins season 2. Art Director: Alice Tonge. Producer: Jason Delahunty. 15/ Project: Film4 is Free. Director: Kevin Spacey. Producer: Shananne Lane.
16/ Project: Ghosts. Art Directors: Andy Booth, Jim Seath. Photographers: George Kavanagh, Alex Howe. Producers: Keeley Pratt, Louise Oliver. 17/ Project: Shameless – The Last Supper. Photographer: Jim Fiscus. Art Director: Tom Tagholm. Producer: Ed Webster.

Studio Portraits

In the following pages, we present a selection of portraits of graphic design studios from around the world, some contemporary and some from design's historic past.

Today's graphic design studio, whether in São Paulo or Tokyo or South Africa, doesn't seem to change much: Apple Mac computers, shelves sagging with books, chairs built for long hours in front of the screen, scraps of typography stuck to the wall, a bike rack, and books, more books – piles of them.
But if we go back in time – to the pioneering studios of the 1940s (Henrion) and 1960s (Total Design) – we find that studios are less formulaic, less predictable.

And yet, as we enjoy this rare glimpse into the secret world of the studio, a question forms – what will the studio of the future look like? Will we recognize it? Will it even be a physical space? Is the studio of the future virtual?

266 —— 267
Peter Saville
London, UK
2009

268
8vo
London, UK
c.1989

269
8vo
London, UK
c.1989

270
ps.2 arquitetura + design
São Paulo, Brazil
2009

271
Disturbance Design
Durban, South Africa
2009

272
Jan Van Toorn
Amsterdam, Holland
2009

273
Work
Singapore
2009

274
Niklaus Troxler
Willisau, Switzerland
2009

275
Niklaus Troxler
Willisau, Switzerland
2009

276 —— 277
Henrion Design Associates
London, UK
c. 1960s

278 —— 279
Henrion Design Associates
London, UK
c. 1960s

280 —— 281
Winterhouse
Connecticut, USA
2009

282 —— 283
Alan Fletcher
London, UK
2006

284
Alan Fletcher
London, UK
2006

284
Alan Fletcher
London, UK
2006

285
Alan Fletcher
London, UK
2006

285
Alan Fletcher
London, UK
2006

286
Carin Goldberg
NYC, USA
2009

287
Finn Creative
Kununurra, Australia
2009

288 —— 289
Farrow
London, UK
2009

290 —— 291
Ed Fella
California, USA
2009

292
Total Design
Amsterdam, Holland
1983

293
Total Design
Amsterdam, Holland
1980

294 —— 295
Total Design
Amsterdam, Holland
1963

296 —— 297
Pentagram
London, UK
2009

298
Studio Général – Toffe
Paris, France
2009

299
George Hardie
Hampshire, UK
2009

300
Prologue
California, USA
2009

301
Prologue
California, USA
2009

301
Prologue
California, USA
2009

Peter Saville
London, UK
2009

Peter Saville's extensive
archive is stored in the
middle of his live/work
studio.

Photograph courtesy
of Peter Saville

8vo
London, UK
c.1989

The pre-digital studio of
Mark Holt, Simon Johnston
and Hamish Muir, in
London's Covent Garden.

Photographs courtesy
of Hamish Muir.

ps.2 arquitetura + design
São Paulo, Brazil
2009

Studio of leading Brazilian
design company.

Photograph courtesy
of ps.2.

Disturbance Design
Durban, South Africa
2009

Studio of designer and
illustrator Richard Hart.

Photograph courtesy
of Richard Hart.

Jan Van Toorn
Amsterdam, Holland
2009

The studio of Dutch graphic
designer and educator
Jan Van Toorn.

Photograph courtesy of
Jan Van Toorn

Work
Singapore
2009

Studio of designer
Theseus Chan, founder
of Work and publisher
of Werk magazine.

Photograph courtesy
of Theseus Chan.

Niklaus Troxler
Willisau, Switzerland
2009

Studio of Niklaus Troxler.

Photographs courtesy
of Niklaus Troxler.

Henrion Design Associates
London, UK
c. 1960s

FHK Henrion in his studio
in Pond Street, in north
London, where he met with
clients at the long yew
table. The small wooden
cabinet below the KLM
plane held bottles and
glasses for meetings and
chocolates for 'stressy'
days. Henrion occupied the
studio from 1946 until his
death in 1990.

Henrion Design Associates
London, UK
c. 1960s

FHK Henrion at his specially
made hydraulic work table.
Behind him are individually
revolving book and display
cases (designed by Henrion)
doubling the amount of
shelves compared to
ordinary ones.

At the time this photograph
was taken, Henrion
operated under the name
Henrion Design Associates.
Previoulsy, the studio
was called Studio H Ltd.
It became HDA International
in the 1970s.

Photographs courtesy
of Marion Wesel-Henrion.

Winterhouse
Connecticut, USA
2009

The studio of
William Drenttel and
Jessica Helfand.

Photograph courtesy
of Winterhouse

Alan Fletcher
London, UK
2006

The studio of the late
Alan Fletcher.

Photography by Peter Wood

Photographs courtesy
of Raffaella Fletcher and
Paola Fletcher.

Carin Goldberg
NYC, USA
2009

Detail of Carin Goldberg's
Brooklyn studio showing
shelves containing
('idiosyncratic') inspiration
and reference collected
over the years.

Finn Creative
Kununurra, Australia
2009

Studio of Kevin Finn,
graphic designer and
editor/publisher of Open
Manifesto. Finn's studio is
situated in the north west
of Australia.

Photograph courtesy
of Kevin Finn.

Farrow
London, UK
2009

The central London studio
of designer Mark Farrow.

Photograph courtesy
of Mark Farrow.

Ed Fella
California, USA
2009

The only work space for the last 22 years of designer, illustrator and educator Ed Fella. He describes it as 'a room within a room, the larger room being the 14 grad students spaces at CalArts.' This room also holds Fella's entire archive. As he notes: 'Not a very bright idea in earthquake prone California.'

Photograph courtesy of Ed Fella

Total Design
Amsterdam, Holland
c. 1983

Board meeting.
Clockwise: Jelle van der
Toorn Vrijthoff,
Daphne Duyvelshoff,
Ben Bos, Jolijn van de Wouw
and a little bit of
Loek van der Sande.

Photographs courtesy
of Ben Bos.

Total Design
Amsterdam, Holland
1980

Ben Bos's 'team room'
showing his assistant Wim
Verboven. Verboven went on
to became a senior designer
with his own team.

Total Design
Amsterdam, Holland
1963

Management meeting in
Ben Bos's room. Clockwise:
Dick Schwarz, Friso Kramer,
Benno Wissing, Ben Bos,
Paul Schwarz, Wim Crouwel

Pentagram
London, UK
2009

Ground floor of
Pentagram's London office.

Photograph courtesy
of Pentagarm.

Studio Général – Toffe
Paris, France
2009

The studio of designer
Christophe Jacquet,
who works under the
name Toffe.

Photography by
Renan Astier.

Photograph courtesy
of Toffe.

George Hardie
Hampshire, UK
2009

Studio of graphic designer,
illustrator and educator
George Hardie.

Photograph courtesy
of George Hardie.

Prologue
California, USA
2009

The studio of Prologue,
a collection of designers,
filmmakers, and artists.
The studio is mainly
engaged in moving
image work.

Photograph courtesy
of Prologue.

Studio intelligence

Here is a list of some of the numerous topics to be considered when starting, maintaining or developing a graphic design studio. It's a short survival guide to staying solvent and sane at a time when running a studio can sometimes feel like pushing an elephant up a ladder. These entries are prompts to further investigation, and include a number of topics that are often assumed to be understood but that are frequently the source of mystery and confusion.

Most of the information listed below comes under the heading of common sense, and is based on the personal experiences of the publishers, editors and designers of this book. However, it's important to remember that business law and professional protocols vary from country to country, and as in all cases where financial decisions need to be taken, readers are urged to seek professional advice.

Archiving

Archiving (digitally or in cardboard boxes) is essential for two reasons: first, in most countries, businesses are required by law to keep financial records for a number of years; second, clients usually expect the work they commission from design studios to be kept indefinitely (this is mostly an unwritten assumption, but sometimes studios are contractually obliged to retain material). Regardless, it's worth having a policy on archiving and including the details in your Terms and Conditions (see Terms and Conditions, page 312). You should state clearly your policies: for example, are you prepared to keep files indefinitely or only for a specified period of time? Are you prepared to hand over files for an old project so that clients can pass them on to other designers to work on them?

Whenever possible, it's usually worth hanging on to all the key elements of a project because clients can return years after a job has been completed and ask for files to be reused or reworked. If material has been saved it is usually possible to generate new income, either by reworking it or by charging for resupplying it. Some studios make a small charge for retrieving items from an archive. As a general rule, financial records should be kept indefinitely.

Awards schemes

The merits and demerits of design awards are hotly debated among designers. For some, the notion of a jury of designers awarding prizes to design work by other designers is a flawed and inadequate way of evaluating design. For others, jury-awarded prizes are an essential mechanism for promoting design in general, and individual designers and studios in particular.

Even for studios that support the latter view, it is worth remembering that entering awards schemes is an expensive and time-consuming activity. Studios need to decide which schemes to enter, how much to spend on entering, and how much time to allow for the preparation of submissions (material that is improperly submitted can be rejected, and work that is poorly presented can have its chances of winning reduced). Finally, it's important to look at the winners from previous years and ask yourselves – does our work stand comparison? We need to be honest: to be deluded about the quality of our work, or to submit it in the vague hope that the judges might overlook its shortcomings (they won't) is expensive folly.

Budgets

Vast amounts of time can be saved at the outset of a project by the simple act of asking clients how much they have to spend. They won't always tell us, but we can be fairly certain that they will have a figure in mind, since it's rare for a client not to have allocated a sum of money before they start speaking to designers. If they won't name a figure, then we have to prepare a budget based on the time we estimate it will take to do the job, and the likely costs involved.

Showing clearly how we arrived at this figure is essential if we want clients to approve our final invoice. Of course, the more detail we provide the more scope it gives them to nit-pick. But the modern client demands a high degree of detail, and rounded-off figures and 'guesstimates' are rarely acceptable. Once a figure is agreed, clients should be asked for a purchase order that states all the conditions of the project, including agreed payment terms [see Staged payments, page 311]. We should be wary of clients who don't have a purchase order system or aren't prepared to confirm financial arrangements in writing.

Cleaning

For small studios, hiring a cleaner can seem like an unnecessary expense. But a studio that lacks basic cleanliness sends out a signal to staff, visitors and clients that it doesn't care about its working environment, and for a design studio this is a lousy message to broadcast. Design studios are not hospitals, but they need to be clean and functional. Hiring a cleaner is not an extravagance; it is an essential expense that will pay for itself many times over.

We should also treat our cleaners with respect; too often they are invisible contributors who are taken for granted and treated with casual disregard. And of course they need clear guidelines on what is expected of them; they need to be told how to differentiate between rubbish to be thrown away and an experimental paper sculpture that is waiting to be presented to an important client.

Cutting area

An area for making things with our hands is often considered unnecessary in today's all-digital studios. This is a mistake. Design suffers when it loses contact with its made-by-hand, artisan roots. No matter how small the studio, we should try to find space for an area where things can be made, cut, distressed, painted and built. An area for photography is equally useful.

Designing a website

The most important stage in designing a website is the scoping phase, which must take place before any 'pixel-pushing' begins. This is a vital period of discussion and should determine the full functional requirements of the site and lead to a shared and agreed understanding between client and designer. It's far cheaper to build in functionality at the start than to bolt it on later. And it's all too easy to design a site that looks beautiful but that doesn't work as expected.

As you clarify the scope of the project, you'll need to draw up a sitemap, followed by a wireframe version. By creating a purely structural design without the confusion of graphic detail you can quickly see where the different elements should sit, whether you've included everything the user needs, and if everything is in the right place. Don't forget to consider purpose (who is the site for and what should the user be able to do with it?); hierarchy (navigational structure and how 'deep' the site is); and accessibility (colours and type size). Only once the wireframes have been signed off should the graphic part of the design begin.

Talk to your client. Do they need a simple portfolio site, or one driven by a complex database? Will they want to keep it up to date themselves, or are you going to do it for them? Can you program as well as design, or will you need to outsource? Websites require maintenance – both in the technology that drives them and the content that populates them. It's always about time and money, but spending time planning at the beginning of the process can save you money and heartache later on.

Employment contracts

Although employment law in many countries is increasingly complex and tends to favour employees over employers, employment legislation is mostly common sense, and contains principles that most forward-thinking employers subscribe to anyway.

What should an employment contract contain? A good lawyer or business consultant will advise, but as a rough guide it should contain such items as holiday allowance, working hours and meal breaks. It should also list details of salary, frequency of salary reviews, profit-share arrangements, length of probationary period, etc.

Even in well-run studios with an exemplary record in the treatment of design and non-design staff, employment contracts are a necessity; they protect both employer and employee and reduce the likelihood of disputes and disagreements.

Entertainment

Entertaining clients is a complex area. Lavish and frequent lunches used to be an important part of the client/designer relationship, especially in boom times such as the 1980s. There are still a few clients who expect to be bought expensive meals, but fortunately they are a dying breed.

Buying lunch or dinner (breakfast, even) for a client at the end of a successful project can be an effective and pleasant way of saying thank you. A working lunch in the studio during the life of a project can also be effective as a way of showing that we value our clients, and of moving a relationship onto a less formal footing. But using entertainment as a way of winning business (for example, taking a potential client out to lunch before they have given us a job) is a sign that we are desperate, and as a tactic should be used with extreme caution.

Equipment

One of the great joys of setting up a graphic design studio is that it can be done cheaply. A studio can consist of nothing more than a laptop, some software and an internet connection. However, there are a few things that will make life simpler and work easier (though not necessarily better).

Here's a checklist: a computer (usually a Mac, with as much memory as possible); licensed software (Adobe Creative Suite is a good start point, plus any specialist programs); a selection of fonts (bought from reputable foundries); lightweight scanner (A4 is fine, use a bureau for high-res or oversized); printer (laserjet for cheap black and white prints, inkjet for colour run-outs – A4 is OK, A3 a nice luxury that avoids endless hours cutting and sticking); colour swatchbooks; paper samples (manufacturers will gladly send samples); cutting board; steel-edged rule; scalpel; folding bone; digital camera (10 megapixels+); large hard drives to store digital files as part of a regular back-up routine; rigid, light-safe storage for printed work (boxes, plan chests, etc); kettle; fridge; microwave; and, most important of all, books and music.

Furniture

It doesn't take much to furnish a studio: a couple of desks, some chairs, a set of drawers, a few shelves, a meeting table with chairs, a fridge, a kettle and a surface for cutting on. However, because we spend vast amounts of time in our studios it is essential to provide co-workers with proper furniture, functioning equipment and suitable working conditions. Failure to do this might prove costly: debilitating physical side effects such as Repetitive Strain Injury (RSI) can be caused by the prolonged use of computers, and posture-related health problems are a growing area of concern. Guidance should be sought on the correct way to be positioned when working with computer screens. Consideration needs to be given to such factors as optimum distance from the screen, the height of worksurfaces, appropriate chairs, and the need to take regular breaks.

Getting clients

To be a designer is to be locked into a perpetual quest to find, keep and maintain clients. Sometimes we are overwhelmed with too much work; at other times we can't even get clients to reply to our emails. But it's the same for everyone, and don't believe a designer who tells you they never get agitated about getting or keeping clients.

Attracting clients means using all reasonable and honest tactics to call attention to ourselves. The most important tactic is the cultivation of a clear and precise studio identity. A studio identity is more than a chic logo – perhaps persona is a better word – and includes the quality of the work produced, the way that work is presented, and what we might call the studio's ethos, or, to put it another way, what a studio stands for.

After that, we need the usual paraphernalia: websites, portfolios, promotional materials, mail-outs, emailable items, blogs and studio publications. Also, press coverage and media exposure, anything in fact that might help bring us to the attention of potential clients (see Press and media coverage, page 309).

Most designers want to get to a point where clients approach them. And with the help of a well-cultivated reputation and a body of impressive work, this goal can be reached. Some achieve it seemingly without breaking sweat; others struggle. But when clients call, it's never just luck: it is always because studios are doing the right things, even if they are doing them unconsciously.

Getting paid

Finding clients and doing the work are only part of the task facing studios. We also have to get paid. If we want to stay in business and honour our obligations to staff and suppliers, getting paid on time is crucial. Here are a few simple rules to ensure prompt payment: invoice for the project as soon as the work is done; ask if payments can be staged throughout the life of a project to help keep cashflow positive (see Staged payments, page 311); after submitting an invoice, call to make sure it has been received and entered into the payment system; as soon as payment is due, ask to be paid. The client/designer relationship is sensitive, so it is often advisable to have someone else chase payment for you, but it pays to be persistent.

Green issues

It is necessary for designers – just as it is for any other trade or social activity – to think and act responsibly on green issues. Environmental concerns are no longer a matter of individual moral choice; the evidence that we are trashing our planet is incontrovertible. We can argue about the degree to which we are damaging ourselves, but we can't dispute that it is happening. Contributing to the pollution of the world should be avoided in much the same way that we avoid punching strangers: it's not a good idea.

Besides simple morality, there's another reason for acting responsibly in green matters. Increasingly, when design studios are invited to tender or make formal bids for work, they are obliged to demonstrate green credentials. This is especially true of government or publicly funded projects.

Here is a short guide to running a green-aware studio. It is adapted from 'Fact Sheet #1 – The Studio', (www.threetreesdontmakeaforest.org/facts/business.html): use double-sided printing; reuse envelopes; use electronic formats when possible; consider waste disposal at all times; get rid of small waste bins and use communal recycling ones; ask your local authority about recycling services for businesses; turn off computers and screens at the end of each day; use energy-saving light bulbs; replace water coolers with filter or tap water; use public transport; use green-accredited taxi firms and couriers; devise a clear environmental policy that is available to all studio members; set up a 'ride to work' scheme; review all studio purchases, including recycled paper/envelopes/toilet paper, refillable inks, environmentally friendly cleaning products; check out the credentials of printers and ask them about their environmental policies.

Hospitality

How we treat the visitors to our studios says as much about us as our work does. Designers are often so absorbed in their work that they forget about simple front-of-house presentation. Not that this should be lavish or fussy: far from it. It is usually enough to offer our guests a mug of fresh coffee, a cup of tea, or a glass of water.

Many small studios can't afford the luxury of a receptionist or even a reception area, which means that studio personnel need to be vigilant and attentive to the comings and goings of visitors. In many studios, visitors walk off the street straight into the main working area. As long as guests are not ignored, this needn't be a bad thing.

Job descriptions and job titles

Job descriptions and job titles can appear an unnecessary detail. In fact, they serve an important dual function. First, they let clients and collaborators know who they are dealing with; second, they allow studios to have a structure. It's true that while studios remain small they will function perfectly well without a formal structure. But as soon as they grow, employees need to know where they fit in, who they report to, and who they can request to perform tasks. This aspect of studio life needn't be fetishized, and there is rarely any need to have complex hierarchies – studios with relatively flat structures work best. Yet it is perfectly natural to want to have our roles defined, and perfectly natural that we each have a job title. And of course, when it comes to resolving disputes and grievances, a job description, in writing, is an essential document for all concerned.

Kitchen

A clean kitchen equipped with the basics of food production is vital to the smooth functioning and well-being of any studio. Conversely, a messy kitchen is a sign of a creatively unhygienic studio. A communal eating area is also desirable, although in small studios this tends to be a luxury. The value of communal dinning is a recurring theme in the interviews in this book.

Legal

Designers should avoid contact with lawyers; encounters tend to be expensive, time-draining and rarely beneficial to the psychic health of designers. But we live in litigious times, and the number of places where we encounter lawyers and the law grows daily. When setting up a studio it is essential to have a few basic legal documents drawn up. These include agreements between business partners (see Partnership agreements, page 309), contracts of employment (see Employment contracts, page 305), and trading rules and stipulations (see Terms and Conditions, page 312). It is also usual to consult a lawyer before signing a lease (see Property, page 310).

How do we find a lawyer? We ask around and we take recommendations from friends and colleagues (see Professional advisors, page 309). There are some legal practices that specialize in media-related work such as the internet, copyright and intellectual property.

Library

All studios have books. Most studios have books before they have desks and chairs. Smart design firms have a book budget; a sum of money allocated for the purchase of books. This is a good way to build an effective library, especially if different members of the studio take it in turns to purchase new books. Of course, books need to be stored in an accessible way. Shelves are an essential part of any studio, and as with most things in life, it's worth buying the best that budgets allow.

Lighting

Natural light can help turn a dull studio into a pleasant and productive workspace. If there isn't much natural light, painting walls white will increase the amount of reflected light. Yet many studios don't have any natural light, which means that the quality and type of artificial lighting needs to be carefully considered. Thought must be given to the correct positioning of light fittings, as badly positioned lights cause glare or deep shadows. Good lighting has a direct effect on morale, productivity and efficiency. Conversely, poor lighting can cause eye-strain, headaches and inefficiency.

Although designers mostly work at computer monitors, they constantly need to check colours off-screen, and for this they need natural light. If none is available, the use of daylight-balanced fluorescent bulbs is recommended. As a rule, it is advisable to check colours under as many different light sources as possible.

Meeting rooms

A separate room where work can be presented to clients, and where private discussions can be held, is a useful asset for any studio. Yet as Milton Glaser points out in these pages (see Milton Glaser, pages 130–137), meetings behind closed doors can erode a studio's culture of openness. One way to avoid this is to have a meeting room with an internal window or glass wall that allows others to see what is happening (even if they can't hear what is being said). This contributes to a sense of transparency while at the same time accommodating the occasional need for privacy.

Music

Music can aid concentration, promote well-being and provide creative stimuli; conversely, it can irritate, distract and spread bad feeling. One person's fondness for the dark roar of Black Sabbath, the avant-garde scrapings of John Cage or the yelping of the latest R&B sensation may be another person's idea of audio torture. For studios that elect to play music for the benefit of everyone, there needs to be a high degree of unanimity in musical taste, otherwise people will resort to headphones, or fighting over the off-switch. Designers with headphones clamped to their ears can seem remote and cut off; some studio heads resent the use of these contraptions, regarding them as a hindrance to studio communication. Each studio has to decide what is an acceptable music policy for them. There are no rules; only a volume control and an on/off button.

Not for profit/pro bono work

The rise of graphic design as a well-paid and well-regarded occupation is due to its integral role in modern commercial life. Today's market-based economies are dependent on designers to provide the messaging and communication needed to promote and sustain consumption. Yet many graphic designers have come to question their complicity in this culture of persuasion, and have looked for ways to use their skills for the benefit of non-commercial activities.

Many designers choose to work for not-for-profit organizations, and others undertake pro bono projects – a way of operating that is defined as work undertaken voluntarily and without payment as a public service. Pro bono working is common in other areas of professional life: in the US, for example, the American Bar Association recommends that lawyers undertake at least 50 hours of pro bono service per year.

Pro bono work is a matter for individuals and studios to decide for themselves. However, it is still professional work, and many of the rules of normal commercial life need to be applied. To avoid exploitation and unrealistic expectations, it is advisable to agree the parameters of each pro bono project and to exchange letters and contracts exactly as if it were a normal commercial transaction.

Partnership agreements

Like pre-nuptial agreements, partnership agreements between the founders of design studios can appear to go against the spirit of comradeship and shared endeavour with which most studios begin life. But when working relationships go wrong, it soon becomes clear that written agreements are essential. Oddly enough, problems often start when studios are successful. Suddenly, the way the firm's profits are shared becomes a burning issue, and the person who we thought was a friend turns into a rancorous, litigious adversary. This is rare, but it happens, which is why we need to draw up partnership agreements at the outset. An accountant, lawyer or business advisor will help with this, but it is a step that we omit at our peril (see Professional advisors, page 309).

Press and media coverage

If you want to tell the world about yourself, you can launch a blog, make a Facebook page or open a Twitter account. But if you want to be noticed by reputable publications and credible blogs, you have to approach them correctly and – most important of all – you need to have something interesting to show or say. Here are some Dos and Don'ts for designers to keep in mind when approaching magazines and websites.

First, the dos: do send interesting work (preferably by email) with a short description of the content and circumstance surrounding its creation; do prepare the work in a way that shows it to its best advantage and makes it easy to use in magazine or web layouts; do make sure you have your client's approval to submit work for publication; do credit everyone who worked on the project. Now the don'ts: don't assume every editor of every magazine or blog is waiting for your work; don't assume that just because you have submitted material it will be automatically included; don't treat journalists and editors as if they were your PR team waiting to promote your work – they have opinions and views that are as valid as yours; don't send material to more than one publication or site at a time – choose a place that you think will appreciate your work and send it there (if it is rejected, send it to the next name on your list); don't send material that is out of date – editors and journalists are usually only interested in the new and the unseen.

Finally, it should be remembered that exposure in the design media rarely results in clients queuing outside your door waving their cheque books. This hardly ever happens. But it is always gratifying to see your work featured and commented on, and it contributes to building a studio profile within the design world which, over time, will seep out into the wider world of clients and non-designers.

Professional advisors

Most studios can survive happily with only an external accountant and the occasional use of a lawyer. It's rare to need the services of any other professional advisors, and a good accountant should be able to provide most of the advice and practical help that a small to medium-sized studio needs. An accountant will advise on all aspects of finance: tax, financial planning, payroll, profit and loss reporting, cashflow and fiscal compliance.

How do we find a good advisor? We ask friends and other designers for recommendations. It's unlikely that an accountancy firm with hundreds of partners and offices around the world will be suitable for a two-person studio; but there are many solo accountants and small accountancy practices offering a personal service. We also need to meet the person who is going to be navigating us through one of the most treacherous areas of professional life. We don't need our accountant to be our best friend – sometimes a bit of old-fashioned detachment can be beneficial – but we do need someone who we can talk to and trust, and someone who doesn't treat us with condescension or baffle us with financial gobbledygook. We also need to know how much their services will cost over a year. Accountants are not cheap, but a good one will save us more money than they cost us. If not, dump them.

Property

One of the great benefits of graphic design is that it can be done pretty much anywhere. Designers can begin trading from their bedrooms. This tactic won't necessarily impress potential clients (some won't mind), but it's better than committing to a commercial lease that puts an unbearable strain on a fledgling business. Another common interim step that many studios take is to share space with other designers or compatible businesses. Yet again, this can be a useful stepping stone prior to signing a full commercial lease. Plus, if you can squeeze into a corner of an existing studio, or related business, there are often spin-off benefits to be had beyond the obvious advantage of a reduced rent; it is often possible to pick up referrals, for example.

Property laws and the protocols surrounding commercial leases vary from country to country. As a rule, however, new studios and studios in the first few years of their existence should not commit to a long lease. Most property owners – and their agents – will try to persuade tenants to take a longer lease than is necessary. This should be resisted. For a studio start-up, a one-year lease with the option to renew is a sensible arrangement. For more established studios, committing to more than five years can be risky.

To find property, you should comb the internet and keep eyes open for signs on buildings saying 'For Rent'. You can also call property agents in the location you want to work in: you risk being trampled to death in their rush to send you details, but you will find out what's available.

Finally, in many countries, national and local governments offer grants and financial aid to business start-ups. This sometimes takes the form of assistance with the rent of premises. It's worth checking to see what's on offer in your region.

Recessions

Recessions happen regularly in Western economies. About once every decade we can be sure that the economic heartbeat of nations will flatline. And since all economies are globally linked, any downturn will occur simultaneously pretty much everywhere in the world. When this happens, clients stop spending money, or drastically reduce the amount of cash they are willing to part with. Projects get cancelled and work becomes scarce. Banks stop lending money, and the national mood dips.

The most obvious way to deal with the inevitability of recessions is to resist the temptation to overreach ourselves when times are good. For example, after a couple of good years we should not rush to sign a long lease on a lavishly appointed studio that we will not be able to afford if our income is halved in a future recession.

Recessions are hell for everyone caught up in them, yet there is a good side to them. During periods of global economic decline we reacquaint ourselves with the fundamentals of business life, and we relearn lessons that are easily forgotten in boom times. Running a business in a recession makes us hyper-aware of the risks of overstretching ourselves, and reminds us that even tiny amounts of expenditure need to be controlled.

Signage

Since lots of design studios are in shared buildings they should, at least, have the studio's name clearly visible next to a buzzer or doorbell. Visitors turning up at a multi-occupancy building often find it hard to locate the place or person they want to visit. But there's no excuse for design groups having poor signage. Since design is fundamentally about the presentation of information, we should start by showing that we know how to present ourselves, and by demonstrating that we can use graphic design to help visitors find us rather than asking them to take part in a treasure hunt.

But signage is not just about names on doors and directional aids. The way a studio handles the labelling of box files and internal messaging is a sure-fire indicator of its attitude to design. As Erik Spiekermann notes in these pages (see Erik Spiekermann, pages 76–85), it is unacceptable to use Comic Sans even for a simple notice reminding people to remove staples from documents before photocopying them. Spiekermann has designed a typeface for each of the studios he has run, and insists on their use for every sort of printed communication, no matter how mundane.

Software

Designers need software like fish need water. It is impossible to function effectively in the commercial arena without up-to-date legal software. Requirements will vary from studio to studio: some studios will have modest software needs, others will require vast amounts.

For studio start-ups, software is one of the main items of expenditure, and it is likely to remain so until open-source software reaches the design world. Advocates of open source envisage a future where software is developed collectively rather than by commercial organizations. As one advocate puts it, open source offers the promise of 'better quality, higher reliability, more flexibility, lower cost and an end to predatory vendor lock-in.' The open-source movement has millions of commercial and private users. It is estimated that there are 40 to 50 million users of Linux, the free Unix-type open source operating system, and the browser Firefox is said to have more than 250 million users. The list of graphic freeware and free applications is also growing, but as yet there are few viable alternatives to the main commercial graphics software packages. Until this changes, designers have no choice but to buy legal software and pay for upgrades.

Space planning

Serious space planning is something to contemplate after a studio has been in existence for more than a year or two. The way studios start off is rarely the way they continue, so it is unwise to implement any rigid structuring in the early days of a studio's lifespan. Most designers can plan the spatial layout of a studio to suit their needs, but a friendly architect or professional space planner can make a valuable contribution.

Specifying a print job

Not every job fits simple categorization – you need to think through every aspect, including the obvious. Never assume that someone else sees what you see. If there's any room for doubt, include a sketch, or photos of your own mock-up. If it's a complicated job, talk to the printer face-to-face – good printers are always happy to discuss work in fine detail. If they're not then you might want to find someone who is. If you address all the points below you'll have covered the basics.

Job title – for consistent reference between you and the printer; page size; extent – number of pages (and for books, in how many sections: to calculate this you'll need to know the size of sheet being printed and how many pages will fit on it); material – what's used where; print – quantity and type of colours (are they the same throughout or in specific sections?); quantity – number to be produced and additional run-on (an additional quantity printed at the same time); finish – sealing, trimming, folding, special finishes (foils, varnishes, drilling, stickers, etc); delivery – where and when (local, national, international).

Staged payments

The convention in the design world is to invoice for services once a project has been completed. For a small studio, this can impose an intolerable financial burden, so always ask for staged payments. Most reasonable clients will agree to a polite request. If they refuse, we can be justifiably wary of their ability and willingness to honour their debts.

Dividing a fee into three parts is a sensible way to organize staged payments: one third in advance, one third halfway through the project, and the final third on competition.

Studio name and identity

Choosing a studio name is never easy.
The matter of naming a studio has been
complicated by the dominance of the internet,
and the ever-increasing importance of online
search engines. All simple URLs have long
since gone, and it's no good having a name
that isn't search-engine-friendly, so we must
be ultra-clever in the way we name ourselves.
Registering a URL and ensuring that
ownership of it is not allowed to lapse is also
vital. Registering a name for legal reasons is
more problematic, and varies from country
to country.

Creating a studio's visual identity can be
tortuous. Designers who are capable of bold
decision-making on behalf of their clients
suddenly become creatively tongue-tied when
it comes to working for themselves. With this
in mind it can often be advantageous to treat
it as if it were an external brief with normal
time and budgetary restraints.

Yet the question remains – what sort of name
do we want, and what sort of face do we want
to present to the world? Many choose
a neutral-sounding name and adopt a neutral
visual appearance. Others use the creation of
a studio name and identity as an opportunity
to produce a striking statement. Regardless
of the approach, a studio's name and identity
needs to be a truthful reflection of the
studio's ethos and capabilities.

Terms and conditions

When we have disputes or come up against
unscrupulous clients, we soon realize how
important a set of Terms and Conditions can
be. They are defined as 'general and special
arrangements, provisions, requirements,
rules, specifications, and standards that form
an integral part of an agreement or contract.'
In other words, they are the fundamental
details of how we conduct business.

Where do we obtain a set of Terms and
Conditions? We can ask a lawyer to draw
them up for us; this will mean they are specific
to us and our circumstances, but it will be
a costly exercise. A number of professional
bodies – such as AIGA in the US – offer basic
Terms and Conditions that can be altered to
suit the needs of individual studios. Another
option is to search the internet for adaptable
templates; they are widely available.

However, the most important thing to
remember about Terms and Conditions is that
they are not worth a mung bean unless they
are seen by the people they are intended for
– clients, suppliers, joint venture partners,
etc. It used to be enough that they were
printed on the back of invoices, but now, when
invoices are often sent digitally, our Terms
and Conditions need to be available as PDFs
and accessible via the internet. It is not our
job to make our clients or suppliers read
them, but it is our job to make sure they have
them in a readable format.

Timeline

The timeline for a project illustrates when the
job is expected to be completed. It should be
punctuated by presentation and approval
dates, when content needs to be supplied
and by whom. The more detailed a timeline can
be, the more control we have over a job. It
provides us with a structure and enables us
to see if the job is taking longer to complete
and therefore costing us more. It also helps
to identify who – or what – is holding the job
up and why. Clients find timelines reassuring
and take them as a sign that we are treating
their projects seriously.

Training

There's a sense in which a career in design is really one long training and learning session. When designers stop wanting to acquire new knowledge, it's generally a sign that they are past their peak. But designers tend to be naturally inquisitive and keen to absorb new knowledge. For any designer who wants to keep doing meaningful work, a constant programme of learning and education is obligatory.

Studios that actively encourage, facilitate or pay for training and learning will benefit in many ways; staff who receive instruction in practical skills such as software, coding, animation, management and so on will boost the studio's capabilities as well as expanding their own personal horizons. There are other types of learning that have less tangible benefits such as drawing, craft and foreign language classes. Yet here again the individual and the group benefit from an enlargement of the studio's knowledge pool.

There is no shortage of individuals, private companies and public bodies offering training in all aspects of business and cultural life. National and local government agencies offer help and guidance to anyone looking for training. Of course, studios have to be financially stable before they can offer to pay for staff to go on courses. Some studios build training and personal development expenditure into their remuneration framework; in other words, training is paid for as part of a bonus or profit share scheme.

Unpaid pitching/spec work

It is now routine for designers to be asked by clients to take part in unpaid competitive pitches and to submit creative work on a purely speculative basis. After receiving submissions from a number of studios, the client selects their favoured proposal and the winning studio – or individual – is paid a fee to do the job. The losers get nothing. Sometimes they don't even get a 'thanks but no thanks' – just silence.

In modern business culture, unpaid competitive pitching has become nearly ubiquitous; even governmental and publicly funded clients think it is acceptable to ask groups of competing designers to submit ideas at no charge, and then choose the proposal they like best. Some companies and public bodies have it built into their constitutions that they will put all work out for unpaid competitive tendering.

Studios must decide for themselves whether it is right or wrong to work for clients who demand ideas that they refuse to pay for. Many studios say no to all invitations to pitch ideas on a speculative basis, and most of them survive, too. In fact, many of the most successful studios have a no unpaid pitching policy, proving that it is possible to take a stand on this question.

But if you decide to take part in speculative pitches, you should at least try to humanize the process. Demand a meeting with the potential client and learn about the specific requirements of the project. The more you can develop a personal relationship, the more relevant your response will be and the more chance you'll have of success. Always ask how many designers are being invited to take part – some clients ask six or seven (sometimes more) studios to take part, and this greatly reduces your chance of success. Finally, always ask for a fee, even if there is none on offer. By doing this you remind thoughtless clients that they are asking for a service that has cost implications for the provider of that service. And if you are met with silence after submitting a lot of hard work, ring them up and embarrass them by asking why you haven't heard from them. That makes them squirm.

Text by the editors, except Designing a website and Specifying a print job by Patrick Eley.

DATE DUE